Mastering Communication Skills and Soft Skills

A Learner's Guide to Life Skills

Mastering Communication Skills and Soft Skills

A Learner's Guide to Life Skills

N Krishnaswamy
Former Professor, EFL University, Hyderabad

Manju Dhariwal
Associate Professor, LNMIIT, Jaipur

Lalitha Krishnaswamy
Educational Consultant

In collaboration
with
The LNM Institute of Information Technology, Jaipur

LNMIIT
The LNM Institute of Information Technology

B L O O M S B U R Y
NEW DELHI • LONDON • OXFORD • NEW YORK • SYDNEY

Bloomsbury Publishing India Pvt. Ltd.
DDA Complex LSC, Building No.4
Second Floor, Pocket C-6&7, Vasant Kunj
New Delhi 110070

Bloomsbury is a trademark of Bloomsbury Publishing Plc

ISBN: 978-93-85436-27-7
10 9 8 7 6 5 4 3 2 1

Typeset by Manmohan Kumar
Printed by : Sree Vinayaga Screens, Madurai, INDIA

Contents

INTRODUCTION ix
Salient Features of the Book xi

ABOUT THE AUTHORS xiii

ACKNOWLEDGEMENTS xv

UNIT I – BASICS OF COMMUNICATION: THEORY 1
Points to Remember 1
The Six Star Strategy (5 W's & 1 H) 5
UNIT I – PRACTICE 7
What's the difference? 7
Sign Language 7
Body Language (Kinesics) 8
Time: Chronemics 8
Touch: Haptics 9
Eye Contact: Oculesics 9
Case Study for Discussion 11

UNIT II – COMMUNICOLOGY AND HUMAN LANGUAGE: THEORY 12
Points to Remember 12
Animal Communication and Human Language 16
UNIT II – PRACTICE 20
Case Study for Discussion 22

UNIT III – BARRIERS TO COMMUNICATION: THEORY 24
Points to Remember 24
Pragmatics 26
UNIT III – PRACTICE 28
Communication Mishaps 29
Case Study for Discussion 31

UNIT IV – COMMUNICATION AND LANGUAGE SKILLS: THEORY 33
Study the diagram 33
Listening 34
Speaking: The Gift of the Gab 35
Reading 36
Writing 36
UNIT IV – PRACTICE 39
Listening 41
Speaking 42
Reading 42
Writing 43
Case Study for Discussion 43

UNIT V – COMMUNICATING IN A GLOBAL LANGUAGE: THEORY 45
UNIT V – PRACTICE 54
Case Study for Discussion 62

UNIT VI – SOFT SKILLS: THEORY 64
A. Big five Personality Traits 65
D. Some traits of Inter-personal skills 67
UNIT VI – PRACTICE 74
Test 1 to 6 74
Case Study for Discussion 86

UNIT VII – RESUMES AND COVER LETTERS: THEORY 88
Your Life on a Page 90
UNIT VII – PRACTICE 100
Read the following advertisement and try to understand it: 100
Case Study for Discussion 103

UNIT VIII – GROUP DISCUSSIONS AND INTERVIEWS: THEORY 105
Tips for Effective GD 105
At the Interview 107
Closing the Show 115
UNIT VIII – PRACTICE 117
Group Discussion 117
Case Study for Discussion 122

UNIT IX – BUSINESS COMMUNICATION: THEORY 123
Oral: Presentation 123
Memos and Memo Letters 125

Reports, Proposals, Abstracts 133
Technical Writing 136
UNIT IX – PRACTICE 138
Part I: Business Communication 138
Part II: Study Skills 140
Activity 1 – Note-taking 141
Activity 2 – Note-making 142
Case Study for Discussion 150

UNIT X – INTERCULTURAL COMMUNICATION: THEORY 151
Points to Remember 151
UNIT X – PRACTICE 158
Case Study for Discussion 160

UNIT XI – PROFESSIONAL COMMUNICATION: THEORY 161
UNIT XI – PRACTICE 172
Case Study for Discussion 174

APPENDIX I: EMPOWER YOUR ENGLISH 176
APPENDIX I: ANSWER KEY 201
APPENDIX II: TOWARDS GENDER-SENSITIVE COMMUNICATION 210

Introduction

There is a story in the Hebrew Bible about 'The **Tower of Babel**'.

According to the story, all human beings of the generations following the Great Floods spoke a single language and migrated from the East, came to the land of Shinar.

And they said, "Come, let us build ourselves a city, and a tower whose top is in the heavens; let us make a name for ourselves, lest we be scattered abroad over the face of the whole earth."

But the Lord came down to see the city and the tower which the sons of men had built.

And the Lord said, "Indeed the people are one and they all have one language, and this is what they begin to do; now nothing that they propose to do will be withheld from them.

Come, let us go down and there confuse their language, that they may not understand one another's speech."

So the Lord scattered them abroad from there over the face of all the earth, and they ceased building the city.

Therefore its name is called Babel, because there the Lord confused the language of all the earth; and from there the Lord scattered them abroad over the face of all the earth.

– *Genesis* 11:4–9

The tower was never built and the Lord confused the language of all the earth! Not only Gods confused our language but also human beings through lack of definitive meaning in language! Language itself is confusing, unstable, and slippery! That is why the expression 'The Tower of Babel' is also used to denote babbling, a scene of confused and noisy talking, misinterpretation and misunderstanding; the confusion is caused not only by multiple languages that are mutually incomprehensible and unintelligible but also within a given language. Communication is very complex because of all kinds of variations in cultural norms, and linguistic variations in idiolect, dialect (regional, class, caste, gender, race, etc.), register, and style.

Communication is a complex process; conveying information is only 'giving out' but communication is 'getting through'. Communication is very creative as well as extremely delicate; it is an art as well as a science. More often than not, it fails to communicate what is intended. George Bernard Shaw aptly remarks, 'The single biggest problem in communication is the illusion that it has taken place.' Some thinkers feel that all communication is 'miscommunication'! Communication is not 'just talking' and talking. Robert Frost, the well known poet, says, 'Half the world is composed of people who have something to say and can't, and the other half have nothing to say but keep on saying it'. Those who keep talking without anything to communicate are the bores!

It is often said that the world has become a 'Tower of Babel', so, it has become absolutely essential to learn communication skills, not only within one language and culture but also inter-culturally.

Earlier where people lived in small communities, personal communication was easy and simple because of mutual proximity and intimacy. Now, though the world has become 'a global village', people are scattered all over and there is very little face-to face communication; now, technological communication has replaced personal communication since it reduces the limitations of space, making communication faster. Moreover, economic globalization and expanding business by multi-national companies necessitate inter-cultural communication too. However, though faster, except in audio-video supported communication, some essential aspects like body language, tone and emotions are lost in technological communication. Hence there is a need for training in personal communication to minimize cultural and linguistic miscommunication and to enhance effective interaction. The market demands it and all companies insist on the need for communication skills and soft skills.

The essence of being human is language and only through language one's personality, etiquette, and cultured behaviour is created; in that sense, it is language that creates and shapes what are called 'soft skills' in computer jargon. Language has the power and energy to help, to heal, to hurt, to harm, to humiliate, to humble, and to be a cultured and noble human being. We must cultivate the ability to communicate in a humane way. We must remember that communication too is a skill that you can learn like riding a bicycle or a two-wheeler, driving a car, or typing. If you are willing to work at it, you can rapidly learn and improve the quality of every aspect of your life.

This book, **Mastering Communication Skills and Soft Skills**, is an attempt to give practical, hands-on experience, for the learners interested in learning the essentials of life skills. This book is not just presenting only the theory part but gives the necessary practice in communication skills in the global language, English; it is more of a workbook with minimal theory since there are many books on the theory of communication. The approach is very practical with an emphasis on communication in English and career communication.

This book can be used as a textbook in engineering colleges, IITs, and IIMs, and in MBA and BBA programmes, depending on their requirements The authors hope learners and teachers find it useful and effective.

Salient features of the book: Mastering Communication Skills and Soft Skills – a Learner's Guide to Life Skills

- It is a theory-cum-practice book on communication skills and soft skills (i.e. life skills/people's skills/human skills)
- It gives the essential aspects of the theory to enable the learner to work through the practical problems
- It uses a problem-solving technique to teach communication skills and poses problems in the form of case studies too
- It covers all aspects of communication skills, soft skills, career communication, and the basics of the English Language
- It is meant for Indian learners since it is based on Indian situations
- It also concentrates on inter-cultural communication
- It is user-friendly and uses simple and easy-to-understand language

- It teaches English usage in addition to communication skills and soft skills
- It is suitable as a textbook for courses like BBA and MBA, and engineering colleges, IITs, IIMs where courses on communication are taught
- Corporate companies can use the book in their training programmes on communication skills and soft skills

About the authors

N Krishnaswamy is a former Professor, EFL University, Hyderabad, and a well-known author of several scholarly books, trend-setting text books, and articles. His latest book "ECO ENGLISH" (Bloomsbury) is a different kind of anthology focusing on ESP (English for Social Purposes).

Manju Dhariwal is Associate Professor in the Department of Humanities and Social Sciences at the LNM Institute of Information Technology (LNMIIT), a Deemed to be University, Jaipur. She has presented papers in a number of international and national conferences, authored several journal papers and guided Ph.D. research.

Lalitha Krishnaswamy is a former Professor of Education, educational consultant and author of many books. She has co-authored "ECO ENGLISH" with Prof Krishnaswamy.

Acknowledgements

Our heartfelt thanks to

Dr. Sriraman, Former Professor, EFL University, Hyderabad, for carefully editing the script, which has greatly improved the quality of the book. Any mistakes remaining are only ours.

Mr. Nithianandan, Regional Head, Bloomsbury Publishing India, for the special care taken in getting the final copy ready for publication.

The following students of LNMIIT, Jaipur, for providing valuable feedback and rendering technical skills in arranging the material:

Shubham Sahu
Aqib Mohammad Khan
Kimmi Khurana
Aditya Deswal
Diwakar Redhu
Sai Krishna

Unit I – Basics of Communication

Half the world is composed of people who have something to say and can't, and the other half who have nothing to say and keep on saying it.

Robert Frost

OBJECTIVES

After reading this unit, you will be able to

- ✓ Understand the process of communication
- ✓ Identify modes and styles of communication
- ✓ Appreciate the role of culture in the act of communication

I Points to Remember

1. Communication is a **symbolic, interpretive, transactional, contextual process in which people create shared meanings**. It is a meaning-making and meaning-sharing/exchanging process. Information, knowledge, ideas, emotions, perceptions, feelings, personality traits and images are **conveyed, exchanged or shared** between two persons (dyadic mode) and among people (i.e. group communication) through **signals, signs, symbols and languages** in formal or informal (physical, social, and cultural) – settings for a specific purpose or purposes.
2. Communication is **not a static act** but a **dynamic process** of interaction among people towards a desired goal.
3. Communication is not just message transmission or transference but an **effective tool** for making the **receiver** understand and do certain things that are intended by the **sender** to fulfil his/her motives.
4. Communication is essential for a whole gamut of functions ranging from cultural, social, political, commercial, scientific and artistic to the day-to-day physical and mental well-being of individuals.
5. Communication evolves according to the needs of a given community and it changes, depending on the time, space and culture in which it evolves.
6. Communication may be of three types:
   i. **Intra-personal Communication or Contemplative Communication:** It takes place within an individual

Unit I: Figure 1

Source: www.meetup.com

in the form of **thinking, reflection and interior monologue** to formulate ideas before one engages in social communication or **exterior** communication and self-realization. It happens inside the mind all the time. It happens, particularly, in meditation, prayer, and thinking.

ii. **Inter-personal Communication**: It is exterior communication or person (s) to person (s) communication, in the form of language, body-language, and verbal combined with non-verbal interaction, with or without technical devices.

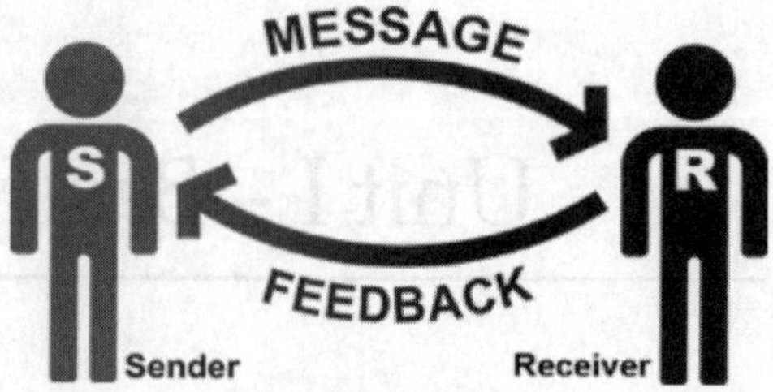

Unit I: Figure 2

Source:www.humanpotentialnow.com

iii. **Mass communication**: Communication with a large population or audience of even anonymous or heterogeneous nature. Example: The electronic media like the internet, social network systems like Facebook and Twitter, TV, radio, films, mobile phones, audio-video devices, print media like newspapers, magazines, journals, posters, etc.

Unit I: Figure 3

www.studentcaring.com

7. **Communication Modes and Means:**
   i. Messages can be conveyed through verbal or non-verbal means, or a combination of both.
   ii. The non-verbal is more effective; it conveys 55% of the message.
   iii. It is said that supra-segmental (features such as stress, tone, or word juncture that accompany over consonants and vowels) and voice communicate 38% and actual words only 7%. The verbal accounts for 45% only. A combination is more effective. For example-Saying 'Thank You' with a smile.
   iv. The verbal consists of the supra-segmental, voice language and a combination of these. Supra-segmentals include stress (word-stress, sentence-stress and emphatic stress,

intonation (i.e. tone), pause, the voice quality, speaking rate, etc.). Conversation through language can be in the spoken mode or written mode.

v. The style can range from frozen (like in a very, very formal or ceremonial situation) to intimate. It is a continuum.

vi. **Grapevine** (a form of informal communication in which people communicate with each other without any formal line of communication. It is called Grapevine because like that of a grape vine, it is impossible to find the origin of information which results in spread of rumours) or the gossip mill is also an effective communication channel in speech.

8. **Kinesics** is the study of body-language in different cultures. Kinesics is concerned with the following:
   i. **Emblems**: Those who have a direct verbal counterpart such as arm waving to express 'goodbye' or 'hello'; thumb and finger held in a circle to express 'OK'.
   ii. **Illustrators:** Directly tied to verbal but accompanied by verbal like saying 'huge' and at the same time lifting arms and moving them in half circle.
   iii. **Affect displays**: Facial and body movements that show emotions like surprise, sadness, etc.
   iv. **Regulators**: Turn-taking cues like pausing and looking in the middle of a talk or conversation
   v. **Adaptors**: Body movements like tapping, fidgeting, scratching, shaking legs to show discomfort or tension.
9. **Chronemics** studies time as an element of culture that communicates. For example, punctuality communicates. Time can also be used as an indicator of status like a VIP or a politician coming late for a meeting. There are past-oriented cultures that take pride in past glory, present-oriented cultures that live in the present (South American cultures), future-oriented cultures like North America.
10. **Proxemics** is the study of space as an element of culture that communicates.In most Western cultures, intimate space (loving, protecting, etc.) is about 0 to 1 and a half inches, personal space (intimate among friends, etc.) is 1 and a half to 4', social space (social gatherings, etc.) is 4 to 12', and public space (in meetings, lectures, etc.) is 12 feet upwards.
11. **Haptics** is the study of touch patterns in societies. South American cultures, Southern Europe and the Middle East have the touch culture like hugging, patting, etc. In India, touch is generally avoided.

    Note: *The difference between '**channel**' and '**medium**' – A channel is a way, course, or direction along which information travels. A medium requires a material substance (air, gas, liquid, solid) that propagates or sends out energy waves. Some TV's have 300 channels; the TV is an electronic medium*
12. **Loudness:** Some cultures use a loud voice; according to some Westerners, Indians are very noisy. Even within India, some linguistic communities use a very loud voice when compared to others. Perceptions differ.
13. **Other non-verbal** code systems include
    a) **Dermal** code systems like blushing, skin tone, etc.
    b) **Chemical** code systems like body odour, gas, etc. Meat eaters have a distinct body odour and tropical people sweat a lot.

14. **Often verbal and non-verbal** behaviours are synchronized. They are used simultaneously.
15. **Silence** is also used to convey messages like the wife not talking to her husband to show unhappiness or the mother not talking to her children to show disapproval. Silence is often used as a weapon to correct wrong behaviour.
16. **Communication settings, Styles and Modes**: The setting may be the work-place, the market-place, a club, outer-space, home, a library, a bed-room etc. Styles may range from frozen, formal, semi-formal, casual, informal, intimate, etc. The modes may be visual, verbal or non-verbal; may be face-to-face, telephonic etc.

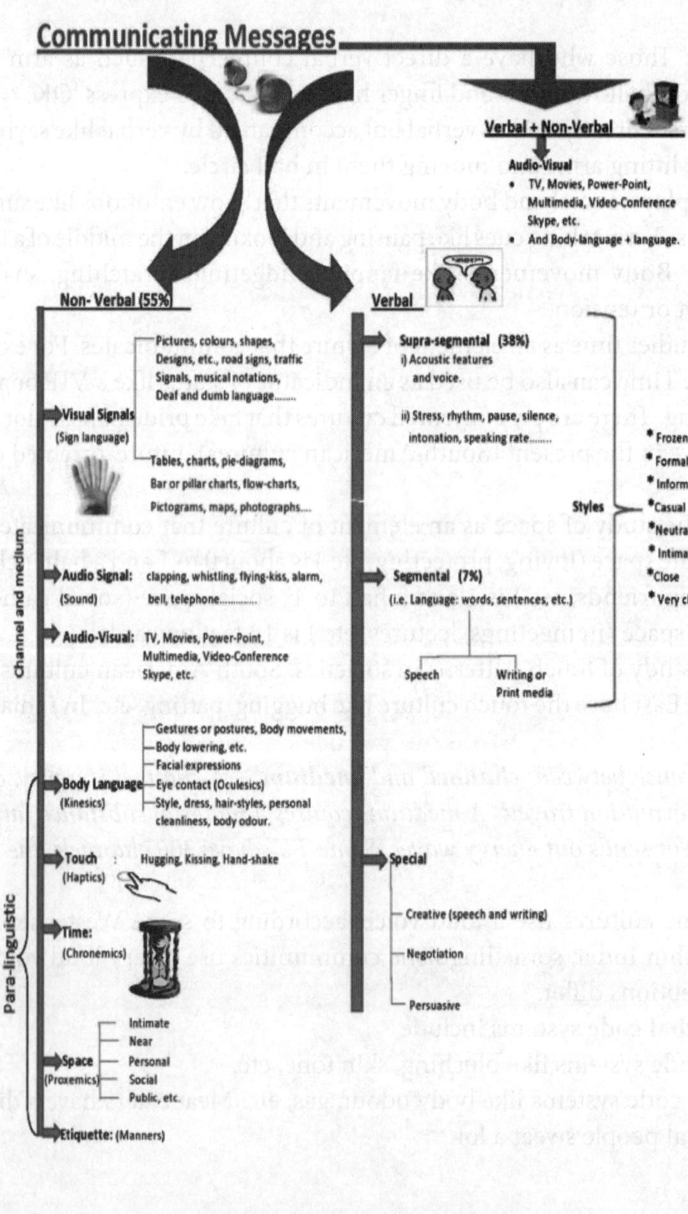

II Don't Forget

i. Communication is a complex process of give and take with innumerable intricacies and dimensions. It's a jungle and you have to find your way. It is a two-way street if properly understood.

ii. Everything we do communicates. **The medium is the message** – Visual, Voice, Words.

iii. The way we begin our message often determines the outcome of the communication process. A good beginning sets the tone. The way a message is delivered always affects the way the message is received.

iv. For effective communication, more than language, what is needed is an **attitude**, willingness to give and take, to open up to others and accept others, to have **empathy** and a capacity to look at situations from varied perspectives.

- The real communication is the **message received, not the message intended**. Always remember that there is not just **expression** alone but **impression** too and that there is a lot of **suppression** between **expression** and **impression**. One's intention may be good but that has to be conveyed and received properly. There can be a mismatch between intention and expression, expression and impression.

v. Communication is a two-way process and not a one way street. Empathy is the quality that will allow one to understand the mental and psychological state of the person we are communicating with.

vi. Creativity in day-to-day communication is one's ability togo beyond stereotypes and see beyond the accepted pattern.

vii. Plan your communication at least mentally. Think and then say/write

III The Six Star Strategy (5 W's And 1 H)

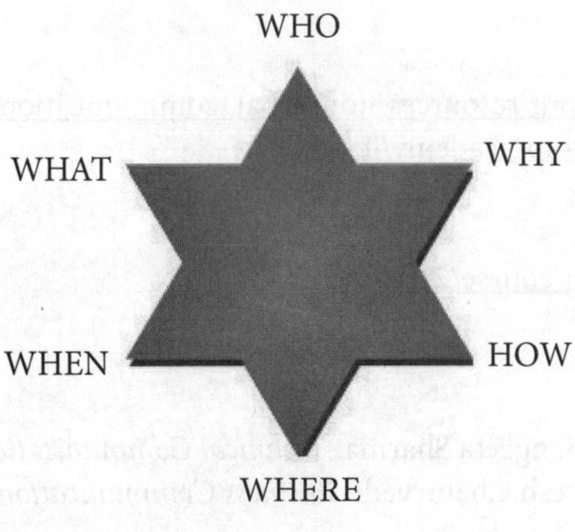

➢ **Who** is your audience/hearer? Think of their/his/her age, gender (mixed), education level, their attitude, their expectation, what offends them, and how well you know them.

➢ **Why** are you saying what you want to say?

- **Where** is the setting – home, club, office, etc.?
- **When** is the time – a sense of timing? Time to speak and, time to be silent.
- **What** is the content – the level of details, their interest, etc.?
- **How** best can you communicate – Diction, Strategy, etc.?

In public and official presentations, the factors mentioned above are very important.

In presentations, prepare notes – the essential, necessary but not essential, and the stand-by; plan well.

IV Recollect the following factors:

	Informal	**Formal**
Setting	club, library, shop, office, home, bus stop	office meeting
Topic	TV programme, weather, cricket match, travel	business, career
Social relationship	friend, stranger	boss
Mental make-up or attitude	relaxed, light-hearted, no strong feelings	seminar

"All the world's a stage. And all men and women merely players."

– Shakespeare in A*s You Like It.*

Communicative competence is a skill that you have to cultivate and sharpen; it is like practising for a play. The more you rehearse, the better your performance will be. Voice cultivation, body language and language skills are to be integrated and practised; their function is synergic.

Online Resources

1. http://www.creducation.org/resources/nonverbal_communication
2. http://education-portal.com/academy/lesson
3. http://www.colorado.edu
4. http://www.forbes.com/
5. https://www.coursera.org/course/21stcencom

Select Bibliography

1. Raman, Meenakshi and Sangeeta Sharma. *Technical Communication*. New Delhi: OUP, 2011.
2. Chaturvedi P D and Mukesh Chaturvedi. *Business Communication*. Delhi: Pearson Education, 2005.
3. Pease, Barbara and Allan Pease. *The Definitive Book of Body Language*. New York: Bentam, 2006.
4. Carnegie, Dale. *How To Win Friends and Influence People*. New York: Simon & Schuster, Reissue edition, 2009.

Unit I – Practice

I. What's the difference?

Signal and Sign; Sign and Symbol

Give examples.

II. Sign language-What do the following convey?

i. On the road

A B C D E

ii. What do they represent?.

A B C D E

Colour – Here are some colour expressions. Say what they mean?

i. Put it in black and white
ii. Out of the blue
iii. To be caught red-handed
iv. A white lie
v. To black mail
vi. The black sheep
vii. A red letter day
viii. Red tape
ix. Off colour
x. In the pink of health
xi. A fair copy
xii. To show one's colour
xiii. A golden opportunity
xiv. A yellow journal
xv. A green belt
xvi. A red alert
xvii. White revolution
xviii. Black magic
xix. Grey market

III. Body language (Kinesics)

What do they mean?

A. The ring gesture

B. V sign

1. Raised eyebrows
2. Furrowed forehead
3. Turning up the nose
4. The dead pan face
5. Nodding the head
6. Turning the head from side to side
7. The thumbs-up gesture
8. Open hands
9. Rubbing the palm together
10. The shoulder shrug
11. Straddling the chair
12. Arm cross
13. Cracking the knuckles
14. Placing the hands on the hip
15. Fidgeting
16. Shaking the leg vigorously

IV. Why do you think that dress, hairstyle, body odour and overall demeanour add to successful communication? Give reasons.

V. The movement of the body and eyes reveal one's emotional status – Comment.

VI. 'A candidate's personality is evaluated on the basis of his/her appearance' – Do you agree? Give reasons.

VII. Space: Body distance (Proxemics)

A. Mention the approximate distance to be maintained-

i. Comfort zone
ii. Intimate distance
iii. Personal distance
iv. Social distance
v. Public distance

B. The perception of space can vary from culture to culture. Do you agree? Give examples.

VIII.

A. Time: Chronemics

Comment on the following instances.

✓ A British businessman in Saudi Arabia is keen to secure an important deal. He can't afford to waste any time. But he has to wait for ages to get an appointment with his Saudi partner. Meetings never start on time and when they do, there are frequent interruptions.

✓ In the USA, the future is more important than the past, whereas in India the importance of past is emphasised.

✓ Time perspectives like punctuality vary between the East and the West.

B. Touch: Haptics

In some cultures, hugging or kissing, tapping on the shoulder or shaking hands often are appropriate.

What about India? Comment on kissing and hugging.

C. Eye contact: Oculesics

i. A US manager says, 'I asked my Indian staff on how the project was going and, of course, not much has been done. I was suspicious when they didn't even look at me in the eye.'

ii. In some cultures looking someone in the eye is taken as a sign of disrespect. What about India?

iii. There are many expressions in English that show the importance of the eye:

a. The Evil Eye
b. 'Snake eyes'
c. 'Shifty eyes'
d. Tell-tale eyes'
e. 'Batty-eyes'
f. To look daggers at someone
g. An eye for an eye
h. To keep an eye on someone
i. Eying someone
j. More than meets the eye
k. To have an eye
l. To be in the public eye
m. 'Blue eyes'
n. To catch someone's eye
o. Look a person in the eye

iv. What do they mean and what do they signify?

✓ Why do people wear dark glasses? Any reasons?
✓ Why do women use eye make-up?
✓ Young lovers look deeply into each other's eyes. Why?

IX. **Para language-**

Comment: It is not only words used that convey a message, but also a range of other factors, such as the tone or the voice, the speed and the pitch of what we say.

X. **Turn-taking**

The way turn taking works in a conversation and the role of silence are important. In some cultures it is alright to interrupt but not in other cultures. Do you agree?

XI. Do you think what is called grapevine (also called the 'gossip mill') is also useful in certain respects? Give reasons and illustrate your answer with examples.

XII. In the United States, the knife is held in the right hand and the fork in the left (if you are right-handed). Once the food is cut, the fork is transferred to the right-hand. In most European countries, the fork remains in the left hand. Do you think Indians should follow such table manners?

XIII. **Do you know the origins of the following words-**

1. Etiquette
2. Mister
3. Madam/madam
4. Netiquette

XIV. 'Charity does begin at home and so do good manners.' What does it mean? Explain.

XV. It is said that 'Thank you', 'Sorry' and 'Please' are the magic words in English. Do you agree? Give reasons.

XVI. **Comment on the following habits:**

i. Picking one's nose in public

ii. Chewing and spitting in public places

iii. Swearing or talking uproariously

iv. Lack of respect for elderly people

v. Loud and boisterous laughter.

Can you list five more annoying habits?

XVII. **Directness**

i. Sometimes the language used can be seen as too 'direct'. Some can be sarcastic or polite, depending on the intonation used.

Put the suggested phrases in the order 'most direct' to 'most indirect'.

You want someone to open the window.

1. Would you be so kind as to open the window?
2. It's hot in here.
3. Please open the window.
4. Open the window.
5. Could you possibly open the window?
6. I was wondering if you could open the window.
7. Would you like to open the window?
8. Don't you think it's a little hot in here?

ii. Try to make the following more polite.

1. You must do this by Monday.
2. Your report contained a lot of mistakes.
3. Give me two teas (ordering at a tea-shop)
4. You forget the sales figures.

XVIII. Are non-verbal signals inborn, genetic, or learned cultural signals? Give reasons for your answer.

XIX. The difficulty with lying is that the sub-conscious mind acts automatically and independently of our verbal lie; so, our body language gives us away. Do you agree? *Give reasons for your answer.*

XX. A. Boss to employees – "I want the report".

B. Boss to employees – "I want the report on my table by end of the day today and the employee who submits the report at the earliest will get a treat from my side at the college cafeteria".

Explain the differences in the effectiveness of communication involved in the two pieces given above.

XXI. The arrangement of chairs and tables in a classroom or conference or club shows power equations. Explain with examples.

XXII. 'Soft skills are not soft' – Do you agree? Give reasons. Many other terms like 'Life Skills', 'Social Skills', 'People's Skills', 'Professional Skills' are also used in the field. Which one do you prefer? Give reasons.

XXIII. Some people say: It is not communication skills but communication kills. Comment on this statement.

XXIV. With examples explain how silence communicates.

Case Study for Discussion

At an undergraduate committee meeting, Manisha, the committee chairperson, presented the items on the agenda to the academic council meeting. During the discussions, she noticed that two team members were showing non-verbal signs of disinterest and disapproval. Sanjay was smirking and shaking his head and Saurabh had folded his arms and had leaned back in his chair.

Manisha stopped what she was saying, turned to Sanjay and Saurabh and said, 'I sense you do not support what I'm saying. Do you want me to clarify anything for you?' Sanjay replied, 'I think you would have got proper feedback if you had circulated the agenda items before the meeting started.' Manisha looked at the other group members for a response and found that the rest of the group members concurred with Sanjay. They said that had they known the agenda items beforehand, they would have looked into the points of discussions and framed opinions regarding each point before the meeting. That would have saved time during actual discussion.

By observing the non-verbal cues of two members, Manisha was able to open up communication amongst the committee. This helped in finding anearly resolution to the non-participation of two members. It also led to open discussion among the committee. Besides, it also pointed out the lacunae in her own preparation. Had she ignored the non-verbal cues, she would not have received the valuable feedback of the committee. This in turn would affect her overall decision.

Questions

1. Assume yourself to be the chairperson of the committee. Collect information on the roles and responsibilities of a chairperson to chair a meeting? Write it in detail.
2. What are the non-verbal cues you'll be looking for as the chairperson of a committee-meeting, for its smooth functioning? How would it help you in steering the direction of the meeting?

Unit II – Communicology and Human Language

Communication is a skill that you can learn. It's like riding a bicycle or typing. If you are willing to work at it, you can rapidly improve the quality of every part of your life.

– Brian Tracy

OBJECTIVES

After reading this unit, you will be able to

- ✓ Analyze different models of communication
- ✓ Differentiate between human and animal communication
- ✓ Understand technology-enabled communication

I. Points to Remember

1. The act of communication is as old as living beings, but our perceptions, the ways and means of communication have greatly changed.
2. Communicology, sociolinguistics, pragmatics and technology are concerned with communication studies as well as language and its communicative and functional aspects. Communicology is the study of communication.
3. The various models given below show the ever-changing perceptions regarding the essentials of communication.

   (a) Aristotle's Model

   This is mainly concerned with public speaking. The speaker plays an important role in public speaking. The speaker must prepare his speech and analyze audience needs before he enters the stage. His words should influence the audience and persuade their thoughts towards him.

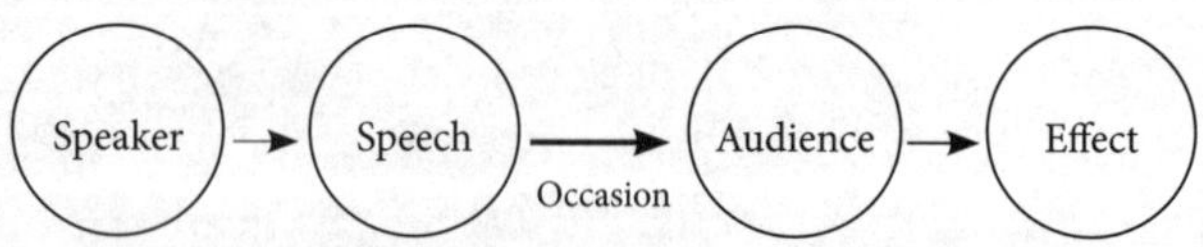

Aristotle's Model of Communication

   Example: Lord Krishna spoke to Arjun to convince him to fight in the Mahabharat war.

   1. Speaker – Lord Krishna
   2. Speech – Krishna persuaded Arjun to fight
   3. Occasion – war of Mahabharat
   4. Audience – Arjun
   5. Effect – Arjun convinced to fight the war

(b) ***Lasswell's Model*** **[Lasswell, 1948)**
who/says what/ in what channel/to whom/ with what effect.
This is described as linear, unidirectional and a one way process.

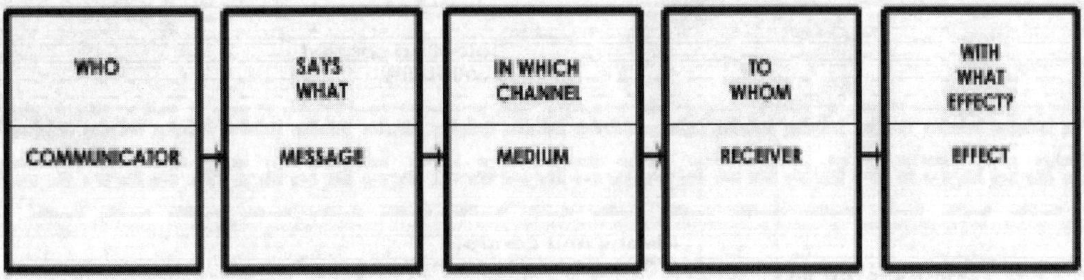

(c) ***Shannon and Weaver Model*** (Shannon and Weaver, 1949)

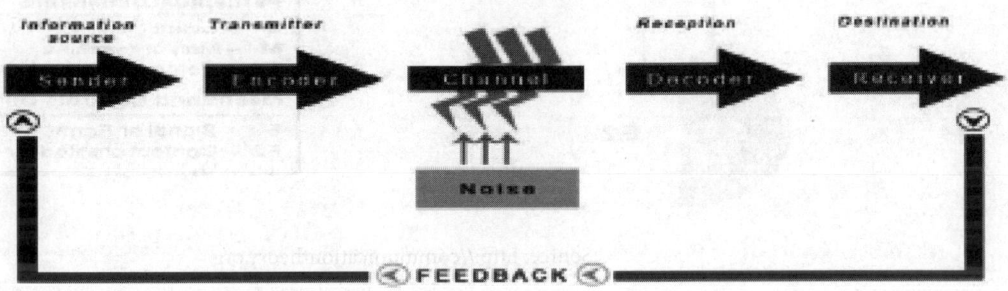

SHANNON-WEAVER'S MODEL OF COMMUNICATION

The Shannon–Weaver model of communication has been called the "mother of all models'

Sender: The originator of message or the information source selects desired message.

Encoder: The transmitter which converts the message into signals.

Decoder: The reception place of the signal which converts signals into message. (A reverse process of encoder.)

Receiver: The destination of the message from sender.

Noise: The messages are transferred from encoder to decoder through channel. During this process, the messages may get distracted due to some form of signal interference and the message received may not be the same as the message sent.

(d) ***Gerbner's Model*** **(Gerbner, 1956)**
Someone/perceives/ an event/ and reacts/ in a situation/ through some means/ to make available materials/ in some form/ and context/conveying content/ of some sequence.

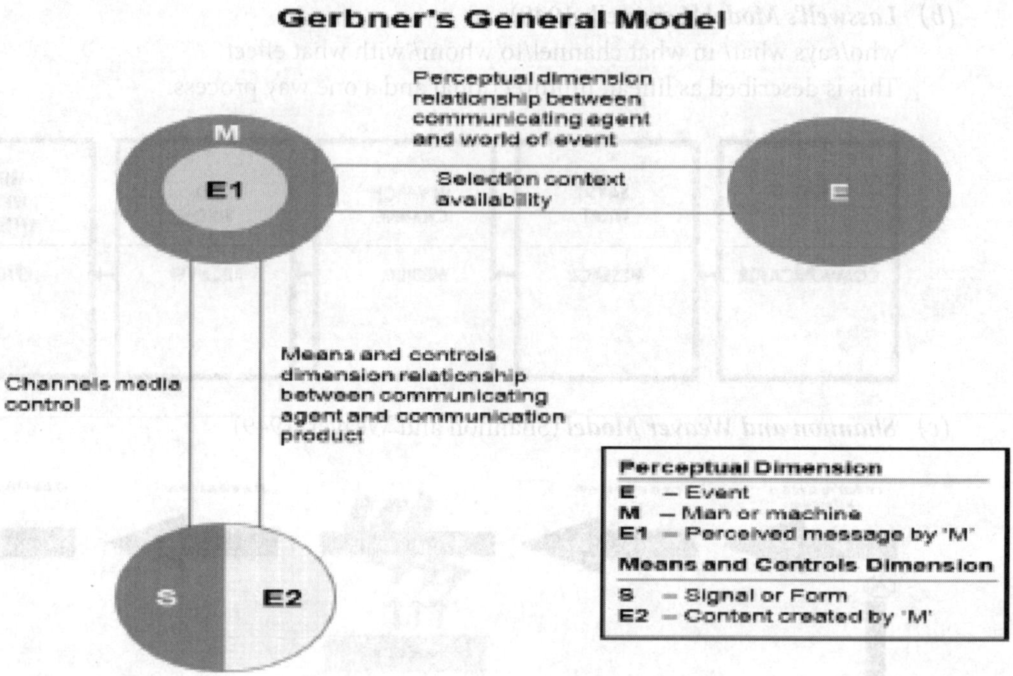

Source: http://communicationtheory.org/

(e) ***Fotheringham's Definition* (1968)**
It is a process involving the selection, production and transmission of signs in such a way as to help a receiver perceive a meaning similar to that in the mind of the communicator.

(f) ***Sociolinguistic Models***
Dell Hymes has formulated the concept of 'communicative competence' (1962, 1970) as an extension of Chomsky's notion of 'linguistic competence'. Communicative competence includes many notions like humour mock-seriousness, role-distance, insolence, respect, etc. which are mostly language-related functions.

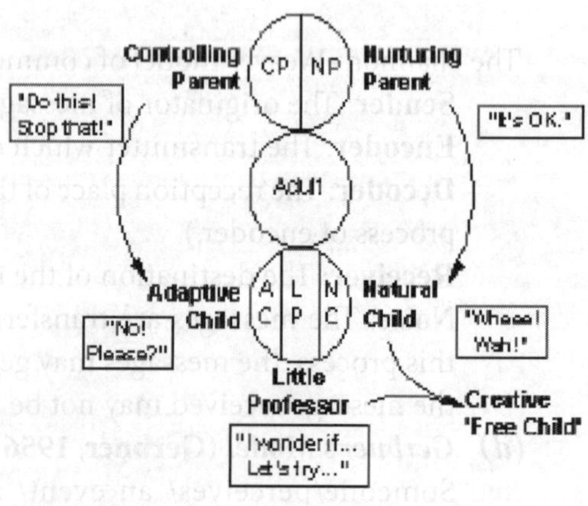

Source: http://changingminds.org/

There are many other models like **Harris' Transactional Analysis**, etc.

The concept of communication is very complex; apart from language, it includes psychological, cultural, social and economical and such other factors. But language is the basis for all other aspects. For example – A diagrammatic representation of Harris' Transactional model is shown.

Different models can be formulated in tabular form as follows:

Model	Comment
Aristotle's Model	Linear model Speaker → Speech → Audience → Effect Represents communication as a static phenomenon
Lasswell's Model	"Who says what in which channel to whom with what effect" Who: The communicator What: The Message Whom: The receiver/Audience Channel: Medium Effect: Response/Feedback
Shannon and Weaver	Shannon and Weaver make a distinction between source and transmitter, and receiver and destination – i.e there are two functions at the transmitting end and two at the receiving end Suggests a definite start and finish to the communication process, which can be at times endless Hence converted into a circular model later by Schramm. Components: Source, Encoder, Message, Channel, Decoder, Receiver, Noise, Feedback
Gerbner	There is a verbal as well as visual formula Someone perceives an event and reacts in a situation through some means to make available materials in some form and context conveying content with some consequence The flexible nature of the model makes it useful. It also allows an emphasis on perception It could explain, for example, the perceptual problems of a witness in court and, in the media; a model which helps us to explore the connection between reality and the stories given on the news

Other Models	Berlo's Model Schramm's Model Helical Model Westley and MacLean's Model Jackson's Model Harris' Transactional Analysis

II. Animal Communication and Human Language

Animals, birds and insects too make noises to communicate with the other members of their group. Human beings also make noises (and or visual marks) to communicate with other human beings. There are however, significant differences between animal communication (also called zoo semiotics) and human languages (also called anthroposemiotics).

(a) **Duality of Patterning**:
Human language displays levels of patterning: sounds, words, phrases, sentences, etc. A stretch of speech in any human language can be analyzed into smaller units and a large number of combinations and meanings can be expressed by means of a limited number of units. Example: English has 44 units (24 consonants + 20 vowels) but unlimited combinations (subject to certain restrictions) are made possible. Similarly, words can be combined in different ways: The mountain kisses the sky; the sky kisses the mountains. (Different combinations and different meanings).
Animal communication consists of meaningful cries that cannot be analyzed into smaller units and combinations are not possible.

(b) **Creativity and recursiveness**:
Since various combinations are possible, human language allows creativity in form as well as meaning. As a result, there is no limit to the length of a sentence and no limit to the number of the sentences.
Example: This is the cow with crumpled horns that tossed the dog that worried the cat that chased the rat (can go on and on). This property of repetition is called recursiveness. Human language is open-ended. This is not possible in animal communication.

(c) **Arbitrariness**:
There is no connection in human language between a sound and the object or emotions.
Example: The object 'dog' is known as 'dog' in English, 'Kukka' in Telugu, 'Kutta' in Hindi, 'Hund' in German, 'Paroo' in Spanish, 'Chren' in French. Human language is arbitrary; it is a system of conventional symbols. There is no one-to-one correspondence in human language; one word may have multiple meanings.
(Example: Bark). Animal communication is not arbitrary.

(d) **Context-free**
Animal communication is context bound and human language is context free. Human beings also can tell lies because human language is context free. As a result, literary creations are

possible only in human language. Animals can communicate only if there is a stimulus; humans can do it without a stimulus. Animal communication has no literature. Donkeys have no Shakespeare or Kalidasa among them!

(e) **Redundancy**

There is a lot of redundancy in human language.

Example: The yes-no type of question in English has two markers: the inversion of the subject and verb and a question mark in writing/a rising tone at the end in speech: Is she still there?

As a result human communication can be vague and ambiguous.

Example: Flying planes can be dangerous.

(f) **Culture-preserving and culture-transmitting:**

'Thanks to language, Man became Man' – Rene Descartes.

Philosophy and other abstract forms are possible only in human language and they are transmitted from generation to generation.

(g) **Dynamism**

Human language keeps changing; each generation modifies it according to their needs and demands.

(h) **Illogicality**

Since language is a human phenomenon, it is often illogical; since it is context-free and arbitrary, it defies logic in the formal sense.

Example: In Hindi 'darhi' (i.e. beard) is feminine but 'moti' (i.e. pearl) is masculine. Why? In English, the plural of 'boy' is 'boys' but the plural of 'child' is 'children'. Why? No logic.

(i) **Brain Structure**

Human brain is different from that of animals. Human brain has an innate capacity for learning language creatively.

III. Machine communication (i.e. between two machines) is different from human communication. It does not have the vagaries of human language.

Modern machine-to-machine communication (M2M) has expanded from one-to-one exchange to a system of networks. Wireless technology is rapidly changing many areas like business, production, utility services, advertisements, transport, home sciences, etc.

IV. In between, there is technology-enabled communication which is becoming common now: Mobile phones, skypes, video conferences, etc.

V. Since human language is the predominant means of communication, it is studied by linguists, neuro-linguists and communicologists. Language is what differentiates humans from all other species. It is language that moulds all life skills of 'head, heart and hand'. Language skills are the basis for all soft skills.

VI. The term 'soft skills', a coinage of the computer age, is a sociological term that refers to the cluster of personality traits, social graces, personal habits and attitudes, professional skills, analytical, critical and creative thinking, behaviour, inter-personal and smart skills, etc.

Soft skills are related to a person's EQ (Emotional Intelligence Quotient) as opposed to the hard skills (part of one's IQ) ; they complement each other. 'It is 'people skills' or social skills because soft skills enhance an individual's interactions with others that understanding oneself and empathizing with others, showing trust, respect, etc. Soft Skills are difficult to measure since they are not visible.

Some others think that soft skills are the easier ones (like the soft option) when compared to the hard skills or mechanical skills required to design and construct a computer or machine.

All these are products of language because without language no human activity is possible; language is woven with every aspect of human behaviour and activity. According to some post-modern theories, there is nothing outside of language. In the present day context, English has become a global phenomenon; so the focus is on the English language.

Remember the following points:

According to communication theory, there are seven traditions in the communication field. These are as follows:

- **The Socio-Psychological tradition**: It epitomizes the scientific and objective perspective of the process of communication.
- **The Cybernetic Tradition**: It examines the role of feedback in completing the process of communication. The word 'cybernetics' was coined by MIT scientist Norbert Wiener and describes the field of artificial intelligence.
- **The Semiotic Tradition**: Semiotics is the study of signs. It sees communication as the process of sharing meaning through signs.
- **The Rhetorical Tradition**: Based on Aristotle's rhetoric, this tradition sees communication as an artful public address in which available means of persuasion like logos, pathos and ethos are employed.
- **The Phenomenological Tradition:** It views communication as the experience of a person of self and others on a day-to-day basis. It lays great emphasis on subjective experience.
- **The Critical Tradition:** Originating from Germany, this tradition perceives communication as a challenge to unjust discourse. The leading proponents of this form of communication were a group of German scholars known as the 'Frankfurt School'.
- **The Socio-Cultural Tradition:** This tradition presupposes that as people talk, they create culture. In other words communication is seen as a process of creation and enactment of social reality.

(*Source: A First Look at Communication Theory* by Em Griffin)

All the theories of communication fall within one of the seven communication traditions. The theories are further grouped under broad categories of Interpersonal Communication, Group and Public Communication, Mass Communication, Gender and Cultural Communication. In a professional set up, as an engineer, manager or leader, one is engaged in communication that operates at various levels; therefore, it is important to understand the dynamics of

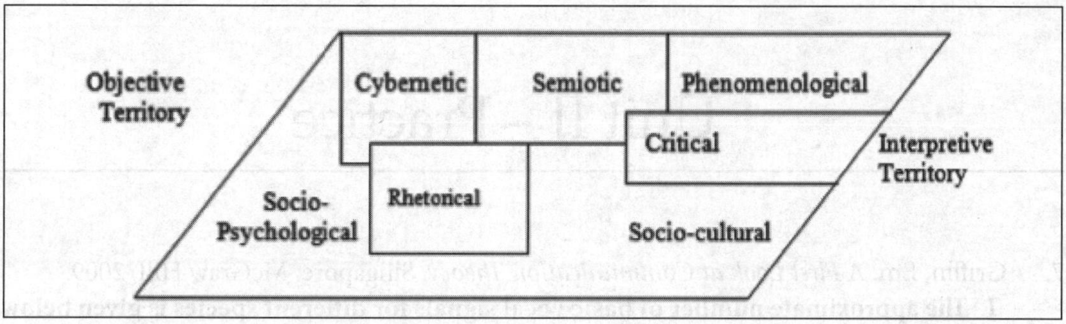

A survey map of Traditions in the field of Communication Theory (Adapted from A First Look at Communication Theory by Em Griffin)

communication appropriate to that level. Knowledge of communication theory and the traditions therein leads to a broader understanding of the communication process and may benefit by drawing from the basic tenets that define it.

Online Resources

1. http://catalogue.pearsoned.co.uk/assets/hip/gb/hip_gb_pearsonhighered/samplechapter/0205930662.pdf
2. http://www.iacact.com/?q=models
3. http://davis.foulger.info/research/unifiedModelOfCommunication.htm
4. http://www.azimuthacademy.com/Azimuth_Soft_skill_courses.asp
5. http://communicationtheory.org/category/cultural-communication/
6. http://www.niit.com/solution/soft-skill-training

Select Bibliography

1. Bhatnagar, Nitin and Mamta Bhatnagar. *Effective Communication and Soft Skills*. New Delhi: Pearson, 2012
2. Seely, John. *Oxford Guide to Effective Writing and Speaking*. London: OUP, 2013
3. Shannon, C. E. A. "*Mathematical Theory of Communication*". *Bell System Technical Journal*, vol. 27, pp. 379–423 and 623–656, July and October, 1948.
4. Adler, R. B., Rosenfeld, L. B., and Towne, N. *Interplay: The Process of Interpersonal Communication.* New York: Harcourt Brace, 1996.
5. Hauser, Marc D. *The Evolution of Communication*. Cambridge: MIT Press, 1996.
6. Anderson, Stephen R. *Doctor Dolittle's Delusion: Animals and the Uniqueness of Human Language.* New Haven: Yale University Press, 2004.

Unit II – Practice

7. Griffin, Em. *A First Look at Communication Theory*. Singapore: McGraw Hill, 2009.

I The approximate number of basic vocal signals for different species is given below:

Species	Number of basic vocal signals
Chickens	20
Cows	8
Foxes	36
Pigs	23
Dogs	10
Dolphins	7–19
Monkeys and apes	10–37
Human beings (For various human languages)	11–80

On the basis of the number of signals alone, can we say that the monkeys that use 37 units are more sophisticated in communication than that of human beings who use a language that have about 30 units? If not, why, not?

II. If smell, touch, taste, etc. are included as part of communication, do you think animals have an advantage over human beings? Illustrate your answer.

III. A mahout, who has trained elephants for a number of years, says that elephants understand only about 40 commands and these commands have not changed in the last 40 years. What does it show?

IV. Animals cannot tell lies and they have no literature. Are the two related? Explain your answer.

V. In what sense 'creativity' is one of the important?

VI. Find out how the following creatures communicate: (i) bees, (ii) ants, (iii) dogs.

VII. Psychologists think that the structure of an ape's vocal throat prevents reproduction of many phonetic elements found in human speech but it can understand and even creatively use language. Comment.

VIII. Give examples of arbitrariness in human language.

IX. Why is human illogical in some respects? If a language is totally logical, what will be the consequence? Explain.

X. Give examples of illogicalities in English spelling, stress, gender, number and meaning.

XI. Without language, what is called 'ego' or 'I' is not possible. Do you agree? Give reasons.

XII. Language is the basis of consciousness. Comment.

XIII. All philosophy, political theories, economic theories, and even what are called soft skills, life skills, smart skills, etc. are based on language because there is nothing beyond language. Explain.

XIV. In English, generally, 'a ship' and 'peace' are feminine but 'time' and 'death' are masculine. What should be the gender of a computer? Speculate and give reasons for your answer. Does it depend on one's perception?

XV. There are many other sign systems like Calculus or Algebra [i.e. $(a+b)^2 = a^2 + b^2 + 2ab$]. Can they be used for human communication? If not, why not?

XVI. The following conversation is from Lewis Carroll's

Then you should say what you mean', the March Hare went on

'I do', Alice hastily replied;

'at least –at least I mean what I say-

that's the same thing, you know';

'Not the same thing a bit', said the Halter.

Can you explain the implications in the conversation?

XVII. Logicians see advantage in abandoning ordinary language in favour of artificial mathematical notations. Do you support them? Give reasons for your answer.

XVIII. 'Knowledge of language' and 'knowledge of real world' are two different things; it is like the rules of a language and the rules of a game. Explain with examples.

XIX. All natural languages are vague and slippery. For example, we cannot define a simple word like 'a city' or 'a man'. Try to define them in absolute terms.

XX. It is the vagueness principle that makes language and life interesting. Discuss.

XXI. Which of the following do you prefer and in what context?

a. Face to face communication
b. M2M communication
c. M enabled communication (Written)
d. M enabled communication (Spoken)
e. Written communication
f. Silence

XXII. Try to find the ambiguities in the following sentences:

i. The committee's appointment is disappointing.
ii. She asked me to leave at 7 o' clock.
iii. Beware of striking workmen.
iv. Would you like to try on that dress in the window?
v. She went to her village to sell the land along with her husband.
vi. I like sweets better than my wife.
vii. We are not teaching machines.

Can you give five more on your own?

XXIII. The word 'soft' has several meanings:

i. Soft: (opposite of hard) a soft pillow
ii. Soft: smooth; as soft as velvet
iii. Soft: without any damage; soft landing
iv. Soft: gentle; a soft voice, a soft breeze
v. Soft: easy; a soft job, a soft option
vi. Soft: sympathetic; a soft spot for her
vii. Soft: non-alcoholic; a soft drink

In what sense do you think, the word 'soft' is used in 'soft skills'?

XXIV. Deaf or dumb persons or persons with brain problems cannot develop soft skills like other normal human beings. Do you agree? Give reasons for your answer.

XXV. Do you think that 'language skills' is to be considered a part of soft skills? Why do we say 'communication skills' and 'soft skills'? Explain.

XXVI. Nowadays, everything (degrees, soft skills, communication skill, etc.) is directed towards money making and corporate employment. Do you think this is the right thing to do? Give reasons for your answer.

XXVII. Communication skills and soft skills are needed for all in a society. Explain and illustrate.

XXVIII. The older generation was not taught communication skills and soft skills in a formal way. Is there any need to teach these skills in the present day context? Give reasons.

XXIX. Economic growth without personal growth is a recipe for disaster. Discuss with reference to the global as well as the Indian context.

XXX. 'Life skills' may be a better term to refer to the communication skills as well as 'soft skills'. Do you agree? Give reasons for your answer.

Case Study for Discussion

People at work are engaged in the process of communication most of the times. They may be sending emails, speaking to someone on the phone or interacting with colleagues face to face. Effective communication helps channelize efforts towards achieving goals in a pre determined time frame.

Techno-sys, is a technical and software solution provider with its head office in Bangalore, India. Its members are spread around the globe in major cities like New York, London, Beijing and Tokyo. To cater to the wide range of interests of its national and international members, it focuses on good communication among its members.

This case study looks at the communication activities of Techno-sys. It shows how a range of methods are adopted by its members to deal with the many issues they face on a day-to-day basis within their workplaces, in the regional and local branches. Each branch has a branch manager who is elected by his or her colleagues. These managers need the information and skills of others to help them perform to the best of their ability.

In order to communicate clearly, people working within Techno-sys try to reduce all the barriers or 'noise'. A transmitter puts data into a form (encoding) which the receiver can understand, such as a textual or visual point. The medium chosen could be a letter, an e-mail or a website. The message is decoded through a process of decoding by the receiver.

As a message flows from the sender to receiver, it is distorted by interruptions or noise and therefore the receiver doesn't get the original message. The following types of barriers may occur:

1. If a message is difficult to understand because it uses badly chosen or illegible language.
2. If there is a cultural difference between the sender and the receiver.
3. If the sender is inept in technical skills or computer skills.

A policy or planning carried out by its employees involves internal as well as external communication. Internal communication takes the form of meeting – minutes, memos, face to face communication and oral presentations.

External communication makes use of letters, reports and proposals. Emails and telephonic communication could be used both internally and externally.

All communication that takes place through well known channels is formal communication. All policy matters are a form of formal communication and are discussed at the higher levels.

All routine matters take the form of informal communication. This type of communication lets people express their ideas and plans and take initiative in their hands. These channels take care of day-to-day problems and concerns of employees.

Questions

1. Amit Mahajan, a new employee of Techno-sys, has strong technical skills but lacks in good English language skills. He is not very confident in speaking English and makes errors while drafting a formal document. According to you, how should he improve his communication skills?
2. The innovation division of Techno-sys is working to develop a new software targeting the health sector. To make it foolproof, it needs inputs from all the other divisions of the company. What measures should it adopt to get this feedback and to launch the product efficiently into the market?
3. To create a sense of oneness and unity among its employees and for the welfare of public at large, what are the other approaches that the company can adopt?

Unit III – Barriers to Communication

The simple biggest problem in communication is the illusion that it has taken place

– George Bernard Shaw

OBJECTIVES:

After reading this unit, you will be able to

- ✓ Identify different types of barriers to communication
- ✓ Analyze contextual communication
- ✓ Understand the role of culture in communication

I. Points to Remember

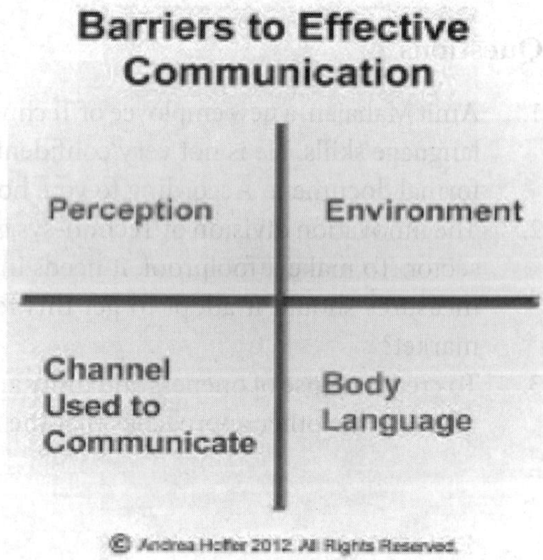

1. **The generation gap**: The generation gap keeps changing due to several factors like technology, globalization, changing mind-set and attitudes. This affects communication between the old and the new, the parents and the children, the teacher and the taught etc. The word 'generation' is difficult to define – number of years or attitudes? So, the 'gap' too is difficult to describe. (See also Appendix II)
2. **Differences in perception**: Even within one generation, perception may differ. Example: Men and women look at life in general differently and there is gender gap in communication. (See also Appendix II)
3. **Differences in the knowledge levels of a given area:** One may be better informed than the other. Example: A computer geek and a computer illiterate.
4. **Stereotyping and jumping to conclusions, assumptions and pre conceptions**: The basis for stereotyping is prejudices, bias and other psychological factors. Example: All god-men are honest; a thief cannot be a gentleman.
5. **Strong emotions**: Example: Love is blind; influence of alcohol: anger
6. **Self-centeredness**: Preoccupied with oneself and one's affairs. Example: I am always correct-results in selective hearing.

7. **Lack of clarity of purpose and lack of presentation skills**: No clarity regarding the aims and objectives of communication in general, and the purpose for that particular instance. Moreover, inability to present the facts properly and logically. To be a good speaker, one also needs to be a good listener.
8. **Plain laziness**: Reluctance to write or poor handwriting or poor listening skills or inattention or even short span of attention.
9. **Lack of Communicative Competence in the language:**
   - inefficiency in the use of verbal and nonverbal use of the language.
   - the wrong choice of channel and mode.
   - the wrong choice of setting and place.
   - lack of language competence (i.e. communication skills).
   - communication over-load.
   - Inability to avoid linguistic ambiguity.
10. **Lack of common code/language**: The sender and receiver must-share the same language/dialect/accent/register/style/topic.
11. **Techology & Communication gap**: There is a communication gap between the technology literate and technology illiterate.
12. **Socio-cultural differences:** Lack of understanding of the concepts of time, space, body language etc.
13. Inability to co-ordinate and synchronize all the factors mentioned above.
14. **Interference**: noise and other interruptions like traffic, etc.

Barriers to Communication

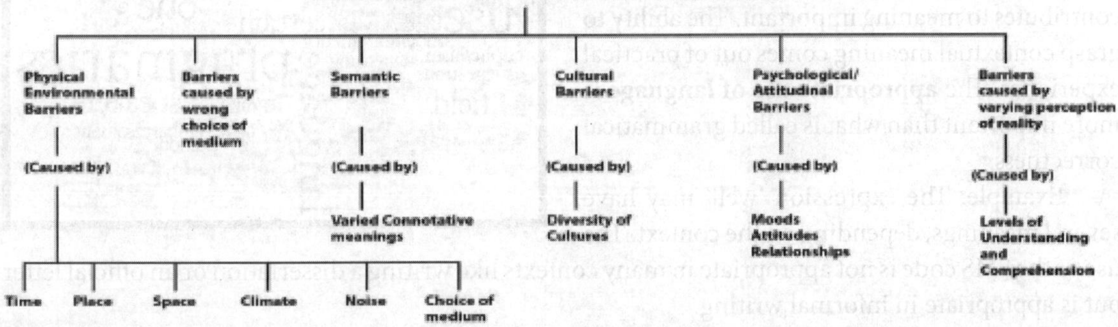

Here are some *do's* and *don'ts* for effective communication:

Do's

- ✓ see others' perspective;
- ✓ select the right channel, mode and setting;
- ✓ make an effort to understand the receiver/audience;

- ✓ cultivate communication skills;
- ✓ allow scope for misunderstanding;
- ✓ mind your tone;
- ✓ plan your communication;
- ✓ learn to listen before you speak;
- ✓ remember that culture is communication;
- ✓ remember that silence also communicates.

(A policeman giving directions has a clear mental image of them, but the man receiving them has a very confused image.)

Source: http://imaginghelp.com/

Don'ts

- ✓ don't become emotional or self-centered;
- ✓ don't stereotype
- ✓ don't take for granted that what you say will be understood;

Inspite of all the barriers, people do communicate and transact because transactional communication is based on practical considerations.

II. Pragmatics

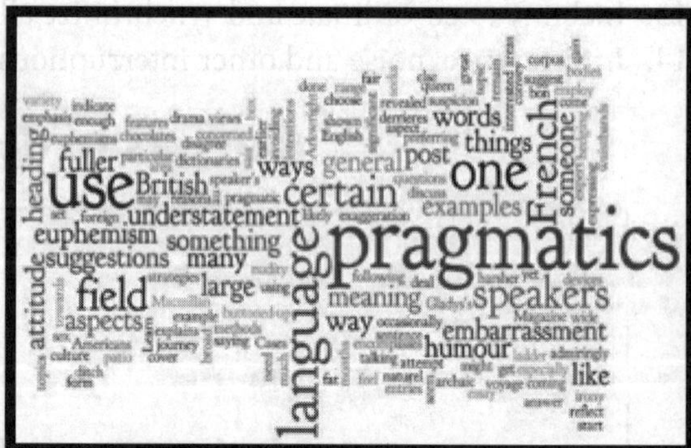

Contextual meaning is very important. Pragmatics studies the ways in which context contributes to meaning important. The ability to grasp contextual meaning comes out of practical experience. The **appropriate use of language** is more important than what is called grammatical correctness.

Example: The expression 'well' may have several meanings, depending on the context. The use of the SMS code is not appropriate in many contexts like writing a dissertation or an official letter but is appropriate in informal writing.

Online Resources

1. https://sielearning.tafensw.edu.au/
2. http://education-portal.com/academy/lesson/barriers-to-effective-communication-definition-examples.html#lesson
3. http://www.yourarticlelibrary.com/business-communication/4-different-types-of-barriers-to-effective-communication
4. http://www.teachit.co.uk/armoore/lang/pragmatics.htm

5. http://colelearning.net/who/module3/page1.html
6. http://2012books.lardbucket.org/attribution.html?utm_source=inline

Select Bibliography

1. Hogan, Kevin, and Ron Stubbs. *Can't Get Through: Eight Barriers to Communication*. Gretna:Pelican, 2003
2. Fielding, Michael. *Effective Communication in Organisations*. Capetown: Juta and Company Ltd, 2005
3. Monipally, Mathukutty M. *Business Communication Strategies,* New Delhi: Tata McGraw Hill, 200.
4. Wood, J. T. *Interpersonal Communication: Everyday Encounters*. Boston:Wadsworth, 2002.
5. Bauer, Talya, andBerrin Erdogan. *An Introduction to Organizational Behavior. Unnamed publisher,* Book Archive, Creative Commons licensed, *2012*

Unit III – Practice

I. Answer the following questions:

1. What, according to you, is the number of years that can be considered to describe the 'generation gap'? Give reasons from your experience.
2. Like the generation gap, is there a 'gender gap'? Explain.
3. Do women and men communicate differently? How? Can you give some examples?
4. Comment on the following stereotypes:
   a. Madarasis are hardworking and clever.
   b. Gujaraties know how to make money.
   c. Bengalies are emotional.
   d. Malayalis are clannish.
   e. Punjabis are not very intelligent.
   f. Westerners are promiscuous.
   g. Boys are good at maths and girls are good at humanities.

   Give more such stereotypes from your experience.
5. Grandfathers generally think that mobile phones are a menace and they should be banned. Do you agree? Give reasons for your answer.
6. Parents think that 'Facebook' is the greatest enemy of education. Comment.
7. In the West, once the time for an action or eventis scheduled, it has to be used as designated. In the Middle East it is 'Insha Allah' (i.e. Allah willing, it will happen) What is the Indian perception of time? Give examples.
8. 'Time is money'. What about time wasted?
9. The street naming and numbering system in India can be a puzzle for any American, who is used to intersections and signs. What about your experience?
10. Have you experienced 'culture shock'? Describe at least one such experience.
11. Do Indians queue up wherever services are offered? Why are they always keen on breaking the line?
12. 'Special changes give a tone to communication, accent it, and at times even override the spoken word':-Edward Hall in 'The Silent Language'. Explain and elaborate.
13. 'Culture is communication'. Not only among various cultures, but also within a given culture, there are sub-cultures. Even between a husband and wife there can be cultural differences. Give your opinion.
14. The arrangement of furniture in classrooms and offices communicates the hierarchy. Explain.

15. The normal conversational distance between people illustrates their relationship. If the distance is crossed, misunderstandings take place. Do you agree? Illustrate your answer.
16. When to shake hands and when to hug is very important. What is your experience? Can you give examples when misunderstandings happen?
17. Your friend says, 'I'll be back in a little while'. What may be 'a little while'?
18. The Hindi word 'Kal' is not very specific. What does it indicate? Illustrate your answer.

II. Read the texts given below and answer the questions.

- Conversation between an American tourist and an American Customs Officer:
  Officer: What's your occupation? (without raising his head)
  Tourist: None.
  Officer: Nun! (Looks at her).
  What went wrong? Explain.
- At home, when I have to consider only my wife sitting within six feet of me at breakfast. I take so little pains with my speech that very often instead of giving me the expected answer, she says, 'Don't mumble; and don't turn your head away when you speak. I can't hear a word you are saying!' And she also is a little careless. Sometimes I have to say 'what' two or three times during our meal; and she suspects me of growing deafer and deafer.

  – G.B. Shaw.

  What does the passage given above tell you about the nature of communication.
- What does the passages given below illustrate? Explain
  Pandit Nehru went to Madras (Chennai) during the anti-Hindi agitation and addressed a public meeting, attended by thousands of people.He said, 'All this talk about imposing Hindi on Tamilians is nonsense.The next day, the newspapers in Tamil Nadu carried the following headline: 'Nehru says Tamilians have no sense.'Is it just funny or does it indicate a barrier in communication? How?
- A senior American linguist came to India and gave a speech on the linguistic theory of Noam Chomsky. An Indian professor argued that he was wrong.
  The American said, 'It's all bullshit.'
  The next day the local papers flashed:
  American professor insults Indian professors.
  Do you agree? If so why? If not why?

III. Communication mishaps. Re-word to make the intended meaning clear.

1. Outside a shop a notice says:
   We exchange anything – Washing machines, TVs, Cookers, etc.
   Please bring your wife/husband along and get a wonderful bargain.
2. In an office
   After the tea-break, staff should empty the tea-pot and stand upside down on the draining board.

3. In an office
   Toilet out of order. Please use floor below.
4. Before marriage you are unfinished. After marriage you are finished.
5. In an essay on 'Indian Women'
   Indian women eat their husbands before they eat themselves.
6. In China, near a swimming pool -
   Fall into the water carefully.

IV. Say how the following Indian values and practices are perceived by Westerners:

1. Throwing garbage in public
2. Urinating on the roadside
3. Cattle on the road
4. Jumping the red signal and keep blowing the horn
5. Strong group affiliation (i.e. region, caste, etc.)
6. Respect for age and seniority
7. Doing personal favours to officials and politicians
8. Absence of punctuality or Indian punctuality
9. Lack of discipline in public life
10. Body odours VIP culture
11. Feudal mentality
12. Arranged marriages
13. Yoga and meditation
14. Tradition

V. Say how the Western values are perceived by Indians

1. Individuality and freedom
2. Self-reliance
3. Equality
4. Efficiency and precision
5. Time
6. Directions
7. Openness
8. Dating
9. Importance attached to privacy
10. Social discipline and order
11. Standing in queue

VI. Look at the following expressions, given in isolation without a context. Imagine at least four or five contexts in which each one can give a different meaning.

1. Not now, darling.
2. Well, well…
3. Shut the door.
4. I declare you husband and wife.
5. How funny.

VII. Comment on the following statements:

1. The message is the medium.
2. The medium is the message.
3. The medium is the massage.
4. The medium massages the massage.
5. The medium mess ages the mass age.

Case-Study for Discussion

It is observed that sometimes it is difficult for people to effectively communicate-even among those who speak the same language. Perceptual, psychological and attitudinal differences can create challenges in successful communication. A case in point might be the stereotypical communication challenges faced between younger and older generation, husbands and wives, or between the employers and the employed.

In the capacity of the Dean, Student Affairs, Arjun worked closely with the Director and one of his IT administrators, a high level computer technician. This technician was responsible for all the IT related issues faced by the students, faculty and staff of the institute which in itself was quite a daunting task. The technician had the ability to accomplish his IT related work successfully, but he was inefficient at communicating student support issues. Lack of skills in these two areas greatly affected his overall performance as an IT administrator and even put his employment in question.

One day the director, the technician and the dean sat down together to see what could be done to solve the communication issues involved in student-support. The director spelt out very clearly his and other stakeholders' expectations to the technician. He asked very general questions on the procedures being followed on the stated issues to which the technician gave reasonable answers. His concurrence on the issue showed that he understood the gravity of the situation and indicated that he would do his best to improve the situation. After the discussions, the dean asked the technician what his strategy would be in handling the student issues in future, to which the technician just gazed at him. He still had no idea how he would tackle the communication of student-support issues and the problem of communicating student related issues to the authorities. This came as a surprise to the dean as well as the director because they had clearly explained to him his job responsibility and ways to carry it out. They had even got concurrence from the technician to that effect. In spite of that, he was unable to define his game-plan for future. This was an example of an unsuccessful communication event.

The dean then took it upon himself to resolve this problem. He asked the technician to prepare a flow chart of his work from morning to evening and asked him to elaborate on the issues he handles in a day. He was asked to show a copy of his correspondence with students to see what he was writing. This was then analyzed for content and form; i.e., the kind of words and metaphors he was using in a particular context. The dean then pointed out his mistakes and underscored the expectations. The technician was then asked to create measures of success in relation to the defined parameters. With a clear and defined picture of work in his mind now, he was able to chart out his strategy for future. Over a period of time, evidence indicated that the technician had indeed learned some new communication skills which helped him in his job and his relations with the student body also improved considerably.

Afterwards, the director called another debriefing meeting. He and the Dean discussed different communication and management styles. They wondered how sometimes messages, very clearly worded and clearly sent, are not the messages received or understood. They vowed to check for understanding more often and to eliminate breakdown of communication, if any. It was felt that it is the responsibility of the person delivering a message that the message received is the same as the message intended. In the case of the technician, the director needed to reframe his message so that it made sense to the technician, ask him to summarize it, and then review his next steps. This would complete the cycle of communication without any breakdown and at the end of it, both would be at the same point of understanding. There was a lesson in it for the Director. He realized that same communication patterns can't be applied to all people in all situations. The pattern needs to be changed from person to person and from situation to situation to make it meaningful.

Questions

1. As an observer to the stated incident, who would you blame for the breakdown of communication?
2. According to you, what went wrong? Why was the technician not able to provide satisfactory answers to the Director's questions?
3. What more could have been done by the Dean to help the technician?
4. If you were in the technician's place, what measures would you adopt to improve your communication skills?

Unit IV – Communication and Language Skills

The most important thing in communication is to hear what isn't being said.

– **Peter F. Drucker**, American business author

OBJECTIVES

After reading this unit, you will be able to

- ✓ Learn the basic skills of reading, writing, listening and speaking
- ✓ Understand the fundamentals of active listening
- ✓ Interpret different forms and styles of speaking
- ✓ Develop reading skills for comprehension
- ✓ Learn the components of writing

❖ Communicating through language means conveying or sharing a thought or an idea, an emotion, a fact or a piece of information/knowledge or experience. Learning a language means learning how to communicate through the medium of language.

❖ There are four basic skills or abilities that constitute the mastery of a language. They are:

i. Listening	iii. Speaking
ii. Reading	iv. Writing

All the four skills should be acquired with proper ***understanding*** and ***thinking***.

Study the diagram given below:

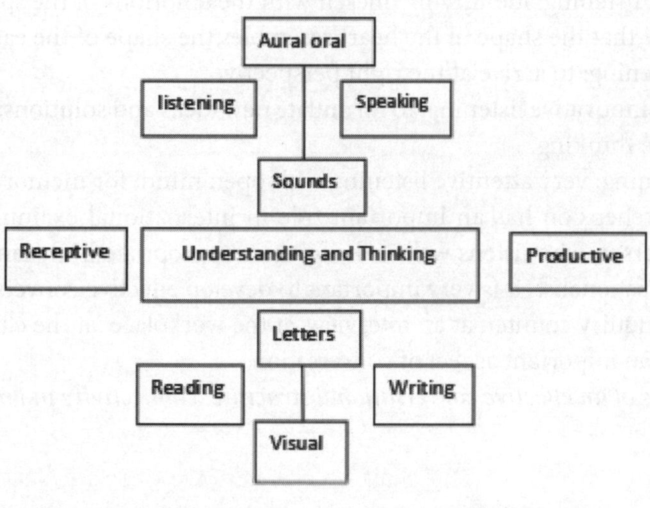

❖ The four skills go in pairs. Without listening, no speaking is possible (that's why the deaf are also dumb) ; without reading, no writing is possible.
  - ✓ In order to speak, one has to listen.
  - ✓ In order to write, one has to read.

"We have two ears, but only one tongue; so listen to others more and speak less."

Listening and speaking come to all human beings (with a well-formed brain) without any effort; they are nature's gift.

Reading and writing are to be learnt; they won't come naturally.

I. Listening

Hearing is primarily a physical act that depends on the ears. If there is a physical disability in hearing, one can get a **hearing**-aid.

But there is no **listening**-aid! Listening is a conscious activity that involves a conscious involvement of the listener, an acknowledgement of understanding and proper response.

➢ **We listen for various purposes such as:**
- ✓ For understanding the content. (maybe for the sake of knowledge, or information, etc.)
- ✓ For taking proper decisions and carrying out transactions
- ✓ For solving problems – one's own/others/institutions/……
- ✓ For pleasure (like listening to music)

➢ **Most people prefer to hear rather than listen and understand**
- ✓ The process of listening involves five stages: receiving, understanding, evaluating, remembering, and responding.
- ✓ Active listening is a communication technique that requires the listeners to provide feedback on what they hear.
- ✓ Three main degrees of active listening are repeating, paraphrasing, and reflecting.

➢ **Some types of listening**:
- ✓ Empathetic listening: identifying oneself with the emotions of the speakers. (Remember that the shape of the heart resembles the shape of the ear).
- ✓ Critical listening: to arrive at the right perspective.
- ✓ Creative or innovative listening: to formulate new ideas and solutions; this involves critical and creative thinking.
- ✓ Active listening: very attentive listening with open mind; for memory and recall.

Listening comprehension has an important role in international examinations and business communication. A person who listens well and engineers appropriate body language in response is seen as a good conversationalist. It is very important to develop effective conversational skills, maybe on the phone, at an enquiry counter, at an interview, at the workplace, at the club, at home, in social meetings; listening is an important aspect of conversation.

Essential features of an effective conversational structure: connectivity in form and content.

a) **Adjacency Pairs:**
It is the sequence of two related pairs by two speakers, the second utterance being an appropriate response to the first or a question provides an answer. This is mostly found in conversations – a greeting of one is returned by the other; a question elicits an answer; a request is followed by compliance or rejection, etc.
Example: A greeting is returned by the other:
A: Good Morning. How are you?
B: Good Morning. Fine, thank you. How are you?
Or
A: How do you do? B: How do you do?

b) **Coherence** refers to the content aspect; it allows ideas to flow smoothly and clearly and makes the text or conversation comprehensible.
Example: 1) A: I went to a movie.
B: But I didn't. I had some other work.
2) A: Did you take the 2o' clock train?
B: I met Gopal on the way.
In the first one there is coherence but in the second one there is no coherence.

c) **Cohesion** refers to the stylistic aspects like smooth transition. It is the glue that holds pieces together; it is grammatical as well as lexical.
Example:
- The earth is round.
- It is a well-known fact.

Conjunctions, pronouns and sentence linkers add to proper cohesion.

d) **Politeness:** Courtesy
Example:
A: Can I help you?
B: No, thanks.
Effective conversation must have a balance between thought and language, sincerity in intention; it avoids all irrelevance.

II. Speaking: The Gift of the Gab

1. Speech abounds in today's world: mobile phones, land lines, the electronic media (talk shows, discussions, walk the talk, skype, video conferences, etc.)
2. The speaking style must be appropriate to the occasion. The style of speaking depends on the following:-
   - The relationship you have with the persons you are talking to (friends, strangers, persons in authority, etc.)
   - The situation you are in (party, official setting, business setting, etc.)
   - The mood of the persons you are talking to (angry, happy, nervous, upset, etc.)
   - What you are talking about (request, complaint, transaction, etc.)

The styles can be:
- **tentative** (If you are talking to a superior, you have to be polite even if you disagree; you can say: I'm not sure….)
- **direct style** (e.g. – you are mistaken)
- **polite style** (e.g. – I'm sorry. But I feel there is a mistake somewhere)
- **formal style** that maintains a social distance (e.g. – official meetings, business meetings, etc.)
- **informal style** usually between friends (e.g. – Cut it out, will you?)
- **strong language or blunt style** (e.g. – I know you are a liar. You can't fool me!)

3. Forms of public speaking
   - Short talks, presentations
   - Briefings, instructions
   - Discussions; group discussions
   - Debates
   - Public meetings
   - Symposiums and seminars
4. Moderate your speed of speaking
5. Use your body language to make others feel at ease.

III. Reading

1. Reading offers inputs to language production, particularly speaking and writing.
2. Reading aloud will be useful in polishing up pronunciation and speech.
3. Styles of reading:
   - ❖ **Scanning** is done for a specified part of a text to find a particular word or a particular detail. For example, you can scan the classified columns of a newspaper to locate a particular advertisement.
   - ❖ **Skimming** is done at a greater speed without reading each sentence. For example, in finding a title for a passage, we skim the text to get the main idea.
   - ❖ **Intensive reading** is done to studya text in great detail. Text books are read in detail.
   - ❖ **Extensive reading** is free reading for pleasure.
   - ❖ **Supplementary reading** is extra reading (e.g.-non-detailed texts)
4. Reading for comprehension is very important to understand an advertisement or a business document globally and in depth. It may be an e-mail, a letter or a report, or a brochure or a memo-it is important to read and understand the message.

IV. Writing

1. Letter writing, paragraph writing, note taking and note-making, describing people, places, processes etc., transfer of information from tables, charts, graphs, writing advertisements, slogans, writing reports and abstracts, creative writing…..the list can be endless. There are various kinds of writing: narrative, descriptive, expository, reflective, etc.

2. Business Communication in writing is the life blood of any organization. Letters, reports, proposals, tenders, minutes, memos, good promotional materials and other financial and commercial correspondence – all of them require effective writing even on the electronic media. Courteous writing is indispensable to be successful in career building.
3. The choice of **form** and **style** is very important, whether it be a memo, a report, a proposal or a letter.
4. Effective writing depends on (a) style and (b) precision and clarity. Coherence and cohesion are achieved by logical reasoning, close organization of ideas, and how they are glued together through unity of language.
5. Avoid jargon and cliché. **Jargon** is a language difficult to understand because it is badly formed or spoken badly. Every trade has its own jargon (e.g. the legal jargon). **Cliché** is an idea or expression that has been used too often and is now outdated. Example: The old cliché says that trouble shows us who our friends really are.
6. Avoid using unnecessary or inelegant abbreviations. Don't use 'prof' for 'professor' or 'vac' for 'vacation'
7. Use proper punctuation and see how meaning changes:
   E.g. –The panda eats, shoots, and leaves/The panda eats shoots and leaves.
   My mother said, "Ram is lazy."/ "My mother, "said Ram, "is lazy."
   A woman – without her, man is nothing/ A woman, without her man, is nothing
   Can you see the difference?
8. Last but not the least is one's handwriting.

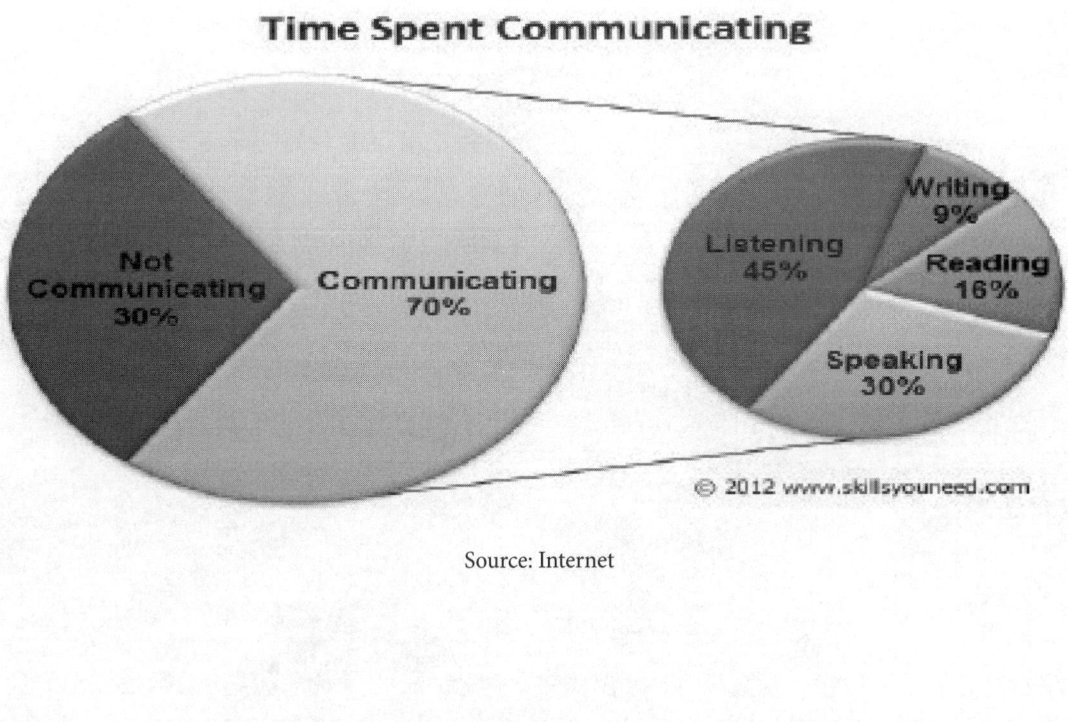

Source: Internet

Online Resources

1. mreader@erfoundation.org
2. http://www.oswego.org/webpages/lstevens/
3. http://www2.warwick.ac.uk/fac/soc/al/learning_english/leap/writing/eapbooks/
4. http://www.librairiemichelfortin.com/doc/cup_integrated_series_readingwritinglistening speaking.pdf
5. http://www.macmillanenglish.com/courses/skillful/
6. https://owl.english.purdue.edu/

Select Bibliography

1. Mukerjee, HorySankar. *Business Communication*. New Delhi: OUP, 2013.
2. Bailey.S.Academic Writing: *A Handbook for International Students*. London and New York: Routledge, 2001
3. Murray, N. *Writing Essays in English Language and Linguistics*.Cambridge: Cambridge University Press, 2012
4. Adler, Mortimer J. *How to Speak How to Listen*, New York: Simon &Schuster, 1997
5. Adler, Mortimer J. and Charles Van Doren. *How to Read a Book: The Classic Guide to Intelligent Reading*, New York:Simon &Schuster, 1972

Unit IV – Practice

Listening

A. *Listen to the passage and complete the activities given:*

For centuries, the principal raw materials for making paper were cotton and linen fibres obtained from rags. Today, these have been replaced by wood pulp. Trees are cut down, taken to the saw mill and chopped up into small pieces. The pieces of wood are then ground and mixed with water to make wood pulp. The wood pulp is then washed to clean impurities. It is then bleached to make the paper white. In the next step, starch or clay may be added to improve the surface of the paper. The pulp is then fed into the paper-making machine. In this machine, the pulp is spread across large wire mesh sheets. Here, the water is drained off. The sheet is then passed between rollers which squeeze out the remaining water. The dry sheet then travels through a series of heated drums. At this stage, a coating may be applied to make the paper smooth and shiny. This process produces a continuous sheet of paper which is wound into giant roles. It is then trimmed to remove the rough edges and cut to the desired width.

Now, complete the flow chart:

Step 1	Small pieces of wood are made into paste and mixed with
Step 2	
Step 3	
Step 4	
Step 5	
Step 6	

B. Listen carefully to the following rules, which apply to students in a college: Rules and regulations, Attendance, Leave etc.

1. Leave will not be granted as a matter of right.
2. All applications for leave with details regarding the period and the reason should be

submitted in the prescribed form, in duplicate, a day before leave is required to the Principal through the Head of the Department concerned.

3. The Principal may give a student leave of absence amounting to not more than 7 days at a time, exclusive of Sundays and other holidays, and not more than 12 days in the year. A student will forfeit one day's leave for every four times he is marked late.
   - A student may be dismissed if s/he is absent without leave for three whole consecutive working days or for a period aggregating five whole days in any one term.
4. In cases where absence without leave is unavoidable, application for leave must be submitted as soon as possible, and never later than the first day of return to the college.
5. Absence without leave for a part of the day and absence without leave for a full day will be counted as absence for one day and two days respectively or the student will be liable to a fine of ten rupees for absence without leave for each day, or part of it.
6. No leave will be granted for any reason in advance or in continuation of Midterm or Dushera holidays or the fortnight before the attendance certificate for the year is completed.
7. The necessary attendance certificate will not be granted, unless the Principal is satisfied that the student's progress and conduct have been satisfactory, and that he has attended three quarters of the number of working days in the academic year.

Answer the following questions about leave: answer in complete sentences

1. What is the maximum number of consecutive days of leave a student may take?
2. If a student has been late 16 times during the year, how many days' leave is he entitled to?
3. If a student is absent without leave for two and a half days, what are the two alternative methods of punishment?
4. In such a case, how is the method of punishment decided?
5. If there are 185 working days in the college year, what is the minimum number of days a student must attend in order to obtain an attendance certificate?
6. In what circumstances do you suppose absence without leave would be recognized as unavoidable?
7. What are the two ways by which a student's casual leave may become reduced?
8. Why do you think leave is not granted before or after the Midterm or Dushera holidays?
9. For Pongal holidays, does the student have to apply for leave?
10. If a student is called suddenly to visit a parent who is seriously ill in hospital, and does not apply for leave before hand, will he lose more leave than he actually took?

C. Supply the adjacency pairs in the following pieces of conversation:

- Mr. Sekar: Good morning. May I know who you are and what I can do for you?
  You:________________________________
- Mr. Govind Sharma: How do you do? My name is Govind.
  You: ________________________________
- Leela: Hi Leena!
  Leena:________________________________
- John: Hello Gopi ! How are you?
  Gopi: ________________________________

- ➢ Sanjay: I think it's going to rain.
  You: ______________________________
- D. Add coherence in the following conversational pieces:
  - ➢ Shyam: What happened at the meeting?
    You: ______________________________
  - ➢ Sales person: Do you prefer the black one or the white one?
    You: ______________________________
  - ➢ Balu: Any chance of borrowing your camera for a few days?
    You: ______________________________
- E. Add **cohesion** in the following conversational pieces:
  - ➢ The clock repairer: Are you going to leave it then?
    You: ______________________________
  - ➢ Sayed: What colour was the bike that hit yours?
    You: ______________________________
  - ➢ You: I was told that the train leaves at 12 o' clock. Is that right?
    Counter clerk: ______________________________
- F. What's wrong:
  - ➢ You: I've lost my wallet somewhere. It's got over five thousand.
    Your friend: No reason to apologise.
  - ➢ You: Excuse me, where's Nehru Park ?
    Passerby: That's quite okay.

I. Listening

- i. Do you think observing body language, gestures and eye movements is also essential in listening? Illustrate your answer.
- ii. While listening, the listener should not violate the 'rule of openness' to the speaker's viewpoint
  Do you agree? Give reasons.
- iii. Taking down notes (i.e. note-taking) will be helpful in listening. Explain.
- iv. Why do people speak more than listen? What are the reasons you can give?
- v. Hearing and listening differ substantially. Explain
- vi. What are the main purposes of listening?
- vii. Do you think attentive listening has several advantages? What are they?
- viii. Do you think that listening is related to critical thinking ? Why?
- ix. Often people respond without listening. Why?
- x. Do you think that listening improves speaking? Give reasons.
- xi. Let a fool hold his tongue and he will pass for a sage. Is this true?
- xii. If speaking is silver, then listening is gold. Do you agree?
- xiii. The best sales people are great listeners – that's how they find out what buyers want. Explain.

xiv. A bore is a person who talks when you wish him to listen – Do you agree? Give reasons:

xv. If A is success, then A equals x + y + z, where x is work, y is play, z is 'shut up'. (Albert Einstein)

Comment:

II. Speaking

i. English spelling is the world's most awesome mess. It affects our speech. Explain and illustrate.

ii. Once Bernard Shaw said that a good way to spell the word 'fish' was 'ghoti'. How? (Think of words like 'laugh', 'women' and 'caution')

iii. Loud reading improves your pronunciation and speaking. Explain.

III. Reading

Skim for information

Read silently (within 3 seconds) the following passage and answer the questions given below the passage.

Communication among animals is an interesting study. Bees, for instance have a remarkable system of communication. When a bee discovers the source of nectar it informs the other bees in the hive through a special 'dance'. The location of the source is communicated by the kind of 'dance', the direction is indicated by the angle of the axis of the dance and the amount of nectar by the vigorousness of the 'dance'. Recently it has been discovered that sea creatures 'talk'. Dolphins emit a distinct noise to seek help, and studies have been undertaken towards achieving communication with these aquatic mammals.

Primitive men drew and painted on cave walls to convey messages; they used signs and symbols. As man's knowledge expanded, writing became necessary in order to transmit information. From writing on animal tissues, men moved on to using paper for writing, following the discovery of paper-making by the Chinese around the 5th century B.C. In the middle of the 15th century A.D., the German printer Johann Guttenberg used the movable type for the first time in Europe to print theBible. This technique widened the opportunities for learning and let in radical changes in man's thinking and living.

Say whether the following statements are True or False:

a) Bees dance when they are happy. ( )

b) Sea creatures communicate with one another. ( )

c) Painting was a forerunner of writing. ( )

d) Dolphins cry for help. ( )

e) Printing paper was first made in Germany. ( )

f) The first printed material was the Bible. ( )

g) Primitive men had the need to communicate. ( )

h) The bee dance conveys a lot of information. ( )

Read aloud the following passage: It is an 'authentic' text with incomplete sentences, pauses, etc.

Now then # what do we want to know about the English dictionary? In fact # what do we want to know about the words # in the English dictionary? Now, in 1860, if someone had asked the question # well, let's start with the year 1806 # that's the year 1806 #. How many words are there in the English dictionary? # Well, I'll tell you. The answer would have been twenty eight # that's # twenty –eight thousand words. But # by 1822 # dictionaries had grown # and by 1822 there were seventy thousand words # about 70, 000 words #. If you ask today # if you had a complete # I mean exhaustive dictionary that would probably, six hundred fifty thousand words in it. That's today # that is a lot of words. But don't worry! Most people don't use six hundred fifty thousand words #. Most people use about sixty thousand words # the most common letter # to begin a word. # is S# has two hundred pages of entries, # the least common is X# only one and a half pages# just eighty one entries.

IV. Writing

1. (Words like **and**, **but**, **too**, **yet**, **then**, **so**, **further**, **similarly**, **thus**, **however**, **therefore**, **actually**, **equally**, **etc.** are often used to connect sentences.)

   Look at the piece of writing about ant-eaters as given below; it is funny.

   Ant-eaters are mammals. Ant-eaters are found in Africa. Ant-eaters have long snouts. Ant-eaters feed on white ants. White ants are also called termites. The ant bear, the three-toed ant-eater, and the silky ant-eaters are common types of ant-eaters. These common types have mouths. The mouths are small. These common ant-eaters have tongues. These tongues are long. The tongues can be extended to catch insects. Ant-eaters have claws. The claws are long. The claws are hooked. The hooking is for digging nests. The claws are strong. They are sharp. The strength and sharpness are for self-defence. The ant-eater sleeps during the day. The ant-eater is a nocturnal animal.

   Rewrite the passage, properly gluing all the sentences to make it natural.
2. Nowadays girls are doing very well in all kinds of examination. If this trend continues, will men become subordinate to women? Write a dialogue between a boy and a girl who are talking about this problem and its consequences.
3. You know what 'generation gap' is. Do you experience it in your family and community? Write a paragraph suggesting some ways of bridging the gap.
4. In the computer –age, handwriting is unimportant. Do you agree? Explain.

Case Study for Discussion

Good business entails good communication, both within and outside the organization. Choice of medium depends on the purpose of communication. If the message is meant for employees of an organization, internal communication could be resorted to, but if the message is intended for the internal as well as the outside world, then external modes of communication are helpful.

Tech–Nation is the Indian branch of **Tech-Global**, a technology solution provider, based in Seattle, USA. Tech-Nation has its office in Hyderabad, India. The company, established in 2003, provides software and hardware solutions to its Indian and overseas clients. For external communication, Tech-Nation typically uses:

- ➢ Written communications dispatched by mail e.g. statements detailing order numbers and payment schedules. Such paper-based correspondence has the advantage of providing a clear document that can be filed for future use. Reports are generated for all the work undertaken and presentations made at appropriate forums.
- ➢ Oral communications: Customers can call with their queries and speak directly to the employee who is managing their account. Oral communication prevents misunderstandings.
- ➢ Online communications. Consumers can view the profile of the company, people in the organization and the services offered by the company. They can post their queries to the person concerned and get suggested solutions online, thereby saving a great deal of time. This is an efficient and quick means of communication. In this way, Tech-Nation is able to communicate effectively with millions of customers worldwide.
- ➢ Face-to-face communications e.g. In cases of emergency, a visit to the local clients' homes with prior arrangement can be made. This provides better understanding of the problem and provides timely solutions.
- ➢ Similar methods are used by Tech-Nation for internal communications. For example
- ➢ Written communications: Internal memos, agenda and minutes of the meetings, notices or posters on staff notice boards.
- ➢ Face-to-face: Board and sectional meetings, presentations, team briefings
- ➢ Oral communications: Phone conversations between employees.
- ➢ Online: internal e-mails and intranet.
- ➢ Face-to-face conversations and oral communications provide transparency and clarity to all issues. Written communications are formal documents providing clear statements of discussions and their outcomes which could be filed and recorded. Online communications have speeded up working by providing instant and economical ways of interacting and generating data that can be easily stored for future use. Online communications can be easily edited and shared between people working together. For example, a customer's order details can be accessed both in the local office as well as in the global office in Seattle, SA, simultaneously.

Questions

1. The manager, customer care office, Tech-Nation, receives an online request from one of its clients. The client wants his existing office management software to be upgraded to the latest version available in the market.
    a. What kind of communication will have to be established in dealing with this request?
    b. A feedback from all employees of the company is needed to get the best solution. How will the manager establish communication with all employees, in India as well as in the Seattle office?
    c. He would like to present this job as a case study to the Board of Governors of the company. How should he proceed?

Unit V – Communicating in a Global Language

The spoken word belongs half to the speaker, and half to the listener

– A French Proverb

OBJECTIVES:

After reading this unit, you will be able to

- ✓ Understand the nuances of global English
- ✓ Identify stress patterns in words and sentences
- ✓ Recognize weak forms in sentences
- ✓ Acquire rules of proper intonation

Basics

I. Remember English has become a global language

a. It is not only international but also global (all over the world)
b. It is the language of the internet
c. 1.5 billion people use English in some form or the other (1/4th of the human race)
d. 340 million use it as L1 [i.e. as their first language] and 400 million as L2[their second language] and 1.5 billion people 'know' English in some form or the other.

II. A language can be learnt in different ways for different purposes.

a. Learning a language as F.L (language + their culture)
b. Learning a language as S.L (language + your culture)
c. Learning a language as G.L (language + your culture + other cultures and their accent for understanding)

III. Cultivate a neutral accent.

One need not match the speech of a British or American speaker but must attempt to be intelligible to most educated speakers in a **multinational** set-up. Clarity in areas like clear articulation, stress, intonation, pause and rhythm is important. A neutral accent cuts across all varieties of English.

IV. Shed regionalisms.

Features unique to particular regions affect universal intelligibility. Your English must be free from regional features like in Bengali English, Punjabi English, Malayali English, etc.

Some hints:

i. Make a distinction between the words in pairs like the following:
   - ❖ cart-cot, shark-shock, cart-caught, part-pot

ii. Distinguish between 'else' and 'yells'; 'east' and 'yeast'; 'ear' and 'year';

iii. Don't double medial consonants:
   - ❖ rubber, dinner, shutter, runner, bigger, sudden, cutter, butter, summer, happy
   - ❖ The medial consonants are pronounced as a single consonant.

iv. Don't sound the r in all places. It should be pronounced only when a vowel sound follows it.
   - ❖ The r is silent in 'shirt', 'form', 'purse', etc.
   - ❖ It is sounded in 'carry', 'sorry', 'bury', etc. because it is followed by the vowel i.

v. Don't add vowels to the initial consonant clusters:
   - ❖ Don't say 'iskool for school', 'istation for station', 'ispray for spray', 'iscrew for screw'.

vi. Avoid spelling pronunciation. The **alphabet of speaking** is different from the **alphabet of writing**. (Example: 'made' and 'maid' has the same pronunciation; 'elite'' is pronounced 'eleet'' and not as 'elight').

Notice the silent letters in the following words:

a. align	(**g** silent)	l. foreign	(**g** silent)
b. almond	(**l** silent)	m. half, calm, palm, balm	(**l** silent)
c. assign	(**g** silent)	n. interesting	(first **e** silent)
d. autumn	(**n** silent)	o. island	(**s** silent)
e. benign	(**g** silent)	p. night	(**gh** silent)
f. biscuit	(**u** silent)	q. often	(**t** silent)
g. building	(**u** silent)	r. receipt	(**p** silent)
h. christmas	(**t** silent)	s. scissors	(**c** silent)
i. doubt	(**b** silent)	t. thumb	(**b** silent)
j. dumb	(**b** silent)	u. wednesday	(**d** silent)
k. February	(**a** silent)	v. whole	(**w** silent)

vii. Distinguish between

a. s and sh/ ʃ /	:	sip-ship; sit-shit; sea-she
b. s and /z/	:	cease-seize; loose-lose; use (N) -use (V)
c. / ʃ/and z/ʒ/	:	shoe-measure;patient-pleasure; fresh-revision; pressure – pleasure; fission – vision
d. f and ph['p' or 'p' aspirated]	:	feel-peel

e. b and v	: bury-very; best-vest.
f. v and w	: vest-west; van-we; give-will; vale-whale, vet-wet.
g. l and r	: play-pray; bloom-broom.
h. /e/and/æ/	: said-sad; bed-bad.
i. /e/and/eɪ/	: fell-fail; tell-tail.
j. /aɪ/ and /ɔɪ /	: tai-toy

viii. Avoid spelling pronunciation:

a. The past tense marker -ed is pronounced differently in different positions. It is pronounced /t/ after voiceless consonants except /t/.
washed-pronounced /t/
talked-pronounced /t/

It is pronounced /d/ after voiced consonants except /d/.
waved-pronounced /d/
tried-pronounced /d/

It is pronounced /Id/ after /t/ and /d/:
waited – pronounced /Id/
decided – pronounced /Id/

b. In the same way, the plural marker s as well as the possessive maker 's is pronounced differently in different positions.
It is pronounced /s/ after voiceless consonants except /s/, / ʃ /, and /t͡ʃ/. tests, desks, tops, Jack's – pronounced /s/
It is pronounced /z/ after voiced consonants except / z /, /ʒ / and /d͡ʒ/.
rings, teachers, keys, John's – pronounced /z/
It is pronounced /Iz/] after /s/, / z /, / ʃ/, / ʒ /, /t͡ʃ/ and /d͡ʒ/.
watches, classes, churches, Ramesh's – pronounced /ɪz/.

V. Stress (also called accent) is the articulation of a syllable with greater force than others.

Learn some tips for improving your accent and for making it neutral.

1. Some common words that are usually mispronounced. Learn the proper stress.

in'form	infor'mation	in'formative
pre'pare	prepa'ration	pre'paratory
'photograph	pho'tography	pho'tographer
a'ppreciate	appreci'ation	a'ppreciative

'atmosphere	'demonstrate	en'vironment.
de'cison	po'lice	'marriage
de'velop	se'mester	se'lection
eng 'gagement	engi'neer	
vice-'chancellor	metho'dology	ex'president

2. In the following words the stress shifts from one syllable to another to change the grammar of the word, and sometimes, meaning too.

'absent (N)	ab'sent (V)	
'convict (N)	con'vict (V)	
'conflict (N)	con'flict (V)	
desert (N)	de'sert (V)	
'export (N)	ex'port (V)	
'import (N)	im'port (V)	
'insult (N)	in'sult (V)	
'increase (N)	in'crease (V)	
'invalid (N)	in'valid (adj)	[the noun meaning a bedridden person]
'object (N)	ob'ject (V)	
'present (N)	pre'sent (V)	
'produce (N)	pro'duce (V)	
'progress (N)	pro'gress (V)	
'project (N)	pro'ject (V)	
'protest (N)	pro'test (V)	
'rebel (N)	re'bel (V)	
'subject (N)	sub'ject (V)	
'academy (N)	aca'demic (V)	
mechanism (N)	me'chanical (V)	

You may use the words above in sentences to notice the change in meaning.

3. **A common stress rule**

Words ending with the following **suffixes** have the stress on the **vowel of the syllable before the suffix.**

-tion	-sion	-ic	-ical	-ically
-ous	-tial	-ity	-ive	-itive
-utive	-ative	-atory	-iatory	-iative
-tomy	-ial	-ially	and others.	

Examples:

tion/-ation

demo'lition	appli'cation	civili'zation
imagi'nation	obser'vation	popu'lation
conver'sation	plan'tation	recipro'cation.

-sion

de'cision o'ccasion di'vision.

-ic

te'rrific	scien'tific	spe'cific
eco'nomic	cata'strophic	e'lectric

-ical

po'litical 'cyclical p'olemical me'chanical

-ically

po'litically 'cyclically po'lemically

-ous

a'trocious de'licious consci'entious

-tial

i'nitial influ'ential confi'dential

-ity

ca'pacity	capa'bility	curi'osity	te'nacity
e'quality	possi'bility	sim'plicity	ne'cessity

-ive

de'v[c]isive contra'ceptive be'lieve per'ceptive

-itive

com'petitive 'partitive 'additive

-utive

e'xecutive cons'ecutive dis'tributive

-tive

in'formative con'templative al'ternative

-atory

pre'paratory lab'oratory ob'servatory

-iatory

re'taliatory con'ciliatory prop'itiatory

-tomy

a'natomy va'sectomy hyste'rectomy

-ial

e'ssential in'dustrial me'morial

-ially

confi'dentially arti'ficially o'fficially

4. **Words with weak prefixes and words that begin with / ə / are accented on the root.**
   Example:

1. a'broad	5. a'cross	9. a'head	13. a'lone
2. al'though	6. be'come	10. a'bout	14. a'gree
3. a'round	7. a'mong	11. a'gain	15. a'sleep
4. a'live	8. a'part	12. a'fraid	16. a'rrive etc.

Vi. Short-grammatical words are functionally important but 'in speech' they do not receive stress.

WORDS	WEAK FORM	EXAMPLE
am	əm, m	I'm
are	ə (r)	You're, We're
is	z, s	He's, It's
was	wəz, wz	He was
were	wə (r)	They were
have	həv, əv, v	They've
has	həz, əz, z, s	He has
had	həd, əd, d	He'd
do	dʊ, də, d	I don't
does	dəz	He doesn't
can	kən	I can
could	kəd, kd	We could
may	meɪ	He may
	ʃ (ə) l̩	
shall	ʃ (ʊ) d, d	I'll
should	l̩	We should
will	əd, d	I'll
would	məst, məs	I'd
must		You must
a	ə	A book
an	ən	An ant
the	ði before vowel	The ant
	ðə before consonant	The
some	sm	Some girls
and	ən, n	Dog and a cat
not	n't	Cannot

A. Other common contractions:

a. here's
b. that's
c. what's
d. where's
e. who'd
f. how's
g. there's
h. when's
i. who's
j. that'd
k. that'll
l. what'll
m. who'll

and the word <u>not</u> when it follows have, do, are, is, was, were, can, could, will, would, etc., is pronounced n't

VII. Prominence given to syllables in words is called word-stress; prominence given to syllables in sentences is called sentence-stress.

i. In speech sentence-stress, rhythm, tone (i.e. pitch variations) intonation and pause are important.
ii. Listen to recorded varieties of spoken English-British, American, Australian, etc. to improve listening comprehension. Also listen to the BBC, CNN, NDTV and such other programmes on the TV and listen to EFL University and IELTS audio tapes.

The following steps may be useful in improving your speech:

i. **Pause:** Pause at the end of each **meaning-unit** within a sentence and finally at the end of the sentence.

//The manager told us/that business communication is not just correspondence/ but total communication/including our speech as well//

There are four meaning units and four pauses. **Speak each meaning-unit at one stretch without stopping in the middle of each unit.**

ii. **Stress:**

1. Pronounce the stressed syllables longer, with greater force.

//The 'manager' ↘told us/that 'human communi' cation is 'not just con-ver'sation/ but 'total communi'↘cation/in'cluding our 'speech as 'well//.

iii. **Rhythm and intonation (i.e. tune):**

1. Don't stress the unstressed parts of the sentence and don't pause in between meaning-units. This will help to maintain the rhythm of the sentence.

//The 'manager '↘told us/that 'human communi'cation is 'not just conver'sation / but' total communi'↘cation/in'cluding our 'speech as'well//.

iv. **Intonation (i.e. tune):** It is the change of the direction of pitch in each meaning-unit within a sentence. Again read the same sentence with proper intonation.

//The 'manager'↘told us/that 'human communi'cation is 'not just conver'↘sation/but 'total communi'↘cation/in'cluding our 'speech as 'well//.

This comes out of practice alone – listening and speaking.

More practice material is given in the worksheet.

v. **Some simple tips for proper intonation/tune:**

Every language has a melody in it; no language is spoken on the same musical note all the time.

a. **The voice can fall or rise on a stressed syllable. The greatest movement of the voice is on a word near the end of a clause/sentence.**

Example: I'll see you next ↘week.

The greatest fall or rise is on the new and important information. Which word is important depends on the context.

Example: our neighbour has bought an ↘Innova. They live in Banga↘lore.

b. Intonation in statements:

❖ A falling tone is normal in a statement.
My brother is a ↘doctor.
I'll see you next ↘week.
Our office starts at ↘nine.

❖ A rising intonation in statements shows that something is incomplete.
In ↗my opinion (it's quite wrong).
It's a long way to ↗walk (I think we should go by bus).

❖ When there is an enumeration of a few things, the rising tone is followed by a falling tone.
↗Gold, ↗Silver and ↗Platinum are very precious ↘metals.
We are visiting ↗Japan, ↗China, ↗Vietnam and ↘Singapore.

❖ In complex sentences, the first half is spoken with a rising tone and the second half with a falling tone.
When the cat is ↗away, the mice will ↘play.
When there's a ↗will, there's is a ↘way.
Unless you try ↗hard, you won't get the ↘job.

❖ Polite requests/invitations/suggestions are made with a rising tone.
Would you like to have some ice ↗cream?
Shall we go for a ↗movie?
Can you please help ↗me?
Would you mind closing the ↗door?

c. Intonation in questions:

❖ A yes/no question is asked with a rising tone.
Will you see me next ↗week?
Do you sell ↗mangoes?
Can you ↗drive?

❖ A 'wh' question usually has a falling tone.
Where do you ↘live?
What will it ↘cost?
How do you spend your ↘time?
What's your ↘name?

❖ The rising tone makes a statement more like a question.

You'll see me next ↗week?

You have got a new ↗job? ↗Oh! ↗Have you? ↗Where?

d. Commands are generally said with a falling tune.

↘Follow me.

↘Shut up.

e. Exclamations are said with a falling tune:

Example: What a lovely ↘day!

What a piece of work is a ↘woman!

What a ↘surprise!

f. Tune can change the meaning:

↘Thank you (sounding grateful)

↗Thank you (business like)

Online Resources

1. http://web.ntpu.edu.tw/~language/workshop/2010-3.pdf
2. https://www.edx.org/course/principles-written-english-part-1-uc-berkeleyx-colwri2-
3. https://www.edx.org/course/purduex/purduex-pncom201501x-communicating-6346#.VKUBgNKUdz8
4. http://www.unc.edu/~jlsmith/pht-url.html
5. http://www.etscanada.ca/toeic_tpospeakingranges.php
6. http://elt.cengage.co.in/homeelt

Bibliography

1. Syal, Pushpender and D.V.Jindal. *An Introduction to Linguistics*. New Delhi: Prentice Hall, 2004.
2. Sethi, J. and P.V.Dhamija. *A Course in Phonetics and Spoken English*. New Delhi: Prentice Hall, 2004.
3. Verma, S.K. and N. Krishnaswamy. *Modern Linguistics*. New Delhi: OUP, 1989.
4. Poldauf, Ian and Rowland Lee. *English word stress: a theory of word-stress patterns in English*. University of Michigan: Pergamon Press, 1984.
5. Akmajian, Adrian et al. *Linguistics: An Introduction to Language and Communication*. New Delhi: Prentice Hall, 2004.
6. Rudanko, Juhani. *Changes in Complementation in British and American English.London:* Palgrave Macmillan, 2011.

Unit V – Practice

Practice will make you perfect.

I. Word stress gives English its characteristic rhythm.

Say aloud the following sets of words with proper stress:

i. Numbers ending in –teen get the stress on –teen.
thirteen, fourteen, fifteen, sixteen, seventeen, eighteen, nineteen.

ii. In all reflexive pronouns, the stress falls on the second syllable.
Example: my'self, your'self, him'self, it'self, our'selves, them'selves.

iii. Some common two syllable (i.e. disyllabic words):
ba'nana, be'cause, be'gin, be'hind, be'fore, be'side, ba'lloon, ca'fe, ca'reer, ca'ssette, de'cline, de'ceive, e'ffect, e'vent, ex'pect, e'xample, e'nough, en'joy, for'get, ga'rage, gui'tar, ho'tel, in'crease, i'dea, Ju'ly, ma'chine, out'line, out'do, per'haps, po'lice, su'ccess, un'less, un'til.

iv. Trisyllabic words with stress on the second syllable.
ag'reement, a'nother, a'ppointement, a'ttention, be'ginning, co'nnection, con'venience, des'tructive, de'velop, di'rection.

v. Trisyllabic words with stress on the third syllable:
after'noon, ciga'rette, coin'cide, decom'pose, disa'ppear, disa'gree, disa'ppoint, engi'neer, over'look, reco'mmend, repro'duce, under'stand.

vi. Four syllable words:
'absolutely, 'comfortable, 'necessary, 'popularly, 'characterise
a'bility, a'pologise, de'velopment, e'fficiency, for'getfulness, in'tentional, o'ccasional, pho'tography, sim'plicity.
acci'dental, circu'lation, diplo'matic, deri'vation, inter'vening, over'crowding, unim'portant.
'after'noon, 'absent-'minded, 'home-'made, 'old-'fashioned, 'second-'hand, 'main-'road, 'middle-'aged.
'anything, 'backbone, 'earthquake, 'shopkeeper, 'eye-witness, 'hand-bag, 'hair-brush, 'tea-party, inter'national, pronunci'ation.

II. Bernard Shaw, a well-known writer in English, once remarked that a good way to spell the word **fish** was ghoti. Do you agree? Why? (f =gh, i=o, sh=ti)

Clues:

gh	=	f in enough, tough and rough etc.
o	=	i in womenfolk- wiminfəuk
sh	=	ti in Nation, notion etc

III. Practise short dialogues like the following. The words which should be stressed have been underlined.

i. I'll <u>meet</u> you at the <u>bank</u>. I'll <u>be</u> there at <u>three.</u>
ii. What <u>time</u> is the <u>show</u>? I think it starts at <u>two.</u>
iii. What <u>time</u> shall we <u>eat?</u> I'd <u>like</u> to eat at <u>ten</u>.
iv. I <u>like</u> your new <u>shirt</u>. I <u>got</u> it on <u>sale</u>.

IV. **Can you mark the proper intonation for the following sentences? Try.**

i. What's your name?
ii. When did you arrive?
iii. The market is not exciting.
iv. Is this the store?
v. The matter is closed.
vi. Is he your teacher?
vii. Can you pass the paper, please?
viii. May I come in?
ix. Please don't mention it.
x. Wish you a happy journey.

Now read each one aloud.

V. **Read the following telephone conversation with proper stress and intonation.**

Receptionist : Hello, good morning. This's Sudha at the receptionist desk, Sagar Nursing Home, Bangalore. May I know your name, please?

Patient : Good morning, Madam. This's Ravi from Kalyan Nagar.
I've an appointment with Dr. Rao at two this afternoon, but, I'm afraid, I won't beable to make it today.

Receptionist : Hello Mr Ravi! I now remember. How are you today? Did you sleep well yesterday night? Do you want a change of the date of appointment with Dr. Rao?

Patient : Thank you, Ma'am. I did sleep well last night. Yes, I would appreciate it if you could get the date of appointment changedto the same time tomorrow.

Receptionist : Well, let me look at his diary. Yes, he is free at that time tomorrow. Shall I block it for you?

Patient : Please do, ma'am. Sorry to bother you.

Receptionist : It is done. Take care. Do call us If you have any discomfort.

Patient : Thank you for the consideration. I'll be there tomorrow at a quarter to two.

Receptionist : Bye now. See you tomorrow.

VI. **Read the following conversation with proper stress and intonation.**

An interview

Counsellor : Will the job you are thinking of help you to do both? What are the work timings?

Kumar : Yes, it will. They have a training wing which simultaneously arranges classes without allowing work to suffer.

Counsellor : Would you like to say how you will manage the visa.

Kumar : Mr Allen, I have applied for it. It is in process. I am confident of obtaining it because I fulfil all the conditions stipulated. At the moment, I do not have it.

Counsellor : Do you intend to immigrate or return after completing the diploma?

Kumar : I don't wish to immigrate. That's the reason why I have not applied for the immigrant visa. Most of my relatives are in the construction industry.

Counsellor : Where are they?

Kumar : In Chennai.

Counsellor : That sounds reasonable but what are your interests in Chennai?

Kumar : I have many. My parents are there. I did my schooling and university under the guardianship of my uncle in Mumbai. I want to be with my parents.

Counsellor : Do you have any other commitment or obligation?

Kumar : Nothing that I can think of.

Counsellor : Well, thank you Mr Kumar. As you seek a non- immigration visa, you may easily get it. Nice talking to you. Wish you good luck. Bye now.

Kumar : Thank you, Mr Allen. Bye.

VII. Do you know what Americans say and write?

- **Spelling**

British	**American**	**British**	**American**
abridgement		encyclopaedia	
acknowledgement		labour	
aesthetic		glamour	
although		industrialisation	
analyse		litre	
apologise		metre (=100 cm)	
realise		neighbour	
organise		practice (N)	
councillor		practise (V)	
signalled		photo	
travelled		programme	
behaviour		pyjamas	
centre		rumour	

cheque (money)		skilful	
catalogue		socks	
counsellor		spelt	
colour		spoilt	
defence		storey (of a house)	
dialogue		theatre	
favour		through	
honour		traveller	
humour		tyre	
jeweller		signalled	
travelling			

- **Vocabulary**

British	**American**	**British**	**American**
assurance		happy	
autumn		pavement	
banknote		petrol pump	
beer/bitter		puncture	
bill		post	
biscuit		queue	
box		railway	
chemist's shop			
(medical shop)		shop	
clever		sweets	
flat (in a building)		taxi	
form		tap	
full stop		tin/container	
hire-purchase		toilet	
lift		torch	
like (N)		town hall	
lodger		tram	
lorry		STD	
rubbish		holiday	
angry		underground	
mad		vest	
match		zip	

Usage

1. **Have –[Have** and **have got.]**

British	:	I've got some money. (Spoken) I have some money. (Written)
American	:	I have some money. [Spoken and Written]

Have in negatives and questions

British	:	I haven't (got) much time. Have you (got) enough time?
American	:	I don't have much time. Do you have enough time?
British	:	You haven't got to go. Have you got to go?
British/American	:	You don't have to go. Do you have to go?
British/American	:	We got the man to bring another shirt.
American	:	We had the man bring another shirt.
British	:	Have you (got) time for a game of chess? (i.e. on a particular occasion) Do you have enough time for cricket? (i.e. generally)
American	:	Do you have enough time for a game of chess/ for cricket? (No distinction is made in American usage)

2. Verbs **be, seem, look, feel**.

British	:	It looks a lovely day.
American	:	It looks like/ looks to be a lovely day.
British	:	She seems (to be) a competent person.
American	:	She seems to be a competent person.

3. Question **tags**

British	:	He likes coffee, doesn't he? She doesn't like you, does she?
American	:	He likes coffee, right? We'll take you there, ok?

4. **Do** for an action:

British	:	You should contact her if you haven't (done) already.
American	:	You should contact her if you haven't done so already.

5. **Do** for emphasis.

British	:	Do have one more glass.
American	:	Have one more glass.

6. **Gone** and **been**:

British	:	Have you ever been to China?
American	:	Have you ever gone to China?

7. **Presentperfect and Past simple:**
   British : I've just met an old friend.
   American : I just met an old friend.
   British : Have you ever seen the Taj Mahal?
   American : Did you ever see the Taj Mahal?
8. **Will** and **Shall**
   The British use **will** and **shall** with first person.
   Americans do not use **shall**.
   British : We will/shall meet you.
   American : We will meet you.
9. **Learned** and **learnt**:
   The irregular form like learnt, dreamt are not generally used in American English. They prefer the regular forms learned, dreamed, etc.
   (Notice : The suit **fitted** him very well. (British)
   The suit **fit** him very well. (American)
   The verbs **dive** and **fit** are regular in British English but irregular in American English.)
   British : My father prefers that I stay/should stay in a hostel.
10. American : My father prefers that I stay in a hostel.
    British : Germany are/is going to win (depending on the meaning)
    American : Germany is going to win.
11. **Group nouns:**
    British : Germany are/is going to win (depending on the meaning)
    American : Germany is going to win.
12. **The** before musical instruments:
    British : the piano, the violin…
    Americans : no **the** (he plays piano)
13. **The** with **hospital** and **university**:
    British : in hospital; at (the) university
    American : in the hospital; at the university
14. **On the telephone:**
    British : Who's **that**?
    American : Who's **this**?
15. British : a **careers** counsellor; an **antiques** dealer
    American : (only singular) a **career** counsellor; an **antique** dealer
16. The pronoun **one**:
    British : One must think of **one's** position
    American : You must think of **your** position.
    They must think of **their** position.
    (Americans do not use **one's** or **oneself**)

17. **Numbers:**
    British : three thousand and fifty
    American : three thousand fifty
18. **Dates:**
    British : the fourth of July/July the fourth
    American : July fourth
19. **well, ill,** etc.
    British/American : My mother is ill.
    Mainly/American : an ill man; an unwell person
    In British : **sick** means **to vomit**.
20. British : That was **really** nice of him.
    American : That was **real** nice of him.
    British : It **certainly** is raining.
    American : It **sure** is raining.
21. **Somewhere**
    British : Let's go **somewhere.**
    American : Let's go **someplace.**
22. **Out** (of) and **round** and **around**:
    British : **Look out of** the window.
    American : Look out the window.
    British : Go **around/ round** the park.
    American : Go **round**the park.
23. **Except for**:
    British : We are all right, **except for** a small problem.
    American : we are all right, **aside from** a small problem.
24. **Through:**
    British : from Monday to Friday
    American : Monday through Friday
    British : We will stay in Delhi from May till/until September.
    American : We will stay in Delhi from May **through** September
25. **Conjunctions:**
    Go/come
    British : Go and take a look there.
    American : **Go take** a look there.
    British : Go quietly **in case** someone notices you.
    Go quietly **so no** one notices you.
    American : Go quietly **lest** anyone notices you.
    British : As soon as I saw her, I recognised her.
    American : Immediately I saw her, I recognised her.

26. **Some idiomatic uses:**

British	**American**
visit someone	visit with someone
talk to someone	talk with someone
write to someone	write someone/ write to someone
ten (minutes) to five	ten (minutes) to/of five
twenty (minutes) past five	twenty (minutes) past/after five
a player **in** the team	a player **on** the team
at the weekend/at weekends	**on** the weekend/on weekends
in Nehru Street	**on** Nehru Street
on MG road	**on** Fifth Avenue
protest about/against something	protest something/about/against something
this is different from that	this is different than/from that
in a train/a station	on a train/station
to act as a chairperson	to chair a meeting

27. **Often**

British	:	She **is often** seen in the library.
American	:	She **often** is seen in the library.

28.

British	:	He is **having** a shower
American	:	He is **taking** a shower.

29. **How to**:

British	:	If I knew **how to** [... to show sentence is incomplete].
American	:	If I knew **how** [... to show sentence is incomplete].

30.

British	:	How **are we to do this?**
American	:	**How to do** this?

31.

British	:	Shall I **do** it immediately?
American	:	Shall I **fix** it right away?

32. **Other expressions:**

British	:	to **write** a book
American	:	to **author** a book.
British	:	to **spend** one's **holidays.**
American	:	to **vacation.**
British	:	to be **a captain** of a team.
American	:	to **captain** a team.
British	:	**Let's not** invite him.
American	:	**Don't** let's invite him.

Case-Study for Discussion

Soft-solutionsis an Indian consultancy company based in Mumbai. The company takes up consultancy projects in India and abroad. The international clients of the company are from America, England and Germany.

Raj joined the company as a PR officer. He was an engineering-cum-management graduate. He had been in the industry for the last seven years and was all set to embark on a challenging and satisfying career.

In **Soft-solutions**, his job responsibility entailed him to act as a liaison, or bridge, between the company and the world, and especially between the company and its clients. As his first assignment, Raj had to renew the contract with an American client, who was a long and trusted client of the company. However, this time, due to certain issues, the American client was not ready to renew the contract. After discussions with the higher management, Raj found out the major grievances of the client. Some of them were the following:

1. Most of the communication was done online. Due to the difference in timeline between America and India, sometimes the response got delayed which ultimately hampered the decision making process.
2. In telephonic conversation, sometimes the main point was missed because of difference in accent, resulting in lack of understanding and interpretation of the messages.
3. There were technical glitches during conference calls or video conferencing between the two sides. This resulted in a lot of frustration to the clients.
4. Lack of action in spite of repeated reminders.

Raj flew to New York, to the American client's office. In a face-to-face communication, he listened carefully to the problem from him as well as from his staff. The client complained of the general apathy and easy-going attitude of some of the employees which resulted in the backlog. He complained of the communication problem too. He also wanted the name of one person as a business point whom they could contact for everything. Raj promised to look into the problem and to meet out all the requirements as suggested. The forthrightness shown by Raj in handling the problem and the positive approach taken by the company in resolving the issue made the client happy. They promised to renew the contract if all their requirements were fulfilled within a specified time.

After coming back, to bring back the American client on board, Raj recommended the following changes to the management:

1. The work-force to be divided into groups. These groups would be allotted day and night shift on a rotation basis. This would ensure quick response to the emails even during night (when it is day in US)
2. A new vendor to be hired to take care of the technical problems during audio and video conferencing.
3. A graduate from an American university to be hired to receive the phone calls from the American and European client. This would reduce misunderstanding due to difference in accent.
4. The frequency of meetings to discuss contentious issues requiring immediate attention to be increased.

5. All issues and complaints needing immediate attention to be routed to a nodal point. A senior and dedicated person to be made in charge of this point.

The management followed up these initiatives. Very soon, they were in a position to renew the contract with the American company as well as build new relationships with other clients. It was a win-win situation for all.

Questions

1. What was going wrong with Soft-solutions and its clients?
2. Who is a liaison? What are the roles and responsibilities of a liaison? Do you think it is a challenging job?
3. What the other measures which Soft-solutions can adopt to improve its relationship with its clients?

Unit VI – Soft Skills

Be sincere, be brief, be seated

Franklin D. Roosvelt

OBJECTIVES

After reading this unit, you will be able to

- ✓ Define and classify soft skills under sub-categories
- ✓ Know about big five personality traits
- ✓ Analyze linguistic and pragmatic approaches to communication
- ✓ Understand phone and email etiquette

- ❖ Soft skills complement Hard skills. So, arm yourself with both.
- ❖ Soft skills not only make you employable but also make you agreeable and successful in life.
- ❖ It is necessary for everyone to be a good human being and a pleasant social being.
- ❖ A person's soft skills are an important part of their own growth as well as success of their organization. That's why companies screen or even train selected candidates for soft skills such as conscientiousness, dependability, agreeableness, emotional stability, etc. since such qualities are important investments for an organization. For this reason, soft skills have become increasingly important in addition to other standard qualifications; *soft skills are the human side of an organization.* In certain areas like public relations, sales, etc. soft skills are more important than hard skills.

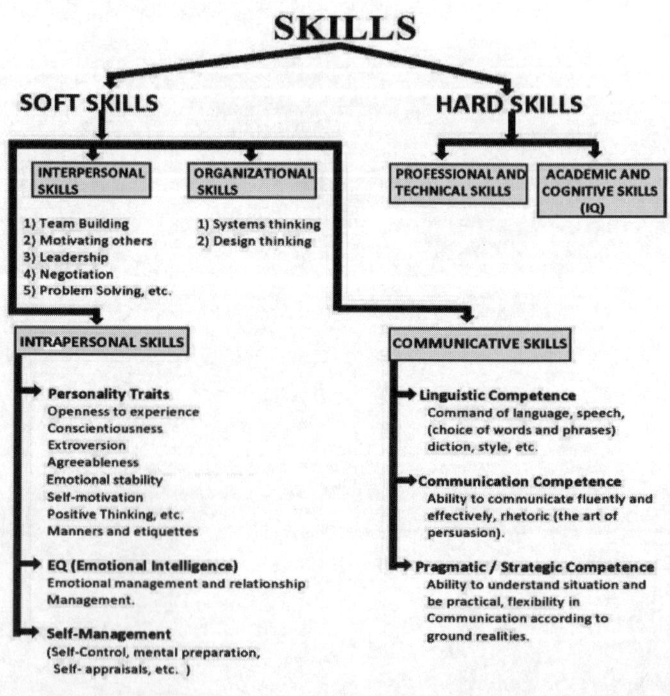

- ❖ If you have the motivation to learn, it is possible to learn soft skills. *It is possible through training to enhance soft skills and groom anyone with proper motivation.* Soft skills are not, unfortunately, included in our curricula. So, there is not much awareness about it and we cannot take it for granted that somehow one will acquire them. So, special training and awareness raising is necessary.

A. Big five Personality Traits

The term personality is used to denote those characteristics of a person that account for consistent patterns of feeling, thinking and behaving; unique and enduring patterns of behaviour and emotional response that make us distinct individuals with good breeding. Researchers have identified five important traits that are very important in one's personality. It is known as the **Five-factor model (FFM).**

1. **Openness to experience:**
   Openness means appreciation of art, emotion, adventure, unusual ideas, curiosity, and varieties of experience.
   Some examples
   ➢ Vivid imagination   Rich vocabulary
   ➢ Sensitive to beauty   Excellent ideas
   ᴺUnconventional responses
   - People who are not very open tend to be more conventional, traditional, plain, suspicious prefer familiarity, and are un-interested in abstractions, and not very imaginative.
2. **Conscientiousness**
   Conscientiousness means a tendency to show self-discipline, act dutifully, and aim for achievement. Such people are well planned and well regulated.
   Some examples
   - Being always prepared
   - Following a schedule
   - Paying attention to details
   - Not shirking duties
   - Being exacting in work
   - Doing things the right way
   - Being organized
   - Doing purposeful planning
3. **Extroversion**
   Extroversion is a trait marked by positive emotions, surgency and the tendency to seek out stimulations and the company of others. Extroverts like engagement with the external world, enjoy being with people, being action-oriented, talkative, assertive and drawing attention to themselves.
   [Note: Surgency is a personality attribute that is part of the Big Five personality traits Surgency involves patterns of behavior often exhibited in group settings and generally concerned with getting ahead in life. Such behavioral patterns often appear when someone is trying to influence or control others. Individuals lower in surgency prefer to work by themselves and have relatively little interest in influencing, controlling, or competing with others.]
   Introverts lack social involvement, lack energy and are shy.

Some examples of Extroversion

- Being comfortable with people around
- Talking to different people
- Talking a lot
- Starting conversations
- Not minding being the centre of attention
- Having a lot to say

4. **Agreeableness**

Agreeableness is the trait of being compassionate, cooperative, getting along with others, considerate, friendly, generous, helpful, optimistic, having faith in the basic human qualities like honesty, decency, etc. and willing to compromise with others.

Disagreeable people are unconcerned with others and place self interest above the interests of others and are suspicious.

Examples of Agreeableness

- Being interested in people
- Feeling others' emotions
- Taking-time for others
- Not insulting insult people
- Havinga soft heart
- Making people feel at ease
- Sympathizing with others' feelings
- Being in others' problems

5. **Emotional Stability (the opposite of Neuroticism)**

Some traits of emotional stability	*Some traits of Neuroticism*
• Not being easily disturbed	Easily disturbed
• Not irritated easily	Highly irritable
• Not upset easily	Easily upset
• Not worrying	Worry about things
• Not moody	Changing moods
• Not stressed out easily	Stressed out easily
• Not feeling blue	Feeling blue
• Relaxed	Not relaxed

➢ It is said that the brain is the hardware and the mind the software since the mind does not exist as a physical entity

➢ Neuroticism is the tendency to experience negative emotions, such as anger, anxiety, or depression. Such people can't think clearly, make decisions, cope effectively with stress or handle difficult situations. People who are emotionally stable are less easily upset, calm and free from negative feelings.

➢ So, one should minimize neuroticism and strive for emotional stability.

B. Emotional Intelligence (EQ)

- Emotional Intelligence refers to the capacity for recognizing our own feelings, as well as those of others, for motivating ourselves and others, and for managing emotions in ourselves and in our relationships. Ability to recognize, name and direct your feelings in positive ways is tested in EQ tests. This is also called emotional literacy. EQ tests help you to perceive, control and evaluate your emotions.
- Questions like 'When I am upset, I can, usually pinpoint exactly why I am distressed and 'While there are some things that I would like to change, I generally like who I am'etc. are asked to test your EQ.
- EQ tests are available online Just take one or two and assess your EQ. Click on 'EQ Tests'.

C. Self-management

- Self-management skills are personal skills like empathy, self-respect, enthusiasm, sense of humour, sincerity, firmness, spontaneity, ability to reflect, self-awareness, time-management, stress-management, self-appraisal, independent learning, ability to create one's specific time-bound goals, plan for and achieve them etc. With mental preparation and getting ready for an event for time-management, you must be able to identify the different demands on your limited time, set priorities, and schedule your time according to your goals. This requires reflection, relaxation, sound life and clean thinking. You must plan properly, evolve realistic strategies and monitor your progress.
- Calm, clear thoughts and quiet confidence are needed for stress-management. A lot depends on how you respond to stress.
  1. Understand stress
  2. Identify the causes of stress job, overwork, environment, etc.
  3. Build defense
  4. Think stress away
  5. Find relaxation techniques like yoga, meditation, deep breathing, reading, aerobic exercises, walking, swimming, etc.
  6. Avoid burnout
  7. Find a hobby
  8. Avoid unhealthy ways
  9. Don't try to change the unchangeable; change your attitude.
  10. Change your life style and alter your mind-set.

D. Some traits of inter-personal skills

1. Team building
2. Providing services
3. Negotiation skills
4. Motivation
5. Problem solving
6. Teaching others

7. Leading a team
8. Uniting a team amidst cultural diversity
9. Decision making
10. Norms of etiquette
11. Diversity tolerance
12. Willingness to discuss, accept other views, and dialoging
13. Listening
14. Politely agreeing or disagreeing
15. Ability to interact in social situations
16. Face-to-face conversations
17. Understanding oneself and moderating responses
18. Being friendly
19. Working with others
20. Ability to engage in small talk and pleasantries
21. Being polite and precise in language
22. Speaking intelligently on any topic
23. Polite conversation on telephone
24. Ability to work within an organization
25. Building relationships
26. Ability to socialize
27. Agglomeration and such other qualities

Negotiation Skills

E. Negotiation can be defined as the process of bargaining between two or **more parties to reach a solution that is acceptable to all parties.**

Negotiation is one of the commonest activities in everyday life; we negotiate for prices, discount, payment terms, options, services, timing, etc. In organizations, negotiation skills are a must for managers and others in decision-making positions. So, it is necessary to consciously learn it and cultivate them in speaking and writing.

A successful negotiation is not always a win-lose situation but actually one that leaves both parties satisfied. Timing is a very important factor in negotiation. Coming up with the right proposal at the right time decides the success of the negotiation activity. To be a successful negotiator, you will have to develop and plan your strategy in advance. Your planning should be based on the strengths and weaknesses of the parties involved, the exact nature of the problem at hand, the issues at stake and the negotiation style.

- Introduce yourself and your team partners.
- Emphasize the importance of reaching an agreement together.
- Give your general views and invite the perspective of the other party.
- Express your interest in their response.
- Emphasize the need for building an understanding.
- Get the right information by asking the right questions at the right time.
- Repeat and paraphrase whenever you think there is no clarity or there is ambiguity.
- Accept corrections wherever necessary.
- Be careful in making and getting concessions. Remember the long term consequences of your actions.

   - ➢ Deal with deadlocks effectively. Try alternatives and suggest ways of dealing with such situations
   - ➢ Apologize if necessary.
   - ➢ Use humour and adjournments to dissipate tension.
- ➢ Table your final offer with conviction.
- ➢ It is important to get the agreement in writing and seek clarifications where necessary. *Remember these: Collaborate, compromise, control, accommodate. Adopt a matter-of-fact or warm style according to the situation. Emphasize long-term benefits and relationships. Don't presume anything. Don't lie. Expect to be probed in depth. Try to build sincerity and warmth. Tailor your details to suit the other party. Look for non-verbal clues. Listen carefully.*
   - **Types of negotiation:**
      - ❖ Negotiation based on compromise
      - ❖ Negotiation based on consensus
      - ❖ Negotiation based on synergy (the result is greater than the sum of the parts). It is a win-win situation.

First of all, the negotiation can overcome problems faster and move forward. But the disadvantage is it might lead to lack of commitment on the part of those who give up something and lead to frustration.

   - Secondly, since all parties agree on the solution, it will lead to better motivation and commitment.
   - Thirdly, it requires a lot of time.

   Culture and negotiation:

   Some cultures take a long time on building relations, before getting to business while others get down to business straightaway.

F. Communicative Skills

Communicative competence means the ability to communicate effectively and appropriately. In addition to the competence in the use of language (i.e. linguistic competence), you need to know how the language is used by the members of a speech community, their idioms, ways of expression, their customs, etc. In addition to linguistic competence and communicative competence (i.e. what is sometimes called' the gift of the gab'), you must also know how to negotiate and get along in actual situations (i.e. pragmatic competence) and in practical life situations.

a. Linguistic aspects include:

proper pronunciation, stress, intonation, tone, rhythm, pause, etc. Linguistic competence enables you to speak properly. Proper writing includes good hand writing, logical arrangement, the right choice of words, ability to handle different types of discourses like dialogues, reports, and different genres such as descriptive, narrative, expository, etc.,

b. Pragmatic aspects include:

- ability to communicate while performing different functions like greeting people, introducing people, asking for information, arguing politely, agreeing/disagreeing, etc.
- ability to interpret social meaning, understand use of different varieties and variations, understand situations, etc.
- ability to initiate conversations, negotiations, understanding and interpreting body language, etc.
- ability to understand behaviourfrom the point of view of culture and to behave appropriately; to understand the social structure, the values and beliefs of people. As the proverb goes, 'While in Rome do as the Romans do'.

There is, in addition, **strategic competence**, which involves how to recognize and repair communication breakdown and how to navigate and get things done.

G. Organizational Skills

Organizational skills are the ability to arrange systematically all activities in every aspect of life. These skills help in attaining a system of order and avert any hassles and problems in getting things done.

1. Make a list
2. Prioritize the list
3. Evaluate results
4. Develop systems-thinking
5. Design thinking

Systems thinking is a holistic approach of seeing system as a whole and finding solutions to the system, taking into account the parts. This involves personal mastery, building shared vision, team learning, pooling ideas, etc.

Organizational skills will help you to organize and plan projects. You should also plan to accommodate last minute changes and course corrections.

If you plan properly, you will be efficient, punctual and reliable since you use a systematic approach.

Note: Some of the traits listed in this section do overlap since they are interrelated. So, don't get worried or confused. For example, telephone skills involve both interpersonal and communicative skills. Communicative competence will help you in presentation, writing, negotiation, etc.

There are different kinds of etiquette, all of which matter for the acquisition of communication skills:

i. Telephone etiquette
ii. Business phone etiquette
iii. Mobile phone etiquette
iv. E-mail etiquette (Netiquette)
v. Conversation etiquette
vi. Social etiquette

i. The features of a good telephone conversation are:

❖ Brevity
❖ Courtesy
❖ Clarity
❖ Precision

The interaction over the phone or e-mail will depend on the relationship between the caller and the receiver. In most situations, courtesy markers are to be used.

Making telephone calls:

- ❖ Think about the proper time to make a call-not during untimely hours.
- ❖ Let the phone ring for a reasonable length of time.
- ❖ When the phone is answered, say 'hello' and greet the person, according to the time of the day.
- ❖ If there is a wrong number say 'sorry' and apologize. Don't just hang up.
- ❖ Identify yourself before starting the conversation and don't use any title before your name.
- ❖ Then ask, "May I know who is on the line?' or 'May I know who I'm speaking to?' or 'May I speak to Mr. -------, please.'
- ❖ Pronounce the words clearly, your voice should reflect courtesy.
- ❖ Your tone and intonation are very important since the other person cannot see your facial expressions.

Example:

A. An **informal** telephone conversation

Leela: ↘Hello, this is Leela calling. Could I talk to Mrs. ↗Kumar, please?

Kala: ↘Hi, Leela, ↘this's Kala. What a ↘surprise! (Say thank you at the end)

B. A **semi-formal** telephone dialogue.

↘Hello, ↘Good morning. ↘This's Renu, ↘Go Air, Bangalore.

May I ↘know ↗who's on the line?

↘Good morning, Ma'am// This's Ram/, ↘PA to MD/ ↘Ram and Sons

Receiving phone calls and answering them.

While answering a phone, don't say 'yes' or 'yeah' or 'yep'; it is curt and inappropriate.

All incoming calls should be answered in a polite manner. Practise good listening skills. It is a good idea to speak a bit slower to ensure clarity.

Example: Answering the phone

Hello, this is Pallavi, receptionist at Oxford Academy. May I know who is calling?

Good morning madam. I'm calling from Hyderabad to inquire f I could join the telephone training programme for the January session. I'm Gobind, an unemployed commerce graduate. I'm calling from Hyderabad, to enquire if I could join the telephone training programme for the January session.

Yes, Mr. Gobind. You can please call at the office before 3 p.m on any working day. Kindly bring with you your transcripts, testimonials and a draft for Rs. 1000/- towards fees. Thank you for calling. Bye.

Thank you Mam. I'll be there tomorrow before 3 p.m. Bye.

ii. Business phone etiquette:

a. Business telephone calls should always be answered with a greeting, the identification of the company and the receiver and 'May I help you'

b. Never put a caller on hold, but if you have to, politely tell them every minute or so and ask if they would like to hold. Speak clearly and loudly; do not mumble or speak fast.

c. Never be rude to a caller

d. Always keep a note pad to take notes, phone numbers etc. Thank the caller for calling at the end of the conversation.

e. If you are making business calls, make the call before the close of office hours. Avoid blunt phrases such as 'we can't do it' etc. When taking down messages, note down the caller's name, phone number, the message, the time and date.

iii. Mobile phone etiquette

- ✓ Speak softly
- ✓ Don't use the mobile phone while driving unless it is 'hands free'.
- ✓ While using mobiles, don't encroach upon somebody's personal space.
- ✓ Keep business private
- ✓ Keep a civil and pleasant tone.
- ✓ Consider your location and don't be an anytime-anywhere caller.
- ✓ Don't be a cell phone bore, whouses the phone in all kinds of places.
- ✓ Don't do multitasking while using the phone.
- ✓ Modulate your voice
- ✓ Use commonsense
- ✓ Limit gossip if you can't avoid it altogether
- ✓ Set your ringtone at a low level
- ✓ Pick your spot and time

iv. E-mail Etiquette (Netiquette)

- ✓ A set of dos and don'ts that are recommended by communication experts.
- ✓ The etiquette depends on whether it is a personal e-mail or a business one.

If it is a business e-mail use

i. Proper capitalization

ii. Punctuation, spelling

iii. Complete sentences in your messages

Remember that in e-mail, only writing (i.e., verbal) plays a 100% role, unlike in face-to-face or telephone communication. So, follow the basic rules.

Select the proper font/colour/size; don't use multi colours. [Ariel is U.K. favourite;Times Roman (US)]; stick to black Don't make the e-mail too long.

Write short sentences. In long sentences, you may go wrong and the ideas may not become clear. Write in a positive tone. Don't use too many abbreviations. Read your message before sending it.

v. Conversational Etiquette:

Don't be a bore or loud mouth or the know-it-all, or the whiner (i.e., airing one's problems), or the ferret (i.e., asking personal questions). Use humour and sarcasm carefully; they are delicate things.

Online Resources

1. https://www.coursera.org/specialization/bizcommunication/15?utm_medium=catalog
2. https://www.coursera.org/learn/publicspeaking
3. http://hrweb.mit.edu/learning-development/learning-topics/comm/articles/basics
4. http://www.skillsyouneed.com/interpersonal-skills.html
5. https://www.coursera.org/course/successfulnegotiation

Select Bibliography

1. Goleman, Daniel. *Emotional Intelligence: Why It Can Matter More Than IQ*. New York: Bantam, 2006
2. McKay, Mathew, Martha Davis and Patrick Fanning. *Messages: The Communication Skills Book*. Oakland: New Harbinger Publications, 2009
3. Hargie, Owen. *The Handbook of Communication Skills.*New York: Routledge, 2006
4. Patterson, Kerry and Joseph Grenny. *Crucial Conversations: Tools for Talking When Stakes Are High. New York:* McGraw-Hill, 2002
5. Strunk William and E.B. White. *The Elements of Style*. Essex: Pearson Education Limited, 2014

Unit VI – Practice

Test 1

You and your image

Work through this quiz with a partner. Do other people see you as you see yourself? It is no good looking into a mirror if you wish to see the person who you really are. The only real test is to see yourself in the same way as other people see you. The following quiz has been psychologically developed to help you to do exactly that.

1. **When do you feel your best**
   a. soon after waking up?
   b. during the afternoon and early evening?
   c. before you go to bed?
2. **Do you usually walk**
   a. quite fast, with long, swinging steps?
   b. quite fast, but with short, quick steps?
   c. not very fast, with your head up, looking at the world?
   d. not very fast, with your head down?
   e. very slowly?
3. **When you are talking to people, do you**
   a. stand with your arms folded?
   b. stand with your hands together in front of you?
   c. stand with one or both hands on your hips?
   d. touch the person you are talking to?
   e. touch your ear or chin or smooth your hair?
   f. have something like a pencil or a cigarette in your hands?
4. **When you are relaxing, do you sit with**
   a. your knees bent and your legs together?
   b. your legs crossed or wrapped round each other?
   c. your legs stretched straight out in front of you?
   d. with one leg curled up underneath you?
5. **When you find something very funny, how doyou react? Do you**
   a. give a loud, appreciative laugh?
   b. laugh, but not very loudly?
   c. laugh softly, under your breath?

d. give a very big smile?
e. smile slowly?

6. **When you go to a party, do you**
   a. make so much noise when you enter that everybody notices you?
   b. walk in quietly, looking for someone you know?
   c. hope that nobody will see you walking in, so you can remain unnoticed?
7. **When you are interrupted while you are working hard, concentrating on something, do you**
   a. feel pleased to be interrupted?
   b. feel very irritated?
   c. feel neither of these reactions very strongly?
8. **Which of the following colours do you like most**
   a. red or orange?
   b. white?
   c. black?
   d. dark blue or purple?
   e. yellow or light blue?
   f. brown, grey or violet?
   g. green?
9. **Just before you go to sleep, when you are lying in bed, do you lie**
   a. flat on your back?
   b. stretched out on your front?
   c. on your side?
   d. with your head under one arm?
   e. with your head under the bed clothes?
10. **Do you often dream that you are**
    a. falling?
    b. involved in a fight?
    c. looking for someone or something?
    d. taking your clothes off or with nothing on at all?
    e. flying or floating?

What your score means.

✓ **Over 60:** Others see you as someone they should handle with care-vain, self centered and extremely domineering. They may admire you and wish they could be more like you; theyare certainly in awe of you, but they don't always trust you and hesitate to become too deeply involved with you.

✓ **From 51 to 60:** Your friends see you as an exciting, highly volatile, rather impulsive personality, a natural leader, quick to make decisions (though not always the right ones). They see you as bold and venturesome, someone who will try anything – well, almost anything – once; someone who takes a chance and enjoys an adventure. They enjoy being in your company because of the excitement you radiate.

✓ **From 41 to 50:** Others see you as fresh, lively, charming, amusing and always interesting; someone who is constantly the centre of attention, but sufficiently well balanced not to let it go to your head. They see you also as kind, considerate and understanding, someone who will cheer them up or help them out as the situation requires.

✓ **From 31 to 40:** Other people see you as sensible, cautious, careful and practical. They see you as clever, gifted or talented, but modest. Not a person who makes friends too quickly or too easily, but someone who is extremely loyal to the friends you do make and who expects the same loyalty in return. Those who really get to know you realize that it takes a lot to shake your trust in your friends, but equally, that it takes you a long time to get over it if that trust is shaken.

✓ **From 21 to 30:** Your friends see you as meticulous and painstaking, perhaps a bit too fussy at times, ultra cautious and ultra careful, a slow, steady plodder. It would surprise them tremendously if you were ever to behave impulsively or do something on the spur of the moment. They expect you to examine everything very carefully from every conceivable angle and then, usually decide against it. They see this sort of reaction on your part as being partly due to your careful nature and partly due to indolence.

✓ **Under 21:** You are seen to be shy, nervous and indecisive, someone who needs looking after, who always leaves it to someone else to make the decisions and prefers never to get too involved with anyone or anything. They see you as something of a worrier, seeing problems which don't exist and crossing bridges long before you come to them. Some people tend to regard you as dull and boring and it takes someone who knows you well to know that you are not. The trouble is that you permit very few people to get that close to you.

Test 2

How honest are you, really?
Answer each question honestly and be honest in noting the score.

a. You find a wallet containing Rs. 1,000 plus an identification card. Will you keep the cash?
No ( ) Maybe ( ) Yes ( )

b. You want something to be done in an office. The clerk concerned refuses to do it first but later hints that for Rs. 100, he will get it done. Will you give him the money?
No ( ) Maybe ( ) Yes ( )

c. You sell your bicycle to a friend who pays you Rs. 1, 500. By reporting only Rs. 1, 000 to your father, you can pocket Rs. 500 Will you do it?
No ( ) Maybe ( ) Yes ( )

d. A book store gives you books worth Rs. 200 butby mistake bills you only for Rs. 25 Will you quietly pay Rs. 25 and walk out with the books?
No ( ) Maybe ( ) Yes ( )

e. In the college laboratory you find a new watch in exactly the design you need. There is no one in the lab. Will you hide it in your bag before you leave?
No ( ) Maybe ( ) Yes ( )

f. You have lunch with your friends in an expensive restaurant. While paying the bill, a friend suggests, 'You are the secretary of our cultural association and you can write it in that account'. Will you?
No ( ) Maybe ( ) Yes ( )

g. You are staying in a hotel and you go to the bath. There you find a gold chain. Will you check out of the hotel with the chain?
No ( ) Maybe ( ) Yes ( )

h. You speed through a stop sign on your bike and dent a car that was coming in the opposite direction. This accident can cost you some money. Will you tella lie to thepoliceman, sayingthat it was the fault of the driver of the car and tell a lie?
No ( ) Maybe ( ) Yes ( )

i. Your bike is for sale and someone agrees to pay the price you name; he gives an advance of Rs. 1, 000 and the two of you shake hands. Later on, another person offers you Rs. 2, 000 more and asks you to tell the first one that you have changed your mind and return the advance. Will you do that?
No ( ) Maybe ( ) Yes ( )
Scoring: Give yourself two points for each No, one point for each Maybe, and no points for each Yes. Then add up and see how your honesty rates.

Test 3

Are you a genius?

There is an international organization, **Mensa**, whose only requirement for membership is an I.Q. in the genius range. Try this test and see if you are eligible. Time yourself: there are bonus points for finishing in less than 15, 20 or 25 minutes.

1. Which of the lower boxes best completes the series on the top?

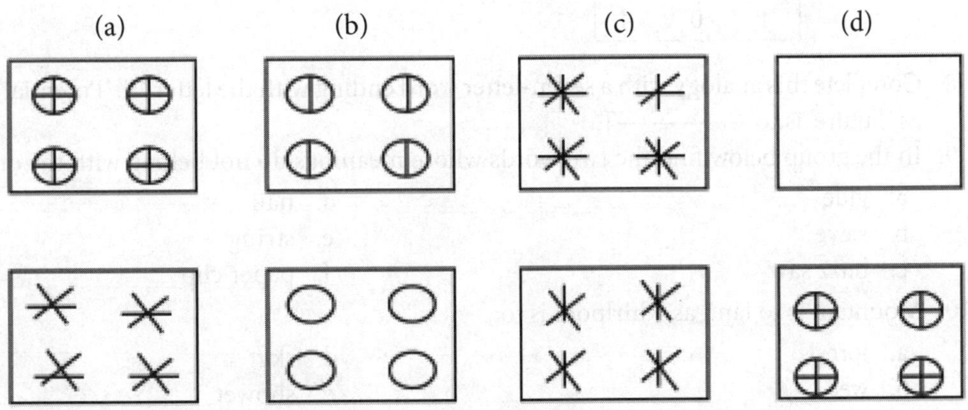

2. I am a man. If Larry's son is my son's father, what relationship do I bear to Larry?
   a. His grandfather
   b. His father
   c. His son
   d. His grandson
   e. I am Larry
   f. His uncle

3. Which does not belong in the following group?
   a. Knife
   b. Swan
   c. Smile
   d. Feather
   e. Lovely
   f. Thought
4. Which two shapes below represent mirror images of the same shape?

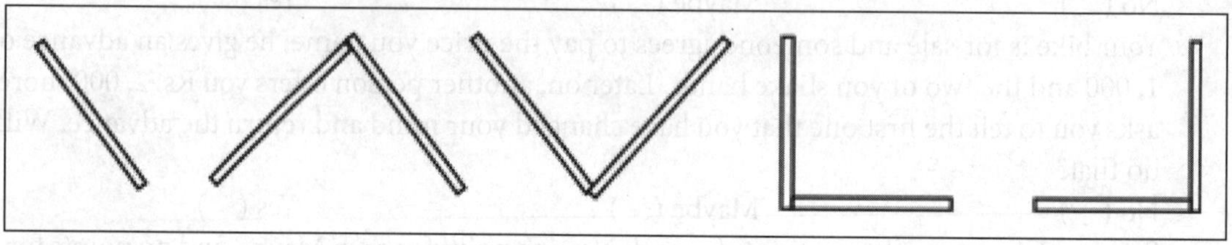

(a) (b) (c) (d) (e)

5. What number comes next in the series?
   9, 16, 25, 36, -----------------------------
6. Complete the analogy with a five-letter word ending with letter 'H'. High is to low as sky is to --------h.
7. In this box below, a rule of arithmetic applies across and down the box so that two of the numbers in a line produce the third. What is the missing number?

6	2	4
2	?	0
4	0	4

8. Complete this analogy with a seven-letter word ending with the letter 'T'. 'Potential' is to 'Actual' as 'Future' is to -------------T.
9. In the group below find the two words whose meanings do not belong with the others.
   a. glue
   b. sieve
   c. buzz saw
   d. nail
   e. string
   f. paper clip
10. Mountain is to land as whirlpool is to:
    a. forest
    b. wet
    c. sea
    d. sky
    e. shower
11. Find the number that logically completes the series:
    2, 3, 5, 9, 17, --------

12. Two of the shapes below represent mirror images of the same shape. Which are they?

(a) (b) (c) (d)

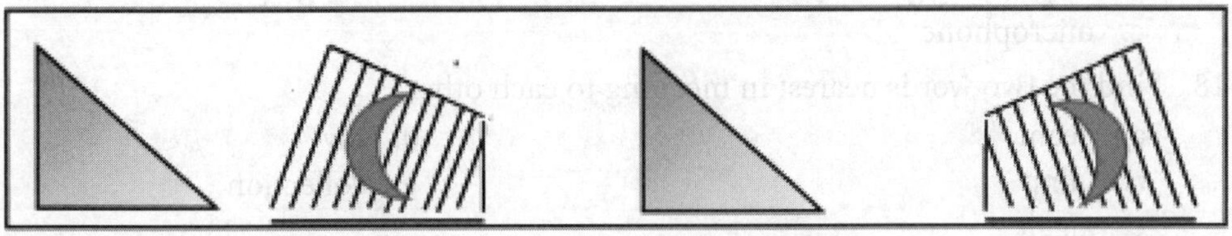

13. Statistics indicate that men drivers are involved in more accidents than women drivers. The only conclusion that can be drawn with certainty from this is that
    a. male chauvinists are wrong, as usual, about women's abilities.
    b. men are actually better drivers but drive more frequently.
    c. men and women drive equally well, but men log more total mileage.
    d. most truck drivers are men
    e. there is not enough information to justify a conclusion.
14. In the box below, a rule of arithmetic applies across and down the box so that two of the numbers in a line produce the third. What is the missing number?

6	2	12
4	5	20
24	10	?

15. If Ax B = 24, CxD = 32, Bx D= 48 and BxC = 24, what does AxBxCxD equal?
    a. 480
    b. 576
    c. 744
    d. 768
    e. 824
16. Which of the four lower selections best completes the series on the top?

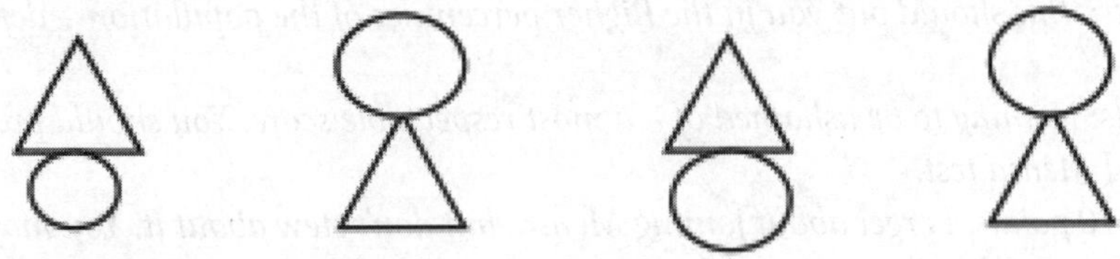

(a) (b) (c) (d)

17. Which word does not belong in this group?
    a. microscope
    b. magnifying glass
    c. microphone
    d. telescope
    e. telegraph
18. Find the two words nearest in meaning to each other.
    a. beam
    b. lump
    c. giggle
    d. ray
    e. collection
19. If Jim turns right or left at the stop sign he will run out of gas before he reaches a service station. He has already gone too far past a service station to return before he runs out of gas. He does not see a sevice station ahead. Only one of the following statements can be positively deduced from this.
    a. He may run out of gas.
    b. He will run out of gas.
    c. He should not have taken this route.
    d. He is lost.
    e. He should turn right at the stop sign.
    f. He should turn left at the stop sign.
20. Complete the following analogy

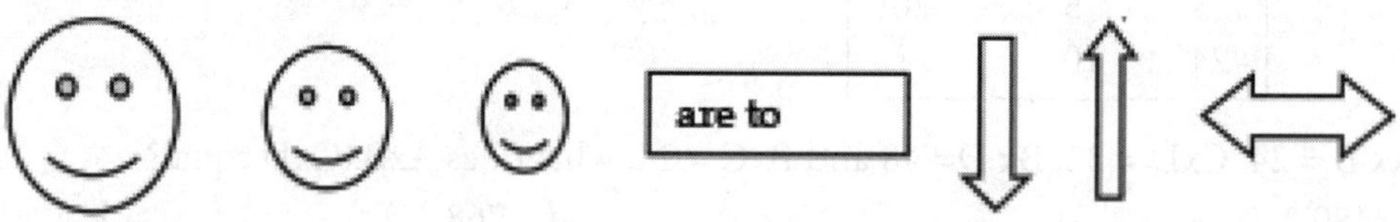

As + – 0 are to:

a. + – 0
b. 0 + –
c. – + 0
d. 0 – +
e. + + 0

How to score:

Give yourself one point for each correct answer. You receive an additional five points if you finished the test in less than 15 minutes, three points if you finished in less than 20 minutes, and two points if you finished in less than 25 minutes. If you scored:

✓ *20–25 points: You are extremely intelligent – a perfect candidate for Mensa*

✓ *15–19 points: This should put you in the higher percentiles of the population – definitely a Mensa candidate.*

✓ *10–14 points: Nothing to be ashamed of – a most respectable score. You should probably complete the standard Mensa test.*

✓ *Fewer than 10 points: Forget about joining Mensa, but don't stew about it. You may be just having a bad day. Some of the most-successful writers, businessmen, artists and other famous people don't have exceptionally high I.Q.s either.*

Test 4

✓ Answer the questionnaire given below to judge the way you feel about certain things or areas. Tick the box that comes closest to expressing your feelings about each question. There are no right or wrong answers, only opinions. Use the scale below to answer.

(A)]Clearly agree; (B) Slightly agree; (C) Neutral;
(D) Slightly disagree; (E) Clearly disagree]

	A	B	C	D	E
1. Entertaining friends at my home is a lot of fun.					
2. Spending money on books is a waste.					
3. A strong long term understanding of each other is necessary.					
4. Prayer is beneficial in seeking solutions to problems					
5. It's imperative that teenagers have some religious training.					
6. I often read religious literature					
7. People who attend religious discourses are generally more honest.					
8. If someone is making a mistake, I'll tell them so.					
9. I enjoy the company of people of my own sex.					
10. I feel that an element of risk adds spice to life.					
11. In a relationship, I feel it is very important to discuss everything openly.					

12. I rarely worry about making a good impression.					
13. I feel I can do things as well as most people.					
14. I do not enjoy being in the public eye.					
15. I have difficulty going to sleep.					

Self-assessment:

i. Based on the answers to the questionnaire, write a paragraph about your strengths and weaknesses; say what sort of a person you are.

ii. Write a paragraph mentioning the qualities that you look for in your friend of the same or opposite sex.

iii. Have you heard of SWOT analysis – a concept used in management?
S-strengths; W-weaknesses; O-Opportunities; T-Threats

Think about these things and write a short paragraph on your understanding of the four concepts mentioned in SWOT analysis.

Test 5

Are you good judge of character?

In sizing up people we all fall back now and then on outward signs of inner character. You can check up on the accuracy of your character readings by marking each of the following common beliefs. 'True' or 'False'.

1. Long slander hands mean an artistic temperament. [ ]
2. A slow learner remembers what he/she has learned better than a fast learner. [ ]
3. A person who does not look you in the eye is likely to be dishonest. [ ]
4. Fat people are typically good natured. [ ]
5. Ears pointed at the top warn of foxiness, selfishness or even dishonesty. [ ]
6. Wrinkles on the outer corners of the eyes show that a person has a sense of humour.
7. Curly hair is a sign of vitality and exuberance. [ ]
8. A high bulging forehead is a sign of superior brain power. [ ]
9. Cold hands are asign ofan affectionate disposition. [ ]
10. Men sleep more soundly than women. [ ]
11. Men's senses are less delicate than women's. [ ]

[Note: There are many more tests available on the internet. Try them on Google. MENSA Tests, Personality Tests, IQ Tests etc.]

Test 6

I. How popular are you?

Do you wonder whether people like you? Here is the answer. This series of questions, based on psychological tests, is designed to give you a general estimate of your personal popularity and your aptitude for making friends. Answer each question with a'yes' or 'no'.

1. Do you express your opinion freely unsought?
2. Do you feel superior to those of your best friends?
3. Do you like to eat alone?
4. Do you read front-page murder stories?
5. Do tests like this interest you?
6. Do you talk about your aspirations, disappointments and problems?
7. Do you borrow often?
8. Are you a 'Dutch treat' addict?
9. When you describe something that has happened, do you give every small detail?
10. Do you like entertaining when it costs money?
11. Do you take pride in your absolute frankness?
12. Do you keep people waiting when you have an appointment with them?
13. Do you honestly like children (of others)?
14. Do you play practical jokes?
15. Do you think it is silly for middle-aged people to fall in love?
16. Do you dislike a gathering of more than seven people?
17. Do you nurse grudges?
18. Do you frequently use such words as 'awfully', 'dreadfully', 'terribly'?
19. Do telephone operators and salespeople irritate you?
20. Do you consider stupid and uninteresting the people who do not share your enthusiasm for music, books, sport?
21. Do you break your word as often as you keep it?
22. Do you criticizeoften, and to their faces, your family, your best friends, and your employees?
23. Do you become depressed or discouraged when things go badly?
24. Are you altogether happy atthe success of your friends (when you are out of luck)?
25. Do you ever indulge in interesting gossip?

II. Who are these people? Give one word for the description given about some personality traits.

i. One who thinks only about himself/herself.
ii. One who boasts about himself/herself.
iii. One who easily moves with others without inhibitions and loves being a sociable person.
iv. One who is closeted with himself/herself.
v. One who has a passion for stealing.
vi. One who suffers from imaginary illnesses.

vii. One who is blindly attached to any opinion or system.
viii. One who is given to thesensual pleasures of life.
ix. One who has excessive enthusiasm about something or faith
x. One who talks too much.
xi. One who enjoys torturing others.
xii. One who constantly doubts.
xiii. One who changes sides often.
xiv. One who is new to a profession.
xv. One who flirts with women.

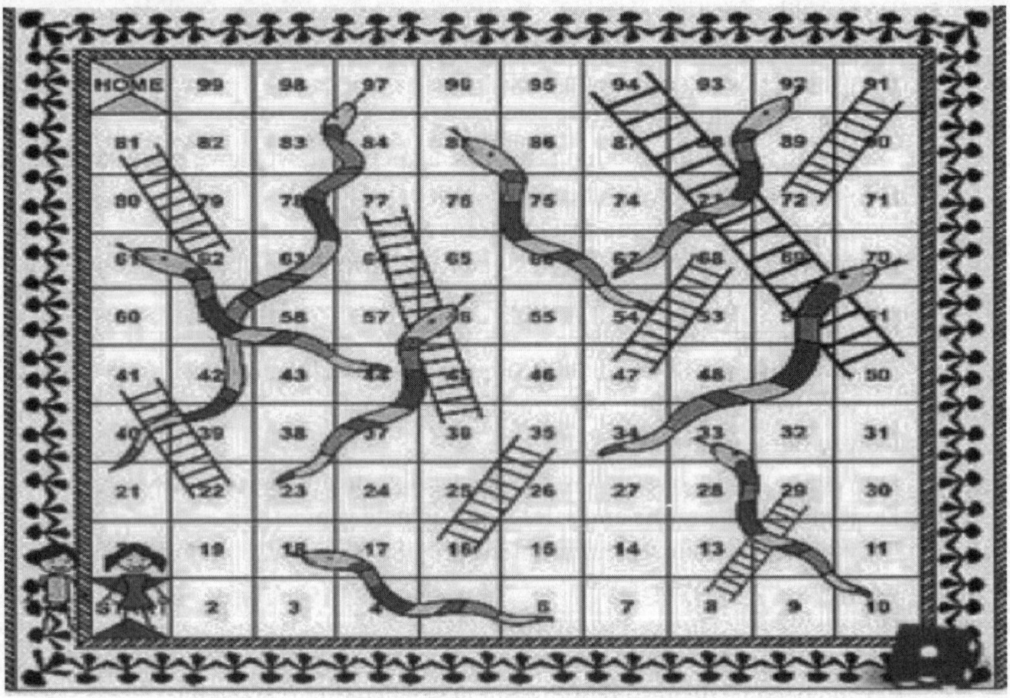

Source: http://www.123peppy.com/

- ❖ Prepare a snake and ladder game to show how one can go up or come down.
- ❖ Use personality traits and other soft skills for the numbers.
- ❖ You can prepare your own chart.
- ❖ What is given is a model/frame.

ANSWERS AND SCORES

Test 1

- You and your image-
- Award yourself points as per the scheme given below. Work out your total score and see what it means.

Points

1.	(a) 2	(b) 4	(c) 6				
2.	(a) 6	(b) 4	(c) 7	(d) 2	(e) 1		
3.	(a) 4	(b) 2	(c) 5	(d) 7	(e) 6	(f) 1	
4.	(a) 4	(b) 6	(c) 2	(d) 1			
5.	(a) 6	(b) 4	(c) 3	(d) 5	(e) 2		
6.	(a) 6	(b) 4	(c) 2				
7.	(a) 6	(b) 2	(c) 4				
8.	(a) 6	(b) 2	(c) 7				
9.	(a) 7	(b) 6	(c) 4	(d) 2	(e) 1		
10.	(a) 4	(b) 2	(c) 3	(d) 7	(e) 5	(f) 6	(g) 1

Test 2

How honest are you really?

- ❖ 18 to 17 — You're a very honest person, straight as an arrow.
- ❖ 12 to 17 — Your honesty is laudable and good.
- ❖ 7 to 11 — Your honesty is selective, a bit shaky.
- ❖ 2 to 6 — You're a self seeker; however, there is hope for change.
- ❖ 1 — You are a thorough cheat.

Test 3

Are you a genius?

- ❖ (c) Omit the horizontal line in the asterisk, as it was omitted in the circle.
- ❖ (c)
- ❖ (e) The other words are nouns
- ❖ (d) and (e)
- ❖ 49; 9 is 3 squared, 16 is 4 squared, 25 is 5 squared, and so on. Also 9+7=16, 16 + 9= 25, 25+11=36, and so on.
- ❖ Earth
- ❖ In each vertical and horizontal row, the second number is subtracted from the first.

- Present
- (b) and (c) All the others hold things together
- (c) A whirlpool is part of the sea as mountain is part of land
- 33. The difference between the numbers is progressively multiplied by 2.
- (b) and (d)
- (e)
- 240. (24 x 10 and 12 x 20 both equal 240)
- 768. It is not necessary to determine the values of A, B, C, D. Simply multiply 24 * 32
- (d) The ball gets larger in each box, while the triangle keep alternating positions.
- (e) The others are all things that increase images or sounds.
- (a) and (d) are synonyms.
- Just the fact that Jim can't see a service station ahead doesn't mean there isn't one.
- Positive and minus change positions: neutral stays in the same place.

Test 5

All are false!

Test 6

1	No	6	Yes	11	No	16	No	21	No
2	No	7	No	12	No	17	No	22	No
3	No	8	No	13	Yes	18	Yes	23	No
4	Yes	9	No	14	No	19	No	24	Yes
5	Yes	10	Yes	15	No	20	No	25	Yes

The highest score is 25. For each answer that agrees with the answers given, give one point. 17 is still good; you are liked.

Case-Study for Discussion

Chennai-based **Apollo Generators** is a national organization selling and servicing diesel-powered generators. In 2012, its Managing Director realized that the company was not earning the expected profit because its sales and accounts managers weren't trained in high-level negotiations. They were giving away unrealistic discounts on valuable products because of lack of negotiation skills which brought down the profit margins of the company. There was a challenge of staying competitive in the market with the broader aim of earning profit for the company. The MD decided to train the managers in fundamental negotiation skills to boost up profits without hurting the interests of the clients. He delegated the task to a local company, Solution-providers, who trained professionals in negotiation and related business-skills.

The solution-providers designed a module for the targeted group in the business/customer interface–the sales and account managers. As a first step, they conducted a workshop for all sales and product managers. They introduced key concepts of negotiation skills to their clients. They taught them how to handle uncomfortable topics in creative, tactful ways without hurting the parties' relationship. They also taught them how to respond effectively to extreme or unrealistic demands of the client without getting offended. They taught them novel approachesto winning and servicing clients, which could help Apollo Generators boost its operating margins. They were taught to incorporate cultural factors in plans for negotiation. They were provided with tools such as planning sheets and frameworks to ensure that they took their new learning into the everyday work place. They were taught to identify different sources of bargaining power. In addition, Solution-providers also helped the company build a culture of learning.

In this way Apollo Generators managers learned the difference between selling and negotiation. They learned how to trade with the counterpart rather than give away advantages easily. The group worked through realistic exercises to apply the new concepts.

As a result, the Managing Director of Apollo Generators reported that his team is achieving better results. They are more confident about addressing previous risks. The account and sales managers are enthused by the process, and are using their new negotiation tools to earn more profit for the company. In this way, a strategic weakness of the company was addressed through timely and decisive intervention.

Questions

1. The MD of Apollo Generators noticed a lacuna in the managers' performance. What was it?
2. What measures did he undertake to address the problem?
3. How did the Solution-providers train the managers? What else could have been done?
4. What was the outcome of the whole exercise?

Unit VII – Resumes and Cover Letters

The art of writing is the artof discovering what you believe.

– Gustave Flaubert

OBJECTIVES:

After reading this unit, you'll be able to

✓ Learn the step-by-step process of writing a resume
✓ Differentiate between bio-data, profiles, CVs and resumes
✓ Write effective cover letters

I. It's time for you to look for a job. Maybe it's your first job, maybe it's a job in a new field or maybe it's an improvement over the slave pit in which you now toil.
Here are some tips and steps to enable you to perfect every aspect of your job hunt.

Step 1 First, read the advertisements carefully. That itself is an exercise in reading comprehension. Modern advertisements provide the first test for you.Read the job advertisement given below and make sense of it:

YOU'RE A GEEK! ***"The sooner you accept that, the better off we'll both be."***
• Hey, to us it's a term of endearment. One that pays homage to your technological talents and passion for what you do. And due to the massive growth in business, we need that talent and passion at Sapient. • We are looking for developers and programmers in Gurgaon and Bangalore with a maximum of 4-6 years of experience in the industries such as commerce, financial services, energy and trading with the following skills:
Java, C++, ATG, QA, Infra. Please visit www.sapient.com/geeks Please send your resume to opportunity@sapient.com

- **How well have you understood the advertisement?**
  a. Who is a geek? Does the word geek have a positive or negative meaning?
  b. What is the difference between a nerd and a geek?

c. Why does the advertisement say that the sooner you accept that the better off "we'll both be"? What does it imply?
d. Why is the word **hey** used in the advertisement? What does it show?
e. What is the meaning of the word 'endearment'? Do they want a geek or not?
f. If selected where will you be placed?
g. Do you want to apply for a position in this company?

Step 2

You must always visit the website of the company you wish to apply to and gather all information about the company before you decide to apply. Study the details about the company and see if you will fit in there and if you would like to work in such a company. Study all aspects – when it was started, its durability, the financial aspects, its image and reputation etc. And then decide. This will help you in the interview too.

Step 3

There are four different words used in the job advertisements of companies and other institutions in India.

a. Bio-data
b. Curriculum Vitae (CV)
c. Resume
d. Profile

In a broad sense, they mean the same thing but the focus is different. The use of the word also reflects the nature of the company or institution. So, study the advertisement carefully and visit the website of the company in which you are thinking of applying for a position.

a. The word **bio-data** is used generally in India; it's not very common in a multinational context. The word means 'biographical information' (not the body data or vital statistics!). It's of Indian origin and is used by small companies and government agencies.
b. The expression **curriculum vitae** is of Latin origin, which means a brief written account of one's education, employment etc. when applying for a job. This is more formal and academic.
c. The word **resume** is of French origin which means 'a summary or abstract'. This is the most widely used one.
d. The word **profile** is of Italian origin and means 'a portrait' or 'a brief biography as given in an article in a periodical'. This is also used by some companies.

All of them, more or less, refer to the same kind of information about a person, but the focus and the format and presentation may be different. It also depends on what the employer wants. So, use the same expression found in the advertisement. (See the ads given in the worksheets.)

If an employer or a government agency uses the word bio-data, you should also use the same word, if the word **resume** is used, you should use the same word.

Step 4

You know that the first impression is the best impression. Your resume is the first entry point into your future workplace. That's why resumes matter a lot.

Your resume is a statement of your career history, your years of education, your commitment to the job, your dreams, all described on a sheet of white paper, titled at the top, with your name.

A resume to be effective must follow one simple rule: information must be delivered in an **attractive, effective** and **easily accessible** manner. A properly prepared resume of a less experienced candidate can trump a poor resume from a more experienced candidate.

Studies show that employers spend about 10–14 seconds, looking at each resume because of the enormous number of resumes that are received; there is no time to go through each resume in detail.

- ❖ So, **distil**, **distil**, and **distil**.
- ❖ Don't write long paragraphs!

Your life on a page

The employers who read your resumes do not know you. They have no idea of your charming personality or your talent or the responsible way you are taking care of your parents! All they have to go byis your resume that is in front of them.

A. Appearance

- ***First of all, take care of the appearance of your resume.***

1. **Font** – Don't get too creative, no decorative designs but a simple easily readable font which shows you mean business. Recommended fonts include Times New Roman or Arial or Verdana with font size 11 or 12.

   Remember what impresses the employer should not be the letters or page but the words.

2. **Paper**

   Don't use colored resumes unless you want to become a fashion designer or a hairdresser. Use whites, light gray or ecru. Use the same paper for your cover letter and the envelope as you use for your resume.

3. **Envelope**

   If your resume is being sent by snail mail, the envelope should be typed.

4. **Scanning**

   Companies have begun scanning resumes into computers so that they can be accessed for future reference. So, use the right font and paper for your resume.

   A good way to test your paper's suitability is to photocopy your resume; if the copy comes out blurred, dark or anything but white, change the paper/font.

B. Sections of the resume

i. **Name**

   Make sure you indicate exactly what you want to be called or you'll run the risk of your co-workers calling you what your grandmother calls you. Don't use any titles like Mr., Mrs., Miss. Ms.etc. as part of your name.Bold or capitalize your name, using letters two to six points larger than the rest of the text.

   Place your name on the first line of the left side of the page. Some prefer to put the name on the center of the page. But many prefer to put it at the **right** so that when the resume is put in a folder, your name is clearly visible.

ii. **Address:**
Make sure the address you are giving is reliable. If you're still in college, give your permanent address in case your resume is considered a few months after you send it in.
E-mail – Give your personal e-mail.
Phone number – A phone number is a must.

iii. **Job Objective**-Don't use the clichés like 'a chance to apply my skills' or 'a challenging opportunity' or 'an opportunity for growth'. They have been used a million times.

The job objective sentence should be brief and no more than two lines long. Generally, job objectives are descriptive or titled. Job adjectives describe the type of job you are interested in, like 'entry level position in sales' or 'to obtain entry level position in an IT company'. Titled job descriptions name the job title like 'banking investigator' or 'engineer in software development and networking' or 'management trainee'.

iv. **Education:** If your academic degrees set you apart from other applicants or link you closely to the position you are applying for, mention them. List the institution (s) you attended, their location and your degree. If you are yet to finish the programme, list the 'anticipated completion date'. Mention only the post graduate or professional degrees that are related to the job. Do not mention B.A, B.Sc.etc. or worse, high school certificates if you have higher qualification. If you have only B.C.A or B.B.A, you can mention that.

Most resume writers put their education section in the last section of their resume (if they have work experience). Recent graduates should have their educational qualifications at the top, below job objective, (if there is no summary of qualifications).

v. **Summary of qualifications**-Avoid clichés like 'self-motivated ' and 'goal oriented' etc. This section highlights your achievements that set you apart from others. The years of experience, the skills you have acquired, your leadership qualities can be stated. Such statements can be bulleted. For example,
   - 3 years IT industry experience/management etc.
   - Proper sales success in IT products.
   - Degrees in information technology.

vi. **Work history or professional experience (if you have any) :**Use bullets to highlight your professional experience. For example,
   - Sales and marketing.
   - Applied marketing skills to increase sales of computers.
   - Cultivated client relationships.
   - Wrote press releases on new computer products.

vii. **Technical skills**
   a. Microsoft Excel
   b. Microsoft Office
   c. Photoshop
   d. HTML
   e. LexisNexis
   f. Database programmes
   g. Typing (55 wpm)

viii. **Additional skills:** Experience in personnel operations and project management.
ix. **Interests:** Develop and edit bimonthly newsletter for in-house circulation.
x. **Language skills:** Fluent German, Spanish, Bengali, Hindi and Telugu.

II. Now let's see how the same information can be presented in different ways

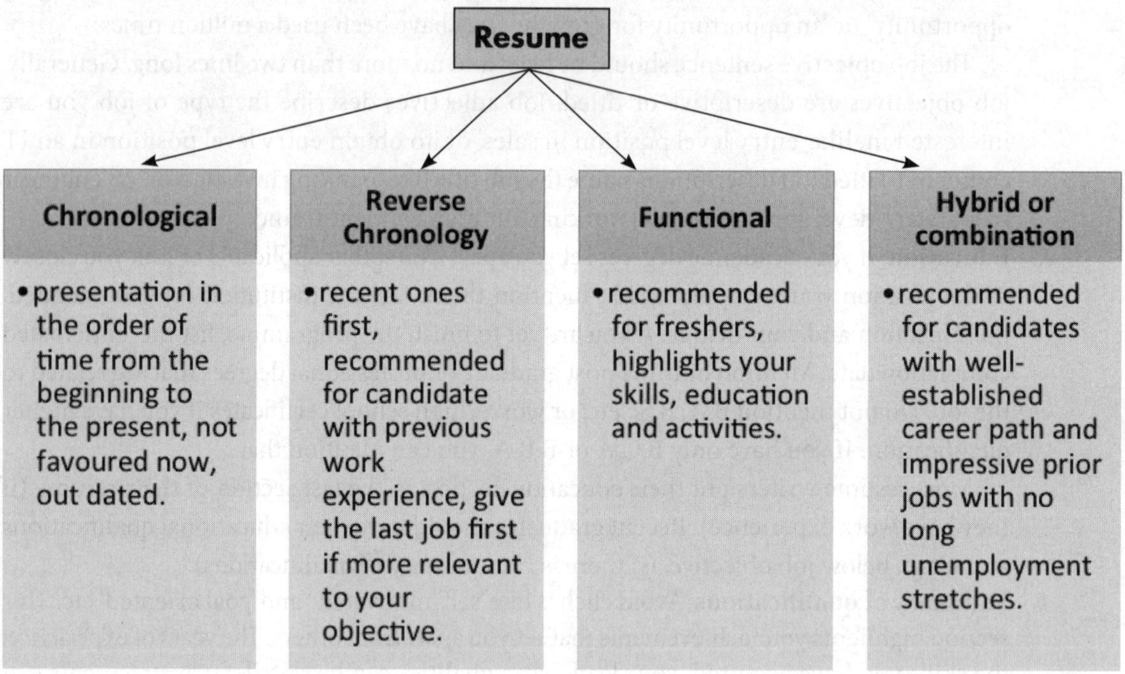

Here are some sample formats for the different kinds of resume. You can fill in your details.

A Reverse Chronological Resume

Name:

Current Address	Permanent Address
____________	____________
____________	____________
Phone:	Phone:
e-mail:	e-mail:

Objective – A junior position in market research

PAGE 1

1. **Job Objective:**
   - _________
   - _________
   - _________
2. **Education:**
   - __________(recent one first)
   - _________
   - _________
3. **Summary of Qualifications**
   - _________
   - _________
   - _________
4. **Professional Experience**
   - __________(recent one first)
   - _________
   - _________
   - _________

PAGE 2

5. **Technical skills**
   - ________
   - ________
6. **Additional Skills**
   - ________
   - ________
   - ________
7. **Interests**
   - ________
   - ________
8. **Languages known**
   - ________
   - ________
9. **Honours**
   - ________
   - ________

Points to note:

1. For your previous experience in a short amount of time, don't include months, give only years: "2004–2005 Senior Web Designer".
2. Give the title of your job or the name of the company, whichever is the most impressive. Be consistent in the format-title of your job or the name of the company. Company names give a better idea of your job.
3. Always remember that your work history should answer the question: 'How will my skill be useful to my employer?'
4. If you have any awards, always say what they are for. If you have produced anything – products, publications, events or agreements, name them to show 'I did this'.

Functional Resume

Name :
Address :
Phone No. :
e-mail :

Objective

To secure a position that will allow me the opportunity to utilize my analytical, interpersonal and communication skills.

Education

___________ (Recent degree first)

____

____

Computer Skills

- IBM and Macintosh formats.
- Microsoft windows 2007.
- Word perfect 5.1 and 6.0
- Microsoft word
- Excel
- LexisNexis

Honours

___________ (recent ones first)

____

____

Activities

- College of Engineering, Senior Class President
- Leadership programme Intern
- University volunteer
- Treasurer, HelpAge
- **Experience**

____

____

____

Points to Remember

1. Functional resumes are useful to list your skills and achievements. Work experience is not emphasized.
2. Your skill list should be organized, divided and bulleted.
3. Put the information you would like to highlight on the **left side** of the page where the employers are most likely to read it. Put information you would least like them to know on the right.

Hybrids

Once you have mastered the fundamentals of resume writing, you can combine the chronological and the functional formats to your advantage. This is recommended for candidates with a good track record and impressive jobs with no long stretches of unemployment. It is good to stress employment experience, abilities and job functions.

II. General Tips:

i. Use spell check and proof-read carefully; there should be no mistakes.
ii. Do not mention expected salary, or details regarding caste, religion unless asked for.
iii. Do not mention family details like spouses, parents etc.
iv. Be specific about interests and do not bluff; mention only those related to the job you are applying for. You can mention your weaknesses as strategies.
v. Make sure that your resume makes you proud.

IV. Cover Letters: *These can be of the following three types:*

- ❖ Covering letter (Indian)
- ❖ Cover letter (standard)
- ❖ Letter of application (Old style British)

i. The cover letter is the first chance to have a conversation with a prospective employer. So, it is as important as your resume. Your cover letter serves as a fuller expression of your personality; your employers are interested in the skills to fit the job and, at the same time, they look for people who can express themselves clearly and in an appealing manner. Careless typos and oddball expressions can spoil your resume and the chances.
ii. Tailoring your letter specifically to the company and the job will impress the prospective employer and give you an edge over others.
iii. In addition to the advertisement, get all the information about the company from the web-site, through web browsers like Google or Yahoo or through LexisNexis.
iv. Avoid cover letter errors
   - ➢ Don't make the cover letter too short. Just one paragraph or two or three sentences will spoil even a good resume. A cover letter should have at least three paragraphs, no paragraphs of over six or seven lines long, with the longest one being the middle and the shortest being the final paragraph.
   - ➢ Don't make your cover letter funny or humorous. Your cover letter must offer a sample of your ability to conduct business-like communication.
   - ➢ Avoid all grammatical or spelling mistakes. Don't totally rely on spell checks because sometimes spell checks may change misspelled words into wrong words. E.g. **Referees** are available on request.
   - ➢ Don't use clichés and don't write overdone sentences, using big, impressive or unfamiliar words and flattering statements.
   - ➢ Don't be egomaniacal. You are writing the letter not to pamper your ego. Nobody likes a self-absorbed narcissist or to work with one. You must give your employees an idea of who you are and what you can do; be sincere.

- ➢ Don't say: 'I would DIE to work in your company' or 'Yours is the most fabulous company and it would be the culmination of my life dream to work with you', etc. Instead you can say: 'I have admired your company's products for some time…'
- ➢ Make sure you're addressing an individual by name or by designation. Avoid addressing HR or just the name of the company. You can always find out the head of the department of the company.

V. The Cover letter Template/Pattern/Format

Your name
Your house no./Apt./Street Address
Your city/town, Zip
Email:
Your phone no.
Fax (if any)

Date

Your prospective employer's name
Designation
Department
Company/Institution address
City/town PIN
Phone:
Fax:

Dear Mr. /Ms. /Sir/Madam (Avoid: Sirs)

The first paragraph tells why you're contacting the person and where you came to know about the job. Also, state briefly who you are. Then say that you've researched knowledge of their company.

The aim: to demonstrate that you're a worthy candidate and to entice them to read further.

The second and third paragraphs are about you, particularly why you're an ideal match for the job by summarising why you are the person they're looking for. You may also clarify some points in your resume.

The last paragraph is your goodbye where you thank the reader of the letter for the time taken. Say you look forward to their reply.

Sincerely/Truly

Your signature

Tips:

- ➢ **Date:** Placement of the date whether centred or to the right is up to you. Usual style is: month, date, year _ July 10, 2009. (Indian and European style is; date, month, year. Writing only numbers will be confusing, 10-7-2009 – the first one month or date?)
- ➢ **Address of the person you're writing**: if not available, give only the designation as in the advertisement. If you know the name, use 'Sincerely' as the complimentary close; if you use the designation, say 'Truly'.
- ➢ **First paragraph:**
  I am writing in response to your advertisement in or website __________ I am a __________ (your identifying characteristics). I am a __________ (your degree/profession). I have worked in__________ (your area of expertise). I am interested in __________ (what position you're looking for).
- ➢ **Middle paragraph:**
  Here, you tell the employer how, based on your qualifications, experience and previous performances, you will perform well in the desired position. Say something like 'My post-graduate degree in computer technology, combined with my __________years of experience, would make a strong addition to your company's team'__________etc.
  - Don't mention the expected salary. If asked to in the advertisement/website put it at the end of the paragraph and mention a range as possible.
  - Don't get overly personal and make touching statements to impress employers.
- ➢ **Final paragraph:**
  - The shortest paragraph in your letter. Here are some examples:
  - Thank you for your time.
  - Thank you for your consideration.
- ➢ **Do not** say: Thanking you in anticipation.
  - A note of confidence is added:
  - I look forward to your reply/response/learning from you/ your call.

VI. Types of cover letters

1. Response to an advertised position – generally in newspapers – mention the exact name of the advertisement, job title, name of the newspaper, the day and 'date of the ad'.
2. Response to the information in the website.
3. Response to networking through friends or through some other contact – In this case, don't mention the contact; simply say what you are looking for: 'I am looking for a position in finance, marketing, __________'
4. Cold mailing: Without any information, just apply to some important companies. Some companies keep the resumes on their file.

VII. Email cover letter etiquette

Email cover letters should not run to more than two or three paragraphs. Don't rehash your resume. In communicating online, you are not exempt from any of the formalities of paper-based communication. Don't write only two or three lines.

If you are keen on getting the job, follow up the e-mailed cover letter and the resume with a hard copy you mail. Make sure your hard copy includes a cover letter that says 'I recently emailed you my resume and I am following it up with this hard copy.' There might be a computer glitch or your attachment doesn't open. In your cover letter, always mention the programme you used to send your attachment (Microsoft word 2000). Always open your attachment to make sure it is updated, error free or virus free. Always save a copy in case you have to resend whatever you send.

VIII. Some useful expressions:

First paragraph:

i. 'I am writing in response to your advertisement in ___________(day, date).
ii. I would like to express my interest in _____(job)_____ field and available ___ (job title)_________ position described in your company's website.
iii. I understand that you might be looking for someone to fill the___ (job) __ position in _____.
iv. I am writing to enquire into the availability of ___(job area) ____ in your company. I have long admired your operations and would like to be associated with them.
v. Enclosed please find my resume which I am sending in response to your advertisement in the *Times of India*, Wednesday, July 10, 2009/ to your company's announcement on its website.
vi. I recently graduated with a ____ (degree in area) and I am extremely interested in beginning my career at ______(name of the company) ____ The impressive growth of your company was the subject of my research paper in the final semester.

Middle paragraph:

i. I have much to offer to the growth of your company that is taking interest in the younger generation of technical people.
ii. I am the founder of a Student Investment Group that was involved in research _______. I have the vision and the multitasking ability to participate in the research and marketing activities of your company.
iii. Much of my work has been crafted for the following companies: (list your activities, internship, etc.)
iv. I graduated in May 2009 from ____ (institution) ___ with a Master's degree in ___ (area) ____.
v. As you can see from my resume, in addition to meeting all the demands of my course work and getting cumulative grade, I have also acquired _________ (years of experience in area).

Last paragraph:

i. I look forward to hearing from you.
Thank you for your time and consideration.

ii. I look forward to the opportunity of meeting you for an interview. Thank you very much for your time and consideration.

iii. Thank you very much for your time spent reading this letter and the enclosed resume. I look forward to hearing from you soon.

iv. I have enclosed my resume for your review. Thank you for your time and consideration.

Online Resources

1. http://www.ocs.fas.harvard.edu/students/materials/resumes_and_cover_letters.pdf
2. http://career-advice.monster.com/resumes-cover-letters/careers.aspx
3. http://www.youthcentral.vic.gov.au/jobs-careers/applying-for-jobs/sample-resumes-and-cover-letters
4. http://careers.theguardian.com/covering-letter-examples
5. https://career.uoregon.edu/sites/default/files/files/resume-cover-letter-guide-revised-6-09.pdf

Select Bibliography

1. McMurrey, David A. *Power Tools for Technical Communication*. Boston:Heinle, 2001
2. Farr Michael. *The quick resume and cover letter book*, Ebook, JIST, 2011
3. Bly, Robert W. *Webster's New WorldTM Letter Writing Handbook*, Indianapolis:Wiley Publishing, 2003
4. McCarthy, Margaret. *Letter Writing Made Easy: v.1: Featuring Sample Letters for Hundreds of Common Occasions*. US: Santa Monica Press, 1998
5. Bly, Robert W. and Regina Anne Kelly. *Encyclopedia of Business Letters, Faxes, and E-mail: Features Hundreds of Model Letters, Faxes and E-mails to Give Your Business Writing the Attention it Deserves*. Franklin Lakes, NJ: Career Press, 2009

Unit VII - Practice

I. Read the following advertisement and try to understand it:

> ***For high fliers, the sky is the limit!***
>
> At ARCIL, the spirit of entrepreneurship is best described by the attitude of doing ethically whatever it takes to achieve the goal.
>
> A heavy blend of individual entrepreneurship skills with team work has enabled ARCIL to deliver customised resolution of non-performing loans.
>
> In our growth trajectory, we are looking for young and dynamic MBAs and **Chartered Accountants** with potential to achieve the best.
>
> Log on to www.arcil.co.in and **open the door to your promising future**.

1. Questions:

a. Who is a high flier?
b. Pronounce the word 'entrepreneur'. Who is an entrepreneur and what is entrepreneurship?
c. What's meant by 'doing ethically'?
d. What's the meaning of the expression 'a heavy blend'?
e. What's meant by 'resolution'?
f. What's 'a non-performing loan?
g. What's meant by 'trajectory'?
h. Who are they looking for?

2. Read the following advertisements:

> Mayden Pharma India Limited, the sister concern of Mayden Vedic Herbal Research and foundation India Private Limited are in search of energetic and disciplined, systematic, result -oriented individuals with proven expertise in the field of pharma marketing.
>
> For the right candidate, salary won't be a constraint. Interested candidates may send their detailed bio-data along with a recent passport size photograph either by post or e-mail to the address given below.
>
> The address is given here.

i. What do you think of the company?
ii. What is your impression of the language used?

> ***Kottakkal Arya Vaidya Sala***
>
> **Requires Marketing Personnel**: Area Managers, Marketing Executives.
>
> Candidates aged below 40 with good communication skills may apply with detailed bio-data and expected emoluments to the General Manager within 10 days from the date of this advertisement.

What is your impression of this ad?

> QA/QC Engineer
> Required for a fabrication workshop: Graduate Mechanical Engineer with at least 4 years of experience in fabrication.
>
> Rush your CVs including experience and certificates to:
> Address given.

Will you apply to this company?

3. Compare the advertisements given above with the ones given below:

➢ It's a job that blends advertising, management and technology.
Let's just say it will challenge both sides of your brain.

Please mail your resume to jobs@google.com
Mention the position and the location you are applying for.

➢ GRUH finance Limited, a subsidiary of HDFC Ltd. Has a retail office network of 89 offices in Gujarat, Maharashtra, Karnataka, M.P., Rajasthan and Tamil Nadu with a customer base of 1 lac families. GRUH is looking for candidates for the following positions:
– – – – – – – –
– – – – – – – –
If the above positions suit your *profile*, kindly send in your resume with a passport size photograph mentioning the position and location on the envelope so as to reach us within 7 days.

➢ How are the words 'profile' and 'resume' used in this ad?

➢ How will you compare this with the ones in 2?

> BOSCH
>
> Invented for life
>
> Dynamic professionals required to drive Bosch Security Systems.
>
> The BOSCH group is a leading supplier of technology and services in the areas of automotive and industrial technology, consumer goods and building technology. The group generated sales 45.1 billion Euros in 2008.
>
> BOSCH security system, India is a division of _______.
>
> We invite promising dynamic professionals for a long term rewarding career to join us.
>
> _______
>
> _______
>
> Interested candidates may send in their profile to careers. security @in.bosch.com (no hard copies). The profile should be in MS word format.

- How is the word **profile** used in this ad?
- What is the specification for sending one's profile?

4. Some companies say 'Eligible candidates may apply online in the application format provided on the 'career' page of our web site'.

Generally the most frequently used expression is **Resume**.

So, get ready to write your resume.

Look at the sections of the resume in the hand-out and the format for **Reverse Chronological Resume and write your resume**.

5. Look at the format of a bio-data given below and comment on it.

- ➢ Name, address, age, date of birth, nationality, place of birth, names of parents, their places of birth, their occupation.
- ➢ Your education: institution attended from school level, qualifications obtained.
- ➢ Extra-curricular activities: NSS, NCC, membership of clubs, sports teams.
- ➢ Skills: musical instruments, dancing, typing, etc.
- ➢ Interests
- ➢ Any courses attended, scholarships, prizes.

6. Some employers, as part of their interviewing technique and selection, ask you to write about yourself – as you see yourself, as others see you, your SWOT (Strengths, Weaknesses, Opportunities, Threats) – a SWOT analysis.

Try to write about yourself, using the hints below:

a. General appearance: do you make a good first impression?
b. Reliability
c. Self-confidence or the lack of it
d. Outlook on life – pessimist/optimist
e. Degree of ambition

f. Popularity with others – getting along with friends/people
g. Your readiness to be friendly
h. General sociability/outward/inward looking personality
i. Relationship with family
j. Any special skills or disabilities
k. Pleasant/unpleasant experiences which might have affected you.
l. Ability to make use of opportunities
m. How do you handle threats?
n. Good qualities / bad qualities
o. Any other facts you want to mention.

7. Look at the ads given in some newspapers and write your resume and a cover letter for any one job, using the hints and the format given in the handout.

   Business Head – Global Delivery

   Company: Azure

   Location: Ahmedabad, Pune, Delhi and NCR
   Date: 20.05.2015
   (Market Research Services). Azure's Market Research & Analytic business is going through a rapid ph

   View full description

Case Study for Discussion

Sanjay, a junior engineer working in a computer graphics company, was assigned the additional charge of maintaining official correspondence with outside agencies. Under this responsibility, he had to write letters on the company letter head to the vendors asking for quotations for new products, placing orders to acquire products and accessories, and claim letters to settle disputes. However.it was noticed by his boss that in most of the cases, he received replies that rejected the proposal or offers made by him. As the situation seemed serious, the boss constituted a committee of three people to examine the reasons for the negative responses to his correspondence. The committee studied the file containing all his correspondence and found out that he did not use reader-friendly language in his correspondence. His letters were seen as hostile and self-aggrandizing by the reader. They realized that use of unfriendly and negative language was the reason for the inadequate responses received by him.

His boss asked the committee to work with him on a corrective course. They had to identify which words and sentences were annoying people and why. The committee underlined all the problematic expressions used by him which could cause offence to a reader, and then asked him to substitute them with a more positive and reader friendly expression. For e.g., instead of writing "You are late in replying " he was asked to try, "I presume you were busy in important matters, so could not write back in the stipulated time', or instead of writing, 'Kindly respond to my letter', it was suggested that he should write, 'Could you kindly consider writing back at an appropriate time' and other such phrases which are reader-friendly and show consideration for the reader's time and convenience. Such correspondence, it was felt, shows respect to the reader and would get positive response by them.

To improve his writing skills, Sanjay studied books on technical and business communication by industry experts. He studied works by Dale Carnegie and Phyllis Weiss, which talked about the ways people express themselves andthe impressions they make. He referred to online resources on the subject.He used the newly acquired skills in communications with his clients. As he could now showcase his ideas and intention through better expression, he got the desired results. He was promoted after a couple of months, and the training and transformation actually carried over to his personal and social life, where he was able to apply his skills in spoken communication as well. As a result, he felt more confident and happier with the way he fitted into his job as well as into his circle of friends.

Questions

1. All business documents have to be reader friendly. Could you give five examples of sentences used in a business document which are not reader friendly? How would you correct them?
2. Imagine yourself in place of Sanjay. What measures would you adopt to improve your business writing skills?
3. Is there any correlation between good writing skills and good speaking skills? Justify your answer.

Unit VIII – Group Discussions and Interviews

Never doubt that a small group of thoughtful, committed citizens can change the world; indeed, it's the only thing that ever has.

– Margaret Mead

OBJECTIVES:

After reading this unit, you will be able to

- ✓ Cultivate group communication skills
- ✓ understand styles of interview
- ✓ improve your interview skills
- ✓ develop personality traits for successful GDs and interviews.

I. Group Discussion

Source: www.openclipart.org

Tips for effective GD

Some of the personality traits that aGD is trying to gauge are:

- ❖ Ability to work in a team.
- ❖ Communication skills
- ❖ Reasoning ability
- ❖ Leadership skills
- ❖ Initiative
- ❖ Assertiveness
- ❖ Flexibility
- ❖ Creativity
- ❖ Ability to think on one's feet

In other words, GD is an effective way of testing one's personality, so it's important to nurture GD skills. Following are some Do's and Don'ts of Group Discussions:

Do's:

- ✓ Define the topic at issue.
- ✓ Analyse its scope and implications.
- ✓ Initiate and generate the discussion.
- ✓ Listen to the views of others.
- ✓ Encourage others also to speak.
- ✓ Turn taking is very important. Wait for your turn.
- ✓ Intervene politely when demanded by the situation.
- ✓ Summarize views of others before presenting your own.
- ✓ Be brief and to the point while presenting your ideas.
- ✓ Concede or agree with others if they have valid points or are reasonable.
- ✓ Try to lead the group to a definite conclusion.
- ✓ Look at the members of the group while addressing them.
- ✓ Speak with proper pronunciation.
- ✓ Stick to the allotted time.
- ✓ Maintain a relaxed and pleasant atmosphere.
- ✓ Summarize the main points at the end.
- ✓ Emphasize the points you consider important.
- ✓ State the conclusions reached.
- ✓ Remember that a group discussion is not a debate.
- ✓ Be careful about your body language.
- ✓ Be yourself. Do not try and be someone you are not.
- ✓ **Try to be the first and also the last to speak**: Initiating and closing a GD will earn you brownie points.

Don'ts:

- ✗ Don't be aggressive in presenting your views
- ✗ Don't dominate the discussion.
- ✗ Don't monopolize the discussion.
- ✗ Don't make personal remarks.
- ✗ Don't enter into arguments.
- ✗ Don't speak for a long time.
- ✗ Don't raise your voice.
- ✗ Don't speak in a monotone.
- ✗ Avoid speech mannerisms.
- ✗ Don't use aggressive body language.
- ✗ Don't recline on your chair or bend forward.
- ✗ Don't ignore other members of the group.
- ✗ Don't use harsh language; always use downtoners: I feel, I think, as far as I know.
- ✗ Don't exceed the time limit.
- ✗ Don't start speaking until you have clearly understood and analyzed the other's view point.
- ✗ Avoid one-to-one discussion or interactions with any of the members in the group, instead involve with everyone present.

Mental preparation or Interior Rehearsal

Prepare yourself and do the rehearsal in your mind. This will make you interview-ready. Many actors do this. Mental preparation will make you feel confident and remove all nervousness and fear.

If possible, also conduct mock interviews and discussions in your mind.

Here are some ways through which you can prepare for your GD:

- ✓ Develop a good reading habit. You should be an avid reader of newspapers and books so that you have sufficient knowledge of what is happening around you and can quote relevant examples in real situation.
- ✓ Develop a habit of holding mock GDs in your mind.

II. Interviews

Source: www.clipartpanda.com

Before the Interview

i. You will not be offered a job without showing your value in a job interview.

Job interviews are like performance in a drama. Job interviews are to be considered performance art; they are showbiz.

So the practice interview is like a dress rehearsal, a close facsimile to the real thing. They are called mock interviews.

No professional climber will attempt to climb Mount Everest without preparations; no cricketer will enter the field without practice; no actor will enter the stage without dress rehearsals. Many universities and institutions offer mock interviews to students (and even the staff on how to conduct interviews). Immediately after the mock interview, your performance is discussed. Sometimes it is taped and replayed so that you can see your performance-things that are never observed such as body language, your nervousness, your voice, the volume and speed of speech etc. Remember, preparation tames panic.

ii. 'Be natural' is poor advice. Natural is not always better! Is combed hair natural?? Trimmed beard? Polished shoes? Not scratching where it itches? So, you should be your Best You. Remember it is a rough-and-tough job world.

iii. Remember more time spent in preparation means less anxiety on the day of the interview. In addition to reducing pre-interview-stress, being prepared has several benefits:
- ❖ It shows the interviewer that you care enough about the position and the company.
- ❖ It suggests that, if employed, you will do a lot of preparation for all the assignments and the meetings.
- ❖ It provides more opportunities to you and the interviewer to have a meaningful dialogue at the time ofthe interview.

iv. Research: Now that the internet is around, the data you needcan be found at the company's website or the home page. A search engine too may help you.
- ❖ What does the company do?
- ❖ Is it global?
- ❖ Is it a conglomerate?
- ❖ What are its divisions and subsidiaries?
- ❖ How many locations does it have?
- ❖ Does it have foreign locations?
- ❖ What is its mission?
- ❖ What are its prospects and problems?
- ❖ What are its priorities?
- ❖ Is it well established?
- ❖ What services or products does it provide?
- ❖ What are its production standards?
- ❖ Is the company in a growing industry?
- ❖ What is its reputation?
- ❖ When and where was it established?
- ❖ Is it public- or private-owned?
- ❖ How quickly has itgrown?
- ❖ What are its earnings?
- ❖ What are its assets?
- ❖ How stable is its financial base?
- ❖ How much of its earnings go to its employees?
- ❖ How far in debt is the company?

And such other details……

All these things will help you to make a decision and pave the way forthe interview.

v. Review your resume

If you can't remember something on your resume, yourinterviewer may think you are lying. Maybe, you left out an important spell of experience in your resume. Put all your certificates and credentials in a neat file with a set of spare copies.

vi. Emotional preparation

Nervousness and other imperfections may mar your performance. Don't get nervous and anxious. If this interview doesn't work, you will have another one; every interview experience will prepare you to perform better in the next one. Even your interviewers were once on the hot seat like you and survived and got the job though their voices trembled a bit and knees knocked a little. Everyone has been through the situation like you.

Make a trial run the day before and ask yourself what you want from the job, what you are good at doing, what people complement you on etc. Sleep well the night before the interview, eat brain food like fruit, vegetable and fibre. Get to the interview site early.

vii. Styles of Interview

Be prepared to face any one of the following:

a. On-campus interview
b. Job-fair interview
c. Telephone interview
d. Screening interview
e. Selection interview
f. Combination interview
g. Behavior-based interview
h. Stress interview
i. Technology-based interviews like computer interviewing, videoconferencing etc.
j. Some companies conduct one-to-one interview, group interview, serial interviews etc.

a. Some employers conduct screening **interviews on campuses** through the career-counselling centres in the university or college. These are only screening interviews.

b. **Job fairs** are conducted where you have screening on the basis of documents-resume or profile. This may take you to an interview.

c. **Telephone interviews** are getting popular as screening interviews. Try hard to get through it to an in-person interview

As preparation for telephone interview, keep the following ready:

- ➢ Latest resumes
- ➢ A list of answers to anticipated questions.
- ➢ A calendar
- ➢ A folder for each company you have applied for with all the documents.
- ➢ A notepad, a pen or a calculator.

While taking a telephone interview, speak loudly – not too fast, not too slow words

- ➢ Use appropriate words and sentences.
- ➢ Avoid pauses.
- ➢ Use an even-tenored voice – neither lower nor high pitched.
- ➢ Put cheer in your voice.

You can practise with the tape recorder and get ready for the telephone interview.

d. **Screening interview**

Screening and selection are the two stages. The purpose of screening interviews is to short-list the best qualified and weed out the rest. Screening interviews are meant to verify your education, experience, skills and track record before putting you to the next interviewing level.

In a screening interview, questions are asked about your skills – ability to do the job, about any inconsistencies in your resume, and questions to show what kind of person you are – whether] reliable, team oriented, result-oriented etc.

e. **Selection interview**

This is a decision interview where you meet people who have the authority to hire you. The following are assessed:

- ❖ Strong presentation of personality: general likeability, motivation to work, blending with others in the company, etc.
- ❖ Qualifications and skills: Can you do the job?
- ❖ Specific details of your job experience and education: Are you trained to do the job?

f. **Combination interview**

- ❖ Small companies do the screening and selection together.
- ❖ Behaviour-based interview.

g. **Behaviour-based** interview lays stress upon 'what did you do when……' and not on "what would you do if..?' there are questions like 'Give an example of your skills in ……' and 'Describe a time when...'

- ❖ What is called a 'STAR' system is used; STAR stands for Situation, Task, Action and Result. Behaviour based interviews look for a person who is optimistic, creative, a leader and a team player.
- ❖ Multiculturalism in the workplace is common now. So, working with people with a variety of cultural backgrounds has become a necessity in the corporate settings. Knowledge of a foreign language is an advantage. You must be prepared to work abroad. You must exhibit your knowledge of the global market. If you have any overseas exposure, it will be an advantage.

h. **Stress interviews**

Stress interviews often consist of:

- ❖ Hour-long waits before the interview to test your patience.
- ❖ Long uncomfortable silences
- ❖ Inconvenient questions
- ❖ A rude interviewer or multiple curt interviewers.
- ❖ Deliberate misinterpretation of your answers and outright insults.

The ability to overcome such hostile responses is very essential in some professions like marketing and sales where you come across rude customers.

You must be calm with unperturbed confidence.

i. **Technology-based interviews** have not yet become very common in India. But they are used to cut travel costs of candidates.

j. **Ono-to-one interviews** are very common. Panel interviews or committee interviews are conducted by a group of people from various departments in the organization. This is all very common in India.

k. In **serial interviews**, you are passed from one screener to the other and finally to the top manager and perhaps about 6 or 7 interviewers in between. Sometimes serial interviews last one to two days. In such interviews consistency counts.

❖ So, rehearse, rehearse and rehearse.This will help you to overcome nervousness and to build a proper attitude against stage fear. In addition, rehearsals will enable you to anticipate interview trapdoors. Even mock computer interviews will help you. Rehearse aloud, atleast five times. You can practice with a camcorder, so that even visuals can be reviewed.

- Watch for leg swinging, tapping or rocking them from side to side.
- Watch fiddling with your hair, or pen or clothes.
- Watch hands getting nervous or shaking.
- Watch your sitting posture, leaning back, arms crossing or shaking your head frequently.
- Forgotten to smile?

Keep these **Don'ts** in mind:

Don't say:

- Uhm…
- Uh…
- Yup or yeah
- You know
- Like
- Well
- Okay
- Pretty good
- I know
- I guess so

Don't:

- Tap feet or fingers
- Pull or rearrange hair
- Fold arms
- Offer a limp handshake
- Displayshy eyes
- Mumble
- Interrupt
- Speak too fast
- Slump
- Twiddle props like pens, paper, paper-weight etc.
- Fidget
- Maintain constant eye contact.

Computer interviewing for **practice is available at:**

a. **E-Spam:** Interview Practice
b. **Student's Centre:** A virtual interview
c. **Kaplan's HotSeat:** A mock interview

Dress Code

- Dress to fit the job and the job's culture.
- Look the part, and the part plays itself.
- No tinted glasses.
- No fad watches.
- A fresh shave is better. No long hair, pony tails, beards and moustaches unless the company culture allows them. You can always grow the hair back after you are hired.

- For men, a suit in navy blue of medium to dark gray and a quality blend tie in conservative stripe.
- Over-the-calf dark socks.
- No bulge in the pockets.
- A good (not tattered) briefcase.
- For women – no heavy makeup, no see-through fabrics, no tight fitting clothing, no sexy dress, no plunging necklines or backs.
- Bathe before interviews.
- Check your hair for cleanliness-dandruff free.
- Be sure that your finger nails are cut and clean.
- Censor your breath – use a mouth wash.
- Ensure your clothing is fresh.
- No scruffy shoes; no running shoes or sneakers.
- Keep scents light.

As part of your research, do some study regarding the dress code of the company. Employers choose candidates similar to employees already working in the company.

Screen test

Hiring mistakes are very costly. So, employers test candidates well before the interview. Pre-employment testing costs less. Institutions can administer **Aptitude Tests** and **Career Interest Tests** to guide students in selecting the right career. Aptitude tests indicate your potential in a given area; for example, a **Scholastic Aptitude Test** shows your learning ability. Career Interests Tests are meant to show what you like to do and to see which occupation will suit your interest profile.

Generally employers administer **Personality Tests, Integrity Tests** and **Skills Tests** or a combination of the three for the evaluation of candidates.

Personality tests attempt to measure and compare your personality traits with other groups of people.

Integrity tests test your honesty, responsibility and reliability. This is also a type of personality test. Skills tests or Performance tests try to measure your performance in the job.

Most tests are computerized. So, get computer experience or else you will be at a disadvantage. Here wrong answers count more against you than no answers do. So, be careful.

TIPS

Select answers that show you in the most positive light. Some, favoured characteristics are:

- Achievement oriented
- Agreeable
- Dependable
- Conscientious
- Emotionally stable
- Responsible
- Tolerant
- Able to speak well

- Imaginative
- Intellectually curious
- Open to new ideas and experiences
- Optimistic
- Sociable
- Trustworthy

➢ **Negative traits are:**

- Can't function under stressful conditions
- Dishonest
- Emotionally unstable
- Poor impulse control
- Irritable
- Prone to theft
- Prone to time theft (leave abuse, lazy, shirker)
- Tense and suspicious
- Negative interpersonal relationship
- Lack of confidence
- Rigid
- Oversensitive
- Violence prone
- Trouble maker
- Fraudulent
- Use of drugs and alcohol

➢ **Some tests include items that test your tolerance level:**

- I have no difficulty in or holding my urine.
- I am strongly attracted by members of my own sex.

Such items may sound rude but they are included deliberately to test your patience. So, don't get upset or irritated. They are meant to test how irritable you are.

A. **Interviewer types**

Try to understand the various types of interviewers so that you can adjust your performance accordingly.

a. Young achiever: A twenty-something, fresh faced, cheerful, positive, and friendly. Show your enthusiasm and leadership qualities.
b. Serious business person: Grey haired, serious and business like. Show your knowledge of the company.
c. Potential boss: Show work experience and a positive attitude. Be humble.
d. Cold contemplator: Methodical, precise, and work-oriented. They love details; so, give them plenty of information so that they have something to analyze.
e. Warm fuzzies: Smiles often, comfortable and thoughtful. Not very skilled at interviewing. Present your qualifications for the job.
f. Incompetent interviewer: Unlike a competent interviewer, the incompetent ones ask irrelevant and even unethical questions. Stay calm and demonstrate your skills in answering such questions.
g. Serious intimidator: Very conservative, neat and organized, work oriented and critical. Don't let them see your fear. Answer to the point.
h. Professional recruiter: Quiet and Confident. They always are the ones that almost always interview candidates. Be specific about your skills, qualifications and accomplishments. Answer confidently and communicate clearly.

i. Talkers: They love talking. They don't listen.So, smile and keep them interested in you.
j. Technical persons: Carry gadgets and a laptop. Don't mix well with others. Focus on technical knowledge and achievements.

B. At the interview

> *Your writing skills were evaluated in the resume, cover letter, in the e-mail and in the tests.*
>
> *All those mistakes, if any, will imply a dangerous lack of attention to detail.*
>
> *At the interview, your oral communication skills, facial expressions/gestures, style and cleanliness, tone of voice, posture, accent, scent, hairstyle and spoken language are tested.*

Questions to be frequently asked:

a. Tell me about yourself: Focus on the **best you**. Prepare a commercial about you and grab the interviewer's interest with a confident statement about yourself – a two minute ad.
   ➢ Some interviewers may use different words for the tell-me-about-yourself question. A lot depends on how you respond.
b. **This question tells the employers:**
   ❖ What you consider important
   ❖ About your values
   ❖ What you have accomplished
   ❖ Whether you are organized, self motivated and focused.
   ❖ Whether you would fit into the company's culture.
c. Questions about the company and the job: To test omit whether you know the industry, whether you show savvy about the company, and whether you understand the job.
d. Questions about your skills: Technical skills and soft skills (people skills/ life skills).
e. Questions about your experience: This is to test if you understand the employer's needs.
f. Questions about your education and training: To test your adaptability and educational experience.
g. Questions about your age: Generally such questions are indirect like "When did you graduate?"
   If young, you can be trained to learn, you will have fresh ideas, can be moulded, comfortable with modern technology, enthusiastic, will tackle less desirable tasks, etc.
h. Brain teasers and questions of general knowledge.
   To test your out-of-the box thinking and creativity. Some general knowledge questions may be asked.
   [Note: Asking questions about your religion, race, marital status, your family matters, and in some cases even about the caste is illegal.]

i. Case questions: To test your analytical ability. They take a long time to answer because they are case studies.

j. The guesstimates: This is to test your ability to guess. No accurate answer is expected.
E.g. How many petrol tanks (gas stations) are there in your town/city?
Think an answer.

k. The salary or bucks question: Delay discussing salary until you are sure you will get the job. Don't talk about it unless you are asked.

C. Closing the show

i. You should know when the interview is over: The interviewer may shuffle papers, glance at a wall clock or watch, or, perhaps, stand up. Some may say, 'Thanks for coming, I'll get back to you'. Some may say, 'Do you have any questions to ask about the company or the position?'
Say 'Thank you, I look forward to hearing from you... Thank you for your time and interest. I learned a lot during the interview'.

ii. Write a Thank-you note.

iii. Write a thank-you note like the following.

Your address
Date
Phone no.
E-mail

Dear Sir/Madam:

Thank you for the opportunity to meet with you yesterday. I enjoyed talking to my interviewers about the company, its future plans, and my possible position there.

Thanks again for your time. I look forward to hearing from you soon.

Yours truly,

Signature
Name

Some don'ts for the interviews

1. Don't blame your teachers, educational institutions where you studied, your previous employers or bosses for your poor performance.
2. Don't discuss personal matters.
3. Don't appear to be too eager to discuss matters regarding working hours, leave rules or salary.
4. Don't adopt a bad posture.
5. Don't let nervousness affect your words and actions.
6. Don't mumble; or speak too loudly, or too fast.

7. Don't give long answers to questions. Be attentive to your questions.
8. Don't fail to answer the questions asked.
9. Don't forget to put on a pleasant look and smile.
10. Don't forget to say thank you when you leave the room.

Online Resources

1. http://www.reed.co.uk/career-advice/blog/2013/february/group-interview-tips-dos-and-don'ts
2. http://www.monstercollege.in/article/article_5.html
3. http://gdpi.ascenteducation.com/india-mba/gd-common-mistake.shtml
4. http://www.freshersworld.com/interview/gd-important
5. https://www.coursera.org/learn/publicspeaking
6. http://www.engineering.cornell.edu/resources/career_services/students/upload/interviewing-skills.pdf

Select Bibliography

1. Rizvi, M Ashraf. *Effective Technical Communication*. New Delhi: Tata McGraw Hill, 2005.
2. Raman, Meenakshi and Prakash Singh. *Business Communication*. New Delhi: OUP, 2006.
3. Deluca, Matthewand Nanette Deluca. *Best Answers to the 201 Most Frequently Asked Interview Questions*, Columbus:McGraw-Hill, 2010.
4. Fry, Ron.*101 Great Answers to the Toughest Interview Questions*. New Delhi: Cengage Learning, 2009.
5. Young, Katherine Sue, and Julia T. Wood. *Group Discussion: A Practical Guide to Participtiion and Leadership*. Long Grove: Waveland PrInc, 2006

Unit VIII - Practice

I. Group discussion

Topics

1. Corporate job or government job.
2. Job in India or overseas.
3. Quality of life is more important than salary package.
4. Being an entrepreneur is better than working for companies.
5. Technical education should be humanized.
6. Global competition is good for India.
7. Technology has reduced all knowledge into mere information.

II. Question bank

A. Questions about you:

1. What are the three things we should know about you?
2. What are your interests?
3. Do you have any hobbies?
4. What books have you read recently?
5. What movies have you seen recently?
6. What is your great strength? Greatest weakness?
7. What is your most memorable accomplishment?
8. Are you a follower or a leader?
9. What is your experience working with teams?
10. Describe your ideal job?
11. What would you like to change about yourself?
12. If you could change some past actions in your life, what would they be?
13. Would you rather work alone or with others?
14. What key assets can you offer in this job?
15. How does this job fit your objectives?
16. Where do you see yourself five years from now?
17. What is your definition of success? Of failure?
18. Why have you been successful?
19. Why should we hire you over the other candidates?
20. Tell us how you deal with unexpected problems problems?
21. You are in customer relations and an dissatisfied customer is complaining bitterly about the product or service. How will you handle the situation?
22. Describe some situations that really bother you.

23. You have been given multiple tasks. There is no way you can complete all of them. What do you do?
24. You are right and you know you are right.. And, yet, everyone is taking issue with you. How do you react?
25. What are your best and worst qualities? How will they relate to the present job?
26. What interests you about this job, industry, organization?
27. How important is winning to you?
28. What is the most unpleasant thing you have ever to do? Why?
29. What motivates you?
30. Is there anything else we should know about you?
31. Which of your past accomplishments are you most proud of?
32. Compare your oral and written communication skills.
33. Have you had any experience with public speaking? Describe it.
34. How will you persuade a person who is unwilling to accept your ideas?
35. What do you find most troubling about writing a research paper or report?
36. Describe some ways in which you have been a leader.
37. What criteria do you use to make important personal decisions?
38. Describe the most creative things you have ever done in your life?
39. What criteria did you use to decide your career path?
40. Do you have a problem doing multiple tasks?
41. What does the word "service" mean to you?
42. Describe some of your strategies fordealing with difficult people.
43. What does the word "team player" mean to you?
44. Can you keep a secret?
45. Have you ever been entrusted with sensitive information? Describe the situation.
46. Describe a time you were loyal to someone even though it was difficult.
47. Describe the process you go through to make a decision.
48. How well do you work with others?
49. So how do you feel working extra hours on occasions?
50. What would make you tell someone this company's secrets?
51. What so far in your life has given you the greatest creative satisfaction?

B. About the job and the company

1. What do you know about this company?
2. What do you know about this job?
3. What do you know about your competitors?
4. What do you see as the direction of this company?
5. What do you think are the challenges facing this company?
6. Why did you apply for this company?
7. How will you help our company?
8. Our company has a mission statement. What is your personal mission statement?

9. Are you willing to work anywhere in India and outside?
10. How did you get to know about our company?

C. About skills:

1. What are soft skills?
2. How will you acquire soft skills?
3. How will you interact with difficult and unpleasant people?
4. What are the soft skills that relate to your career?
5. What do you like most/ least like about researching?
6. How good are you at making oral presentations?
7. How well canyou write a report?
8. Which is better – your oral skills or writing skills?
9. How do you organize your time?
10. How do you involve everyone in your team in a given project?
11. How do you deal with unexpected situations?
12. What do you like most while working with others? What least?
13. What does hard work mean to you?
14. Place hard work in a scale of qualities necessary to do a good job.
15. What would be your optimal schedule?
16. How important are details to you?
17. What does theword "vision" mean to you?
18. What skills do you have to advance in this industry?
19. If you were to employ someone for this job, what skills would you define as being the most desirable and why?
20. If you are looking for a perfect job in this organization, what would be the important qualities for the job?

D. About experience

1. What experience do you have to do this job?
2. You have no work experience. Why should we hire you?
3. What kind of experience do you have to qualify you for this job?
4. Give some specific illustrations of your experience/accomplishments?
5. What do you think will be your broad responsibilities inthe job you have applied for?
6. How long will it take for you to make a significant contribution to our company?
7. How will you discipline a problem employee working with you?
8. Describe how you will make a presentation about the company.
9. Can you work without direct supervision?
10. If a supervisor challenges your decision, how will you respond?

E. Questions about your education and training

1. Tell me how your education is related to the work experience?
2. Why did you select the college/institution where you studied for your higher education?

3. Why did you select (name of the area) for specialization?
4. How has your higher education prepared you for this job?
5. Have you benefitted from your education?
6. What was your grade? Does it reflect your performance?
7. Why didn't you get a better grade?
8. Do you think that your grade indicates how successful you will be in this present job?
9. Describe the skills you have learned in your degree programme?
10. Did you learn any skill outside your course work that can contribute to your job?
11. What extra-curricular activities did you participate in?
12. Did you lead any project or programme?
13. Why didn't you participate in more extracurricular activities?
14. Do you think that your education could have better prepared you for a career? In what areas?
15. What courses did you like best /least?
16. Describe a situation in which you sacrificed your immediate needs for the larger good of a team?
17. What are your hobbies? In what ways can they help you in your career?
18. If you could do it over again, what courses would you take? Would you change your college/university/subject?
19. What did you like about your college/university? What did you dislike?
20. How has your education helped you for the job you have applied for?
21. Are you willing to start at the bottom?
22. Have you worked part-time or in summers? What are they? Give details.
23. Do you like routine tasks, regular hours?
24. Can you work on weekends/overtime?
25. What are the soft skills that you have which may qualify you for this job?

F. About your age (Generally indirect)

1. When did you graduate?
2. Do you think you are too young/old for this job?
3. Do you think you can work with experienced/inexperienced people in your team?

G. Brain-teasers and questions about GK

1. Why are manhole covers round?
2. If you could be an animal, what kind of animal would yoube?
3. Whose birthday is not known and celebrated on the day he died?
4. From what language is the word "coffee" derived?
5. How many zodiac signs are there?
6. Why is a collection of maps is called an atlas?

7. What was the ancient name for Iraq? Why was it so called?
8. Why is Bharat called India?
9. How do chimps greet each other?
10. Who wrote 'Vaishnava Janato'?
11. What is the currency of China called?
12. On which finger of which hand do married men and women wear wedding rings?
13. What is the opposite of 'oriental'?
14. What is the distance between two parallel railway tracks? In metre gauge? In broad gauge?
15. Why is ChetanBhagat's novel called 'Five point someone' and not 'Five point something'?
16. What is the plural of the word 'mouse', as used in computers?
17. What is the world's oldest sport?
18. You have 12 black socks and 12 white socks mixed up in the drawer.No light to see because there is no power. How many socks will you pull out blindly to be sure of getting a matching pair?
19. What is special about the following sequence of numbers?
    8 5 4 9 1 7 6 1 0 3 2 0
    (You can get many more on the internet. Just click 'Brain Teasers' or 'Trivia').
20. You know that 'dogs bark' and 'cats mew', what do camels do?
21. A logician who went to a small village on a thinking holiday, decided to have his hair cut. The village had only two barbers. The logician glanced into one shop and saw that it was very untidy. The barber himself needed a shave and his own hair was hardly cut. The other shop was neat and the barber's hair was neatly cut. The logician returned to the first shop for his hair cut. Why?
22. 'I guarantee, ' said the pet-shop salesman, 'that this parrot will repeat every word it hears'. The customer bought the parrot but found it would not speak a single word. The salesman did not lie. Can you explain?
23. Of all things in the world, I am the shortest and the longest, the swiftest and the slowest. I am the thing that people waste most yet they need me more than anything else for without me nothing can be done. Who am I?
24. I have seven letters. The first two stand for a man. The first three stand for a woman. The first four stand for a brave man. All the letters stand for a brave woman. What is the word?
25. Truth Town is where everyone tells the truth and Liar Town is where everyone tells lies. You are on the road to Truth Town. At a fork in the road, a man is standing as he is from one of these towns. One road leads to Truth Town and another to Liar Town. You want to know where he is from. You can ask only one question. What's the question?

Case-Study for Discussion

You are Pavithra. You have joined an engineering institution, as an Assistant Professor in the Department of Humanities and Social Sciences. It is one of the best engineering institutes in the country which attracts bright students through national level competitive examinations. You teach courses in your specialization and like the work culture of the place. You were the first women hired by the institute and get due respect from colleagues. Of late.you have noticed a few odd things.

A group of male colleagues in your department are often seen in discussions on important matters related to the department. However, you are never invited. As a result, you are unaware of many of the important decisions taken by the department. One of your senior male colleague shows interest in your appearance, complimenting your dress or your new hair style but he never shares anything professional with you. Faculty meetings are convened by the head of the department (HOD), who happens to be a male. In such meetings, whenever you try to raise some important issue, you are either never heard or are frequently interrupted. Your ideas, if expressed by a male colleague, get a prompt response from the HOD.

You find that a new faculty member is hired in the department at a salary Rs 10,000/- higher than yours. Everybody knows that his credentials are much lower than yours. You know that the HOD has quite an influence on the hiring authority. It is evident that the starting salary determines the salary graph in due course of time and this kind of inequality in the beginning could be a major deterrent for one's career in the long term. What should you do? On the one hand, you love your job and feel satisfied with what you are doing; on the other, you know you are being treated unfairly and would like to do something about it.

Questions

1. Imagine yourself to be the hiring authority of the institute.Answer the following questions:
   - ➢ Besides academic qualifications, are there any other criteria followed for faculty selections?
   - ➢ What are your assumptions when hiring female faculty?
   - ➢ Does the university provide equal opportunity to all employees irrespective of gender, caste, religion?
2. If you were in Pavithra's place, how would you deal with the issue of gender discrimination?
3. Supposing you are one of the male faculty members of the HSS department. Would you raise your voice in favour of Pavithra?
4. As a group, discuss the collective responsibilities of all the faculty members for the growth of the department as well as the progress of the institute. What should be the responsibility of the institute administration to maintain harmony in the workplace?

Unit IX – Business Communication

Writing, the art of communicating thoughts to the mind through the eye, is the great invention of the world...enabling us to converse with the dead, the absent, and the unborn, at all distances of time and space.

– Abraham Lincoln

OBJECTIVES:

After reading this unit, you will be able to

- ✓ Draft business e-mails
- ✓ Format official memos and letters
- ✓ Write and present reports and proposals
- ✓ Design professional documents

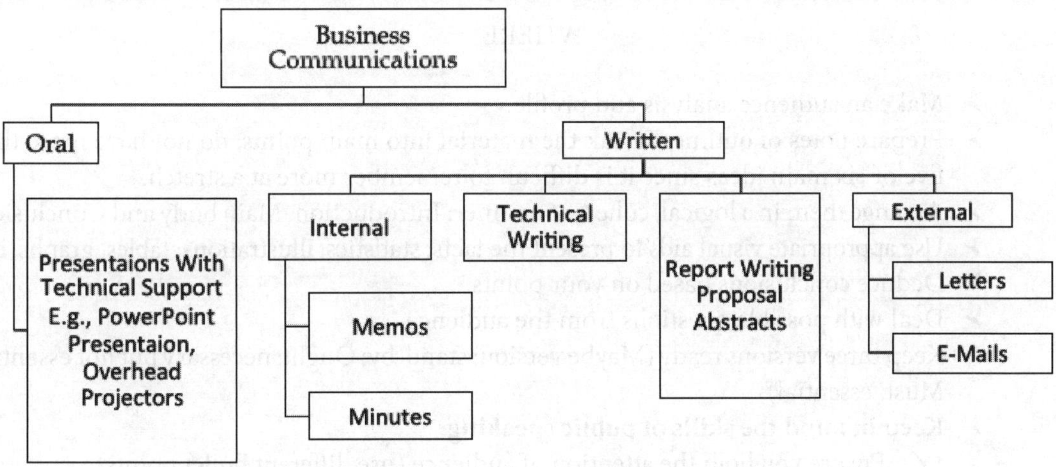

I. Oral: Presentation

- ➢ *Forms: Short talks/Presentations*
- ➢ *Briefings/Instructions*
- ➢ *Discussion/Group discussions*
- ➢ *Debates/Public speaking*
- ➢ *Meeting/Conferences*

- *Seminars/Symposiums*
- *Panel discussion*

Students who are prospective professionals like executive, managers, entrepreneurs, scientists, administrators are required to make presentations in the form of progress reports, research papers, police statements, project proposals, feasibility studies, etc. So, effective oral presentations within and outside organizations have become mandatory for career growth. The ability to plan, organize and present ideas and information effectively is an asset in any profession.
Here are some guidelines:

A. Follow the six star strategy

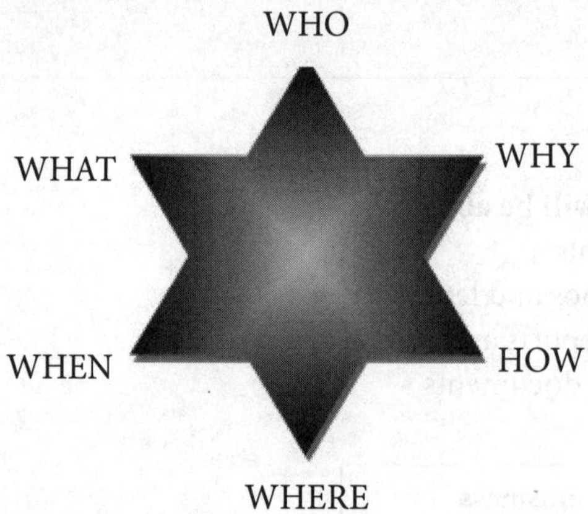

- Make an audience analysis and profile.
- Prepare notes of outlines; break the material into main points; do not have more than five or six main ideas since it is difficult to remember more at a stretch.
- Arrange them in a logical, coherent manner: Introduction, Main body and Conclusion.
- Use appropriate visual aids to present the facts, statistics, illustrations, tables, graphs, etc.
- Deduce conclusions based on your points.
- Deal with possible questions from the audience.
- Keep three versions ready (Maybe version: stand-by; Ought: necessary but not essential; Must: essential)
- **Keep in mind the skills of public speaking.**
  - ✓ Ensure you hold the attention of audience (use different bullet points)
  - ✓ Sustain interest
  - ✓ Inform, instruct, entertain, inspire, persuade.

B. Starting strategy

- Make a startling statement.
- A rhetorical question
- A provocative quote
- An interesting anecdote or a story involving the audience
- A joke
- A statement of the problem and its importance to the audience

C. **Modes of delivery**
- Reading aloud
- Memorizing and speaking from memory
- Speaking from notes
- Extempore speaking

D. **Supporting your presentation**
- White board/Black Board
- Charts
- Power Point
- Overhead Projector (OHP)
- Pictures

E. **Handling questions**
- Don't be impatient.
- Don't be nervous.
- Think and answer.
- Avoid one-to-one arguments.
- Focus on question.
- Do not dodge.
- Rephrase the question if it is not clear.
- Answer questions correctly and relevantly.

F. **In some cases use group dynamics**
- Brain storming
- Collecting ideas
- Setting up teams
- Team roles
- Prioritizing solutions
- Solving by consensus.

G. **Use the right style: formal or informal**

Formal presentations require the appropriate dress and the language. The body language is very important. The presentation has to constantly negotiate the space between you and the audience. Modulate your voice; remember voice, posture, and gesture communicate.

H. **Tips for presentation with electronic support**
- *Limit the content of each slide prepared for presentation.*
- *Limit the number of words to fewer than 40, with not more than six lines of text.*
- *Do not write paragraphs but write effective bullet phrases.*
- *Avoid script or decorative fonts.*
- *Colours make slides look professional. Use dark backgrounds.*
- *Do not apply dramatic slide transitions.*

II. Memos and Memo Letters

A memo is a short form for 'memorandum'. It is derived from the word 'memory'. It is a brief, informal note. It is used within an office as an informal short note, shorter than a letter.

Features of a memo:
- At the top it states to whom it is addressed.
- It does not, however, contain an address.
- It also states to whom a copy is sent.
- It clearly mentions the subject.

- ➢ It does not contain opening salutations and closing is minimal.
- ➢ The paragraphs are short.
- ➢ The format is uniform.
- ➢ The spelling should be correct.
- ➢ Abbreviations, punctuation marks, underlining, capital letters are minimal.

A Typical Memo

To: The Admin head

From: Rakesh Sharma

Date: November 1, 2009

Subject: Ravi and Rakesh Sharma's attendance at the Communication Skills workshop on October 26, 2009.

The Communication Skills workshop was extremely useful and instructive. The resource persons very clearly explained the various aspects that one should learn:

• The language skills	• Group discussion
• Barriers in communication	• Business communication
• Public speaking	• Negotiation

Each subject was taught through practical sessions. We analyzed in detail all the aspects of Professional Communication. We realized after attending the workshop that as a company we are not paying enough attention to communication skills. I believe that our company will benefit a lot by deputing our staff to attend a course like this.

Rakesh Sharma

Memo Letters

Memo lettersare printed forms that provide space for TO, FROM, DATE, SUBJECT and MESSAGE.

There are different kinds of memos like a tentative memo, a decisive memo, memos asking for explanations etc. The tone of the memos will vary. A tentative memo is rambling while a decisive memo identifies the problem clearly and resolves it. It comes straight to the point.

Example:

From: ______
To: The Admin Head
Subject: Wastage of Stationery and New Procedure
The amount that is spent on stationery is increasing because there is no control over the use of stationery. It is kept in the open. With immediate effect, Mrs. KiranVerma is designated as the in-charge of the stationery. Those needing stationery should approach her with an indent. She will keep a record of all the stationery issued.
Thank you for your cooperation.

III. Minutes

A report covering the proceeding of a meeting is called 'minute'. The minutes of a meeting – a company's board meeting, executive committee meeting of an association etc. are written by the secretary of the organization. It is written in the form of resolutions like 'Resolved that……..' The resolutions are ordered in serial numbers. Minutes have to be factually correct and they represent a legal record. The minutes of one meeting are read out at the beginning of thenext meeting and approved by the members before the chairperson signs it.

The following is the general format for recording minutes:

1. The minutes are generally recorded on the letterhead of the organization.
2. At the beginning, there are details such as the day, date, time, venue, and the nature of the meeting and the number of the meeting in the series.
3. This is followed by a list of those present at the meeting.
4. This is followed by an agenda. The major items are given in the agenda.
5. When a person or committee is appointed, it is to be recorded.
6. The first resolution is the confirmation of the minutes of the previous meeting and the last resolution is thevote of thanks.
7. At the end, there is provision for the date and the signature of the chairman.

Model format:

The name of the Company/Organization

Day and Date of the meeting:
Venue:
Nature of the meeting:
Members present:
Mr______ chairman
Mrs______

Mr______
Mrs______
In attendance:
Mr______ Secretary

i. ______ ii. ______
iii. ______ iv. ______
v. ______ vi. Any other matter

Proceedings:

i. Minutes of the previous meeting _____
ii. ______
iii. Resolutions i, ii, iii_____
i. _____
ii. _____
iii. Note of dissent (if any)

Vote of thanks:

Date: Signature of the chairperson
Joke: A committee keeps minutes but loses hours

IV. Letters

Business letters are different from personal letters. Business letters are

- to be courteous
- to be precise
- to be clear
- to be complete
- to be brief
- to be persuasive

The basis is called the AIDA formula.

A= Attention
I = Interest
D = Desire
A= Action

- Get the **attention** of the reader.
- Intensify the **interest** in what you say.
- Convert the interest to **desire** to buy your product or services.
- Give a strong incentive to **act**.

A. Format for Standard Letters

1. Heading
2. Date
3. Addressee name/ designation and address (Inside Address)
4. Salutation
5. Body (i.e. text)
6. Complimentary close or subscription
7. Signature Block

14 November 2009

Dear ------

----------------------------.

Sincerely,

(Name in bold letters)

1. **Heading**: A company or organization will have the printed letterhead with the address, email and fax.
   - ❖ If a letterhead is not used, give only the sender's address. No name is necessary since the name is given at the end, below the signature.
2. **Date**: The standard international convention is: 02 November 2009
   - ❖ (Date, Month, Year; the month is fully spelt).
   - ❖ The standard US convention: November 02, 2009
   - ❖ European convention: 02 November 2009
   - ❖ Other Styles: November 2nd, 2009 OR
   - ❖ 2nd November, 2009
   - ❖ 02/11/09
3. **Inside address**: It is the address of the recipient written in block form aligned to the left margin. **Do not use**'from' and 'to'
   Use the following order:

Name	:
Designation	:
Name of the institution	:
Number and name of the street	:
Locality	:
Town/City and Pincode	:
State and Country	:

In British English sometimes 'Esq.' is used. Esq. means 'Esquire' which is a title of politeness and is written after the name. Do not both Mr. and Esq.

Mr. John Smith OR John Smith Esq.

Messer's (abbreviation for 'Messieurs', which means 'gentlemen' is used if the company has a personal name too:

Messers Ram & Co. Ltd.

4. **Standard Salutations**
   - ❖ *Dear Sir*
   - ❖ *Dear Sirs OR Dear Gentlemen*
   - ❖ *Dear Madam*
   - ❖ *Dear Mr. President*
   - ❖ *Dear Madam Secretary*
   - ❖ Dear Mesdames (all women organizations) in India

- Smt/Sri/Kum/Selvi (Tamil)/Srimati
- Use Ms if marital status is not known
- No full stops after Miss
- Titles other than Mr., Mrs., Miss, Dr. are spelt in full (Dear Professor Verma)
- For a couple: Mr. and Mrs. Rao
- Use state titles before the degree: Mr. Murali Mohan, M.P., M.A.
- Letters addressed to unknown recipients: 'To whom it may concern'.
- Always remember that the salutation sets the tone of the letter.

5. **Body**: The message is written in paragraphs.
   Plain English is the current style and not business jargon.
   Do not use: Hoping to receive your reply.
6. **Complimentary close**: Now, the preference is Sincerely or Cordially
   Other forms used: Yours sincerely, Yours truly, Yours faithfully. Yours does not have an apostrophe. 'Sincerely yours' (no capital letters in 'yours').
   Do not use: I beg to remain OR Your most obedient servant
7. **Signature Block**: Signature and the name in print with designation.

B. Forms of Layouts:

- Indented form (traditional form)
- Hanging indentation
- Block form or box form (current style)
- Modified block form
- Semi block form

i. In the indented form the following conventions are used:

- Sender's address on the right
- Addressee details and salutation: Top **left** position
- First line of each paragraph is indented
- Subscription bottom **right** position

ii. Hanging Indentation

- Addressee details and salutation: **Topleft** position
- Except the first sentence, all other sentences of a paragraph are indented.
- Complimentary close, signature, name: **Right** position.

Addressee details

Dear Sir/madam,

M ____

A ________________________________

R ________________________________

G ____

I ____

N ________________________________

Complimentary close

Signature

Name, Designation

iii. Block Form or Box Form

❖ Addressee details and salutation

❖ All sentences begin from left

❖ Complimentary close: Left

Addressee details

M Dear sir,

A ____

R ____

G ________________________________

I ________________________________

N Complimentary close

Signature

Name

iv. **Modified Block Form**
- ❖ Like the Block Form
- ❖ Only the complimentary close, signature, etc. are on the right.

v. **Semi Block Form**
- ❖ The first sentence of each paragraph is indented.
- ❖ Complimentary close, signature etc. are on the right

C. **Punctuation**

i. Open punctuation style:
- ❖ No punctuation at the end of lines in the inside address.
- ❖ No punctuation following salutations.
- ❖ No punctuations following complimentary close

ii. Mixed punctuation style (Common in business communication)
- ❖ No punctuation at the end of lines inthe inside address.
- ❖ A colon follows the salutation **(e.g. Dear Sir :)**
- ❖ A comma follows the complimentary close.

E.g. Yours sincerely, OR **Sincerely**

D. **Additional Parts**

i. Labels such as 'URGENT', 'CONFIDENTIAL', 'PERSONAL', etc., typed in all capitals must be two spaces above the inside address.

ii. Enclosure notation: Two spaces below the signature, name lines.

Encl: Resume

Say what document is enclosed

iii. Copy notation:

cc: courtesy copy
pc: photocopy
c: copy to Mr. Goel

iv. Give double space between paragraphs.

v. Mailing notation: 'Speed Post', 'Registered letter', etc. at the bottom.

E. **Business e-mail**
- ❖ *E-mail messages can be memos or letters or even reports. E-mail messages may be limited to one screen.*
- ❖ *Stylized texts should be avoided: italics or all capitals or all lower case.*
- ❖ *All capitals is called 'yelling' and all lower cases is 'whispering'.*
- ❖ *Two parts: Header and Body.*
- ❖ *Header is: To:, From:, Subject, Cc (Courtesy copy), Attachments, etc.*
- ❖ *Body is the message.*

V. Reports, Proposals, Abstracts

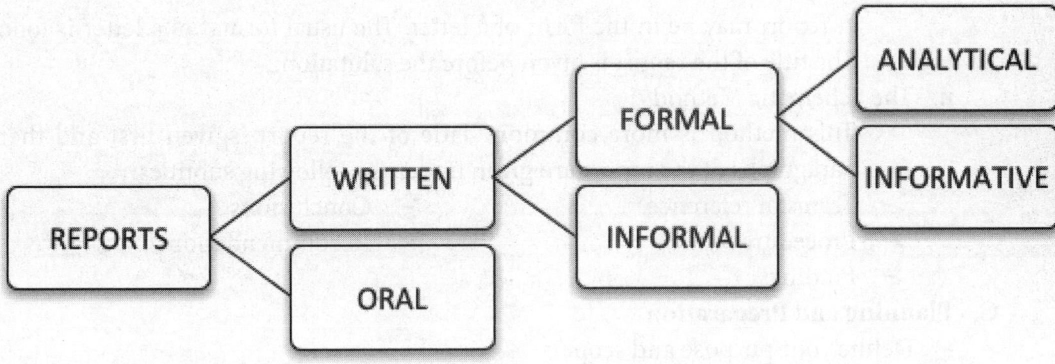

Modern management technique places high value on reports; important decisions are made on the facts and information in reports.

Kinds of reports: interim, final, special, operational, progress, inspection, periodic, partial, preliminary, etc. They may be informational or analytical.

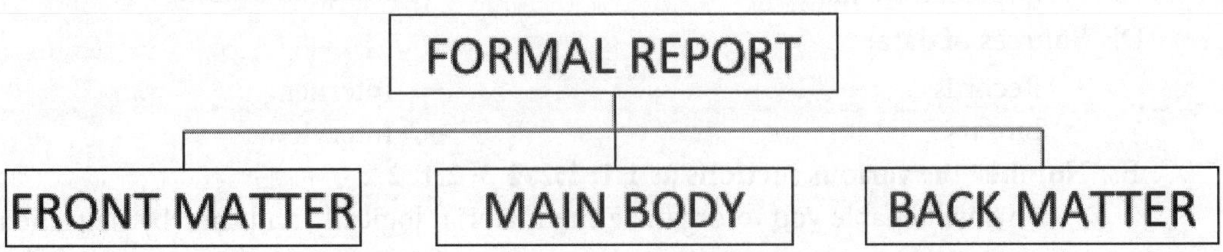

A. Features of a report

- ➢ Cover (*Title number of the report, date*)
- ➢ Title page
- ➢ Forwarding letter
- ➢ Preface
- ➢ Acknowledgements
- ➢ Table of contents
- ➢ List of illustrations
- ➢ An abstract/An executive summary

Main Body

- ➢ Introduction
- ➢ Discussion or description
- ➢ Conclusions
- ➢ Recommendations

Back Matter

- ➢ Appendices
- ➢ List of references
- ➢ Bibliography
- ➢ Glossary
- ➢ Index

B. Methods of Reporting

i. The Letter Method

A report may be in the form of a letter. The usual format of a letter is followed. The title of the report is given before the salutation.

ii. The Schematic Method

This method is more common. Title of the report isgiven first and then the paragraphs of the report are given under the following subtitles:

- Terms of reference
- Procedure
- Findings
- Conclusions
- Recommendations

C. Planning and Preparation

- Define your purpose and scope
- Determine your audience

  Are they superiors, subordinates, public, shareholders, customers, etc.
- Collect the data

  May be direct personal assessment based on observations, interviews (phone or personal), questionnaire, correspondence, meetings and inquiry, investigation, etc.
- Organize the material
- Make an outline

D. Sources of data:

- Records
- Library
- Internet
- Interview

E. **Number the various sections as 1.1, 1.2, 1.3; 2.1, 2.2 ---------**

- This will enable you to organize the material logically and thereby help the reader in easy understanding.

F. **Illustrations** include tables, charts, diagrams etc. to support the statements in the report.

G. **An Informal report** is generally prepared in printed forms. It does not contain the cover, the preface (i.e., transmittal) letter, title page, table of contents or a list of illustrations.

H. **Bibliography: Sample format is given below:**

Krishnaswamy N., et.al., 2015 Eco English-Learning English thro Environmental issues. Delhi Bloomsbury.

(Also see MLA Style Sheet for further guidance.)

I. **Checklist for reports**

- ✓ Does the title reflect the nature of the report?
- ✓ Have you kept the audience in mind?
- ✓ Does the report adhere to the terms of reference?
- ✓ Is the language suitable to the matter?
- ✓ Have you acknowledged all the material taken from various sources?
- ✓ Have you clearly stated in the introduction the purpose, scope and plan of the report?
- ✓ Have you followed the structure and layout of the report?
- ✓ Are the conclusions based on the findings of the investigation?

- ✓ Have you stated the recommendations clearly?
- ✓ Is the numbering properly done?
- ✓ Are there repetitions?
- ✓ Have you given adequate illustrations?
- ✓ Is each illustration referred to in the text?
- ✓ Have you given headings and sub-headings?
- ✓ Is it logically arranged?
- ✓ Have you given proper references? Do the references given at the end agree with the references in the text?
- ✓ Is a glossary of technical terms given at the end?
- ✓ Is there an index of all topics and aspects?
- ✓ Is the page numbering correct?
- ✓ Have you given proper page margin?
- ✓ Is it properly proof-read?
- ✓ Is the paragraph arrangement in accordance with the topic?
- ✓ Have you checked all facts?

J. Oral presentation of reports

- ➢ Mind your body language
- ➢ Be aware of the audience
- ➢ Prepare an outline of the presentation
- ➢ Use visual aids/ or Power point
- ➢ Mind your pronunciation
- ➢ Pay attention to the delivery
- ➢ Give hand-outs
- ➢ Interact with the audience

VI. Proposals

A proposal is a bid to undertake a project for designing or creating something new or modifying an existing method or procedure or system within a specific period of time. It is an offer or a bid to perform a specific job under a contract and a plea for financial support from outside. It is an analytical report making a plea for a research grant from a funding agency.

The parts are similar to a report

- ➢ Title page
- ➢ Table of contents
- ➢ Executive summary
- ➢ Statement of the problem
- ➢ Objectives
- ➢ Technical plan
- ➢ Management plan
- ➢ Cost estimate
- ➢ Conclusion
- ➢ Sample

VII. Abstracts

Abstracts are summaries. They reflect the skill of summarizing. An abstract is a brief summary of a report, article, presentation or proposal. An abstract may be half or a quarter or even one tenth of the original. It generally follows the IMRD plan: Introduction, Methods, Results and Discussions.

- ➢ Title: catchy, concise, and concrete statement.
- ➢ Authors: list of author(s).
- ➢ Abstract (Body).

1. Introduction: Describes the problem and states the motivation and relevance.
2. Methods: Procedure, rules etc.
3. Results or outcomes: States the results concisely
4. Discussion or conclusion

In an abstract, you come to the point directly.

VIII. Technical Writing

Technical writing is the presentation of information that helps the reader to understand and solve a particular problem or issue. Technical writers write, design and/or edit **proposals, manuals, web pages, lab reports, newsletters**, and many other **professional documents**. Technical writers need to have good computer skills.

Every profession has its own special form of writing. Doctors, lawyers, engineers, etc. write specialized reportsand documents. They hire technical writers to prepare documents, reports, surveys, forms, etc. Technical writing and editing involve working with others – researchers, scientists, designers, computer programmers etc.

Technical writing is a form of technical communication used in many fields such as computer hardware and software, finance, robotics, biotechnology, scientific research, consumer technology, etc. Content developers are needed by all IT companies.

Technical writers gather information from existing documents and experts. Technical writers are not subject experts. Technical writers must have very good language and teaching skills and understand the conventions of modern technical communication.

Technical writers must understand

- the audience
- the source material,
- how to make it deliverable and understandable on paper, a webpage or some other medium.

A well-written technical document has to define the objectives at the outset.

- Why is the document being written?
- What exactly is the writing intended to do? This involves identifying the information the readers want the document to provide and determining how the audience will look for the information. This is done by presenting the facts in the form of:
- Points and Sub points
- Tables
- Flow Charts

The writing process involves

- Determining the objective
- Gathering the data
- Recognizing the audience

The writing must *1) be logical, 2) use the proper format, and 3) give a compact summary at the end.*

Technical writers always dothe following:

✓ Pre writing: planning, generating information which involves brainstorming, branching information in terms of nodes and branches, to show the points and sub-points (like a tree-diagram), etc.

✓ Writing: structuring, organizing the data, problem-solving, comparing and presenting information in an acceptable format etc.

✓ Re-writing (time-taken 50%): revising, polishing the draft, adding the missing details, simplifying, deleting the unwanted data, removing errors, prioritizing, checking grammar and spelling, etc.

A report, a proposal or any other matter can be written in the form of technical writing.

Online Resources

1. http://esol.britishcouncil.org/content/learners/skills/writing/writing-formal-letter
2. http://web.mit.edu/me-ugoffice/communication/technical-writing.pdf
3. http://flex.wisconsin.edu/degrees-programs/business-technical-communications/
4. https://owl.english.purdue.edu/owl/resource/590/02/
5. http://www.pearsoned.ca/highered/showcase/hanson/pdf/9780138002688_08.pdf

Select Bibliography

1. Bell, Arthur H. and Dayle M. Smith. *Management Communication.*Delhi: Wiley-India, 2011.
2. Gerson, Sharon J. and Steven M. Gerson. *Technical Writing.* New Delhi: Pearson Prentice Hall, 2007.
3. Sharma, R C and Krishna Mohan. *Business Correspondence and Report Writing.* New Delhi: Tata McGraw-Hill, 2002.
4. Taylor, Shirley. *Model Business Letters, E-mails & Other Business Documents.* New Delhi: Pearson Education, 2004.
5. McMurrey, David A. *Processes in Technical Writing.* MacmillanColl Div, 1988

Unit IX – Practice

Part I: Business Communication

A. Presentation

1. Read the passage given below and prepare a power point presentation on 'Communication: Ways and Means' for a group of final year students of a post-graduate class
2. Read the passage given below. Prepare an OHP presentation for a group of engineering students.

Communication is a multifaceted word that covers everything – interaction with others, casual conversation, persuading, teaching and negotiating. You cannot communicate with a dummy; anything you do is meaningless as it gets no response. When you communicate with another person, you perceive their response and react with your own thoughts and feelings. Your ongoing behaviour is generated by your internal responses to what you see and hear. It is only by paying attention to the other person that you have any idea about what to say or do next.

You communicate with your words, with your voice quality and with your body: postures, gestures and expressions. You cannot not communicate.Some message is conveyed even if you say nothing and keep still. So communication involves a message that passes from one person to another. How do youknow that the message you give is the message they receive? You have probably had the experience of making a neutral remark to someone and being amazed at the meanings they read into it.

Communication is so much more than the words we say. These form only a small part of our expressiveness as human beings. Research shows that in a presentation before a group of people; 55 percent of the impact is determined by your body language-postures, gestures and eye contact; 38 percent by your tone of voice, and only 7 percent by the content of your presentation.

The exact figures will differ in different situations, and clearly body language and tonality make an enormous difference to the impact and meaning of what we say. It's not what we say, but how we say it that makes the difference. Margaret Thatcher spent a great deal of time and effort altering her voice quality. Tonality and body language determine whether the word 'Hello' is a simple recognition, a threat, a put down or a delightful greeting.

Actors do not really work with words; they are trained in tonality and body language. Any actor needs to be able to convey at least a dozen different shades of meaning in everyday conversation and probably also have a dozen different ways to say 'no', only we do not consciously think about them. If the words are the content of the message, then the postures, gestures, expressions and voice tonality are the context in which the message is embedded and together they make the meaning of the communication.

The final truth, however, is that what we communicate is ultimately what we convey. It is very important therefore to strike a rapport with the other person to know how the other person is receiving your message.

B. Memos

i. As the Principal of a college, write a memo to the Heads of Departments and all members of the staff, requesting them to be careful in the use of water, electricity, and stationery in the college.

ii. As Manager of a company, write a memo (an office circular), informing all in the company about a new medical-cum-insurance scheme which has special benefits if at least half the employees join the scheme.

iii. Write an office note (memo) to inform the staff of the revised work timings.

C. Minutes

i. Draft the minutes of the monthly executive meeting of your college association in which, among other things, the annual cultural events and the election of office bearers were on the agenda.

ii. Draft the minutes of the company's board meeting in which the following were on the agenda:

   a. To consider the proposal to increase the bonus amount.

   b. The need for acquiring more equipment for the factory.

D. Report Writing

i. Write a report on the workers' discontent in the factory.

ii. You are the head of the training faculty of a multi-national company. Your task is to train fresh recruits in soft skills and communication skills. You have already conducted 3 or 4 training programmes in the company. There is a need to give training at regular intervals. Write a report to the MD of the company, sharing your training experience and making a case for setting up a training unit in the company.

iii. You are the leader of a team that is going to launch a new consumer product which will change the life-style of working women. You have already tried it in the market and the product has been very well received. Now, you are required to submit a report regarding your market research and finding. Prepare a final report.

iv. Discuss the utility of reports in the decision-making process of an organization.

E. Proposals and Abstracts

A proposal is 'a written offer to solve a problem in a particular way under a specified plan of management, for a specified sum of money'.

i. Write a proposal, offering to solve the problem of internal delay in correspondence in an office.

ii. Write a proposal, offering to tap solar energy for supplying hot water, and electricity to the hostels in your college.

iii. Write bullet notes for making an oral presentation of your project proposal given in E. to a group of students in your class.

iv. 'The present market crash may be attributed to irrational consumerism'. Write an executive summary for this topic.
v. Take a centre page article from the day's newspaper and make an abstract of it.
vi. Write a short essay on the importance of condensed writing in all forms of documentation in business matters.
(*An extreme case of condensation! ha ., ha.....*)

> A visitor to a management college paused to admire a new building on the campus.
> 'It's a pleasure to see a building named after Kalidas, ' he said.
> 'Actually, ' said his guide, 'It's named after Kokila Kalidas. No relation.'
> The visitor was astonished.
> 'Was Kokila Kalidas a writer?'
> 'Yes, indeed, ' said the guide. 'She wrote a cheque!'

F. Letters

i. Write a letter to a computer dealer, requesting a copy of the latest catalogue with current prices to buy computers for your college computer lab.
ii. Write a letter to the editor of a newspaper, complaining about noise pollution caused by loud speakers in the locality where you reside.
iii. An electronic gadget you bought for your department is not giving proper service. Complain to the manufacturer who has given a guarantee for one year.
iv. You agreed to supply intercom telephone to a newly started company by a certain date. Write a letter to the manager of the company, requesting extension of time for supplying the equipment.
v. Draft a business report in the form of a letter on the basis of a consumer survey conducted for your company's new product. (The product may be a Smart Board, a DVD, or any other product of your choice).

G. Technical Writing

i. Write a description of a computer, explaining it to an adult in rural India who has never seen one. Explain its general uses, describe its functions and parts, and point out the advantages in using it.
ii. Write a feasibility report regarding the importance of manufacturing multimedia programs for teaching communication skills in English, pointing out the market potentialities in India.
iii. As a content developer, attempt a write-up on the importance of women's education in India.

Part II: Study Skills

i. **Note-taking**: To be able to take down notes from a lecture or talk is a very useful skill. As you listen to a talk, you should be able to take down the important points of the lecture and, later, when you look into the notes you have made, you should be able to reconstruct the lecture from the notes.

ii. **Note-making**: To be able to read an article, an essay, or even a chapter from a book and make notes so that you can reconstruct the essentials of the text.
- ❖ Decide for what purpose you are making the notes.
- ❖ Skim through the text first (if it is a written text) and get a 'bird's eye view'.
- ❖ Be systematic. Judge the importance of the points made by the speaker or writer and draw your own conclusions. In doing so, you will not be a passive listener or reader.

Activity 1 – Note-taking

Here is a short passage on crossword puzzles. Listen to the passage and take down notes. The teacher should read out the passage). Then, reconstruct the passage.

There are several kinds of crossword puzzles. One kind is the prize competition in which the person who finds the correct answers gets a big prize. But the answers are very hard to find, since several words appear equally appropriate: bad, mad or sad, for example, in the clue sentence, '------- people are seldom popular'. Such competitions attract peoplewho are fond of gambling, because by paying a small entry fee, they can win big prizes.

The second type of crossword puzzle is one in which there is only one possible answer to every clue. But the answer is elusive and calls for some detective work on our part. The clue gives only hints about the word. A clue like 'Mate changes to flush for food' will elude you till you realize that by changing the spelling of mate to **mcat**, you get the answer. Your comprehension and general knowledge are put to test. The effort to solve such crosswords is an intellectual exercise.

The third type of crossword is a straightforward exercise in which words matching the definition given in the clues have to be found and written in the appropriate place in the crossword square. There are no catches or tricks. This type is useful to the study of vocabulary. As simple exercises in problem solving, they provide some entertainment too.

Notes: Crossword Puzzles

1. Prize competitions
    - 1.1 Many answers possible
    - 1.2 Elements of gambling
2. Intellectual Crosswords
    - 2.1 Only one answer to the clue
    - 2.2 Detective work involved
    - 2.3 Intellectual exercise
        - 2.3.1 *Comprehension*
        - 2.3.2 *General knowledge*
3. Educational Crosswords
    - 3.1 Study of vocabulary
    - 3.2 Entertainment

4. If there are more categories, you can use the following notation
   4.1 1.1
   4.2 1.2
   4.3 1.2.1 etc.

Activity 2 – Note-making

Here is passage on acupuncture for note-making. Read it quickly and get the main points. Make notes.

Acupuncture is a system of treatment of diseases which has been practised in China for nearly 5000 years. It consists in the rapid insertion of fine steel needles, about six centimeters long, on particular parts on the body of the patient. After inserting the needle, the doctor twirls the needle between his thumb and forefinger. There are hundreds of acupuncture points on the body. When a puncture is made on the body, energy flows there along lines known as meridians to the diseased organs. This flow of energy helps to restore the balance of the system and thus correct the disorder. The points of treatment may be far from the seat of the disease. For example, to cure a toothache, the acupuncturist may insert a needle on the palm of the patient.

Although China is considered to be the country where acupuncture originated, some forms of treatment resembling it have been reported from other parts of the world by anthropologists. Among some ancient tribes, stones and arrows were used to prick the skin. In another form of treatment, the skin on particular parts of the body was burnt to effect a cure for certain diseases. Whether these kinds of treatment can rightly be classified with acupuncture can be known only after further research.

For long, acupuncture was dismissed by the West as a form of superstition like witchcraft and magic cure. Even in China, admiration for the western system of medicine was so great that the native systems of treatment were neglected or mistrusted. Moreover, the theoretical basis for acupuncture that was propounded in China was a mixture of spirituality, philosophy and psychology. This stood in the way of its acceptance by Chinese scientists.

During the 1960s, acupuncture came to the notice of western scientists, who viewed it with skepticism as well as curiosity. Doctors from Europe went to China to make a firsthand study of this strange form of treatment. They were convinced by what they saw that acupuncture worked. Not only were diseases cured, but even operations were performed after administering anaesthesis by acupuncture. The patient of such an operation could see and know what was being done, but felt no pain. After the operation, he could get up and walk away. Doctors in other parts of the world took acupuncture seriously and some of them trained themselves and set up practice in their countries. In China itself, the status of acupuncture rose when Chairman Mao officially ranked acupuncturists with other physicians.

II. Converting Visual to Verbal and Verbal to Visual mode

A. Often charts, diagram, tables, maps etc. are used to display information. These are called graphic representations.

B. They may be:

2.1 Tables

2.2 The bar charts and histograms

2.3 The pie charts

2.4 The organization charts

2.5 The flow-charts

2.6 Pictograms

2.7 Graphs

2.8 Maps and diagrams

> *Note: Bar charts display data using a number of rectangles of the same width, each of which represents a particular category. Bar charts can be displayed horizontally or vertically. They are usually drawn with a gap between the bars (i.e. rectangles) whereas bars of a histogram are drawn immediately next to each other.*

Bar Chart

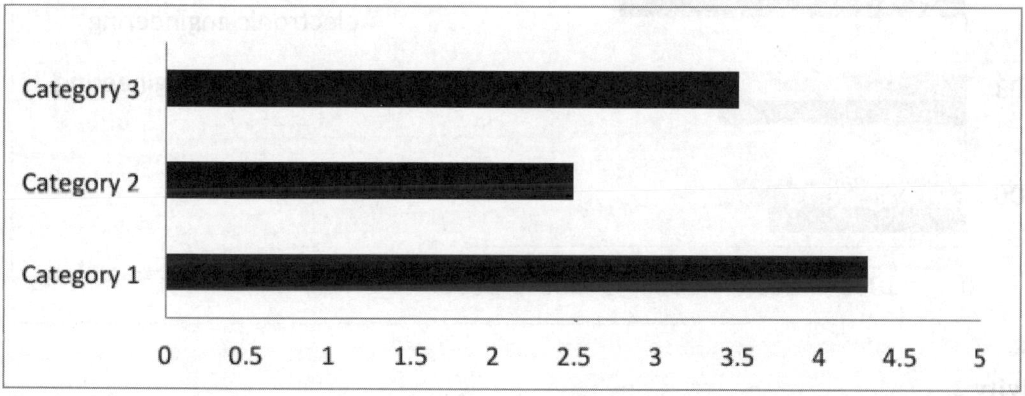

Histogram

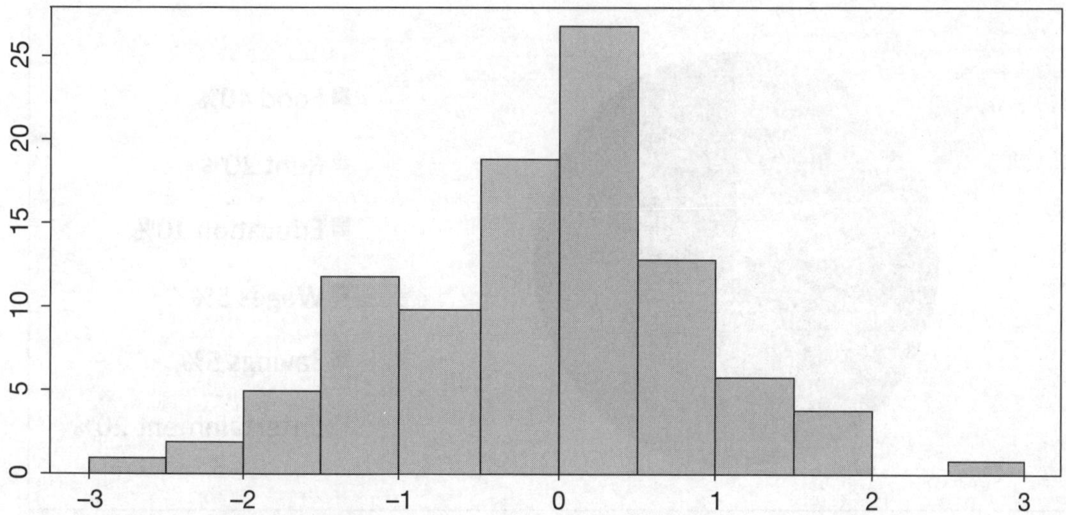

Activity 1

Look at the bar chart below. It helps you compare the popularity of the two courses and the changes that are taking place in technical institutions.

Now write a paragraph comparing the enrolment in the two courses over the years. What conclusion can you draw from the data?

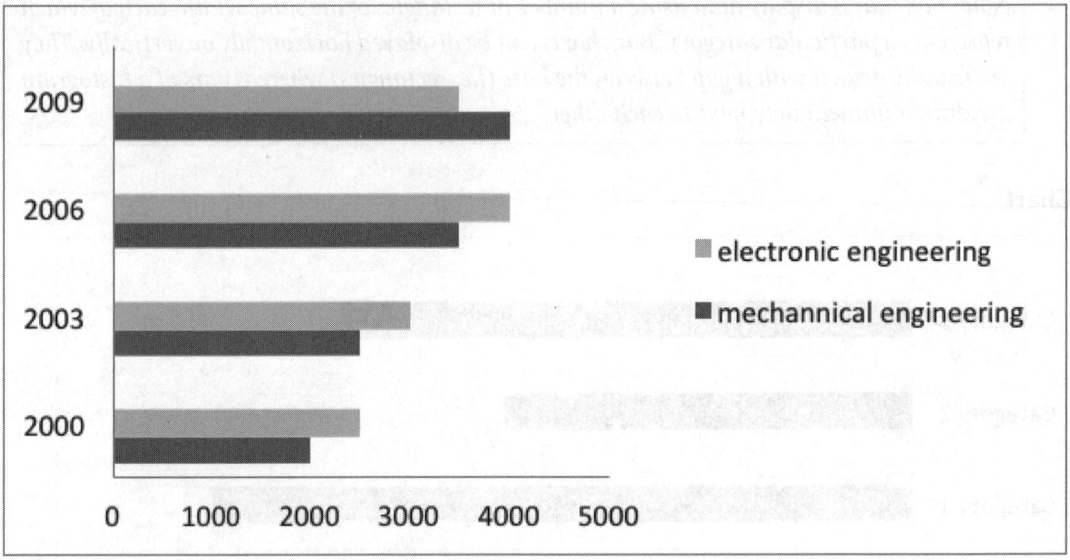

Activity 2

Look at the pie chart given below and write a paragraph about how Mr. Goel's family spends the money.

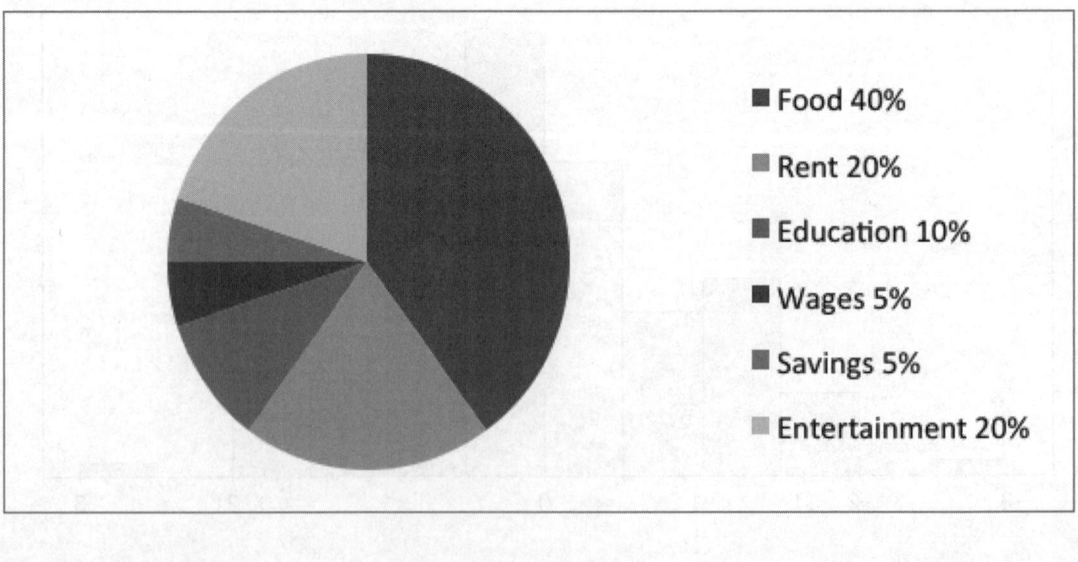

Activity 3

Look at the organizational chart of a company and write a paragraph or two about the company. Give the company a name and say where in the organization you will fit in.

Activity 4

Draw an organizational chart showing the administrative structure of India.

Write one or two paragraphs about the administrative structures of our country.

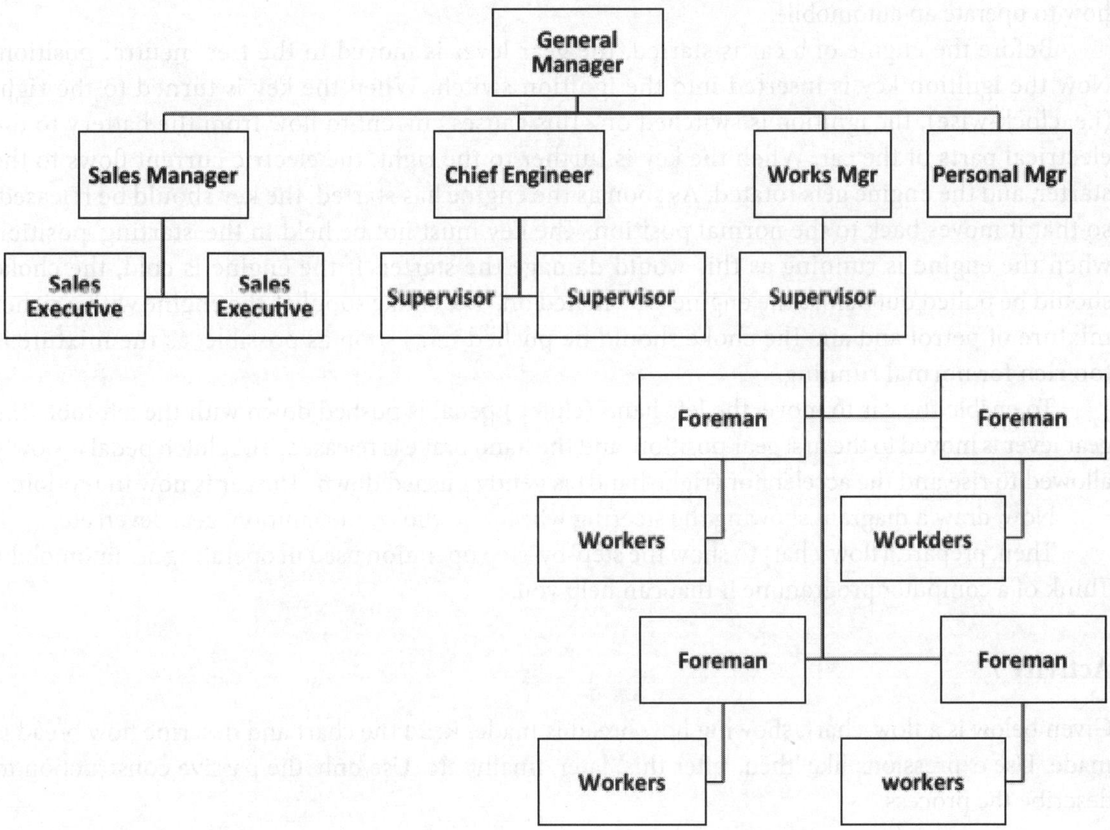

Activity 5

Converting a text into the visual mode.

Leela describes her apartment to her friend Sheela. Draw a diagram showing the plan of the apartment.

As you enter the apartment, the kitchen is on your left and the bathroom is opposite you. The bedroom is on your right, and the living room is to the left, down the passage beyond the kitchen and the bathroom. The two main rooms in the apartment are the living-room and the bedroom. The living room is on the north side and the bedroom is on the south side. There is a big window in the bedroom that has an attached toilet. The window of the bedroom is on the eastside and the window of the living room is on the north side.

Note: First draw a cross with arrow-head to show the directions like N, S, E, and W. Then draw the plan.

Activity 6

Mohinder is the owner of a driving school. He is also the instructor. Often he gives instructions on how to operate an automobile.

Before the engine of a car is started, the gear lever is moved to the free, neutral position. Now the ignition key is inserted into the ignition switch. When the key is turned to the right (i.e. clock-wise), the ignition is switched on. This causes current to flow from the battery to the electrical parts of the car. When the key is further to the right, the electric current flows to the starter, and the engine gets rotated. As soon as the engine has started, the key should be released, so that it moves back to the normal position. The key must not be held in the 'starting' position when the engine is running as this would damage the starter. If the engine is cold, the choke should be pulled out before the engine is switched on. The choke supplies the engine with a richer mixture of petrol and air. The choke should be pushed in as soon as possible, as the mixture is too rich for normal running.

To enable the car to move, the left-hand (clutch) pedal is pushed down with the left foot. The gear lever is moved to the first gear position, and the hand brake is released. The clutch pedal is slowly allowed to rise and the accelerator (right-hand) is gently pushed down. The car is now in motion.

Now, draw a diagram showing the steering wheel, the choke, the ignition, gear-lever, etc.

Then, prepare a flow-chart to show the step-by-step operation used in operating an automobile. Think of a computer programme if that can help you.

Activity 7

Given below is a flow-chart, showing how bread is made. Read the chart and describe how bread is made. Use expressions like 'then', 'after this', later, finally, etc. Use only the passive construction to describe the process.

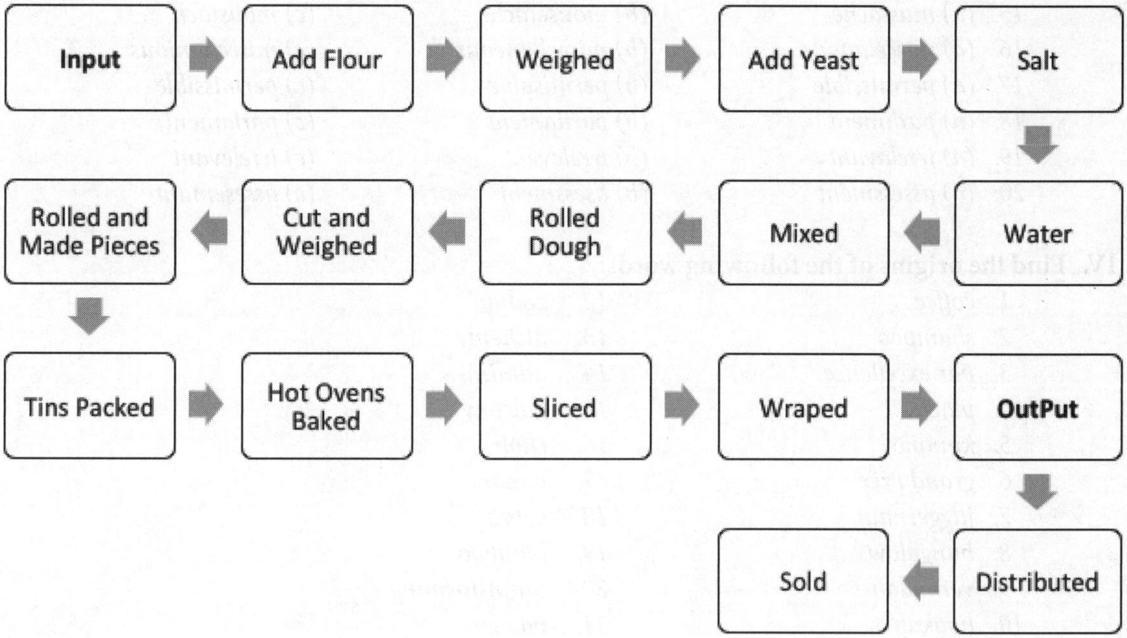

Activity 8

Prepare a flow-chart on how ice-cream is made in factories.

III. Reference Skills

i. Tick the correct spelling

1.	*(a) marriege*	*(b) marriage*	*(c) marige*
2.	*(a) matematician*	*(b) mathematecian*	*(c) mathematician*
3.	*(a) cassete*	*(b) casette*	*(c) cassette*
4.	*(a) cabbage*	*(b) cabbag*	*(c) cabage*
5.	*(a) rafrigerator*	*(b) refrigerater*	*(c) refrigerattor*
6.	*(a) ocupation*	*(b) occupation*	*(c) occupation*
7.	*(a) professer*	*(b) professor*	*(c) profeser*
8.	*(a) grammar*	*(b) grammer*	*(c) gramar*
9.	*(a) business*	*(b) busyness*	*(c) bisness*
10.	*(a) dissappear*	*(b) disappear*	*(c) disapear*
11.	*(a) obitury*	*(b) obituery*	*(c) obituary*
12.	*(a) jellousy*	*(b) jealousy*	*(c) jealousey*
13.	*(a) achievement*	*(b) acievement*	*(c) achievment*
14.	*(a) necessery*	*(b) necessary*	*(c) neccessary*

15. *(a) mustache*	*(b) mousetache*	*(c) moustach*
16. *(a) miscelanous*	*(b) miscellaneous*	*(c) miscellanious*
17. *(a) permissible*	*(b) permisable*	*(c) permissible*
18. *(a) parliment*	*(b) parliament*	*(c) parlament*
19. *(a) irrelavant*	*(b) irrelevent*	*(c) irrelevant*
20. *(a) assessment*	*(b) asessment*	*(c) assesemant*

IV. Find the origins of the following words:

1. *coffee*
2. *shampoo*
3. *par excellence*
4. *plaza*
5. *kimono*
6. *grand prix*
7. *juggernaut*
8. *bungalow*
9. *verandah*
10. *hookah*
11. *hazard*
12. *zodiac*
13. *alchemy*
14. *admiral*
15. *balcony*
16. *choir*
17. *banana*
18. *cobra*
19. *bamboo*
20. *brainstorming*
21. *bazaar*

V. Slogan Writing

A concept has to be expressed in such a way that it sticks in the mind of the audience like a glued sticker. It should be rhythmic, musical, alliterative and catchy.

Look at the following slogans:

i. *Hire me for higher sales*
ii. *Utterly Butterly Delicious*
iii. *Owner's Pride, Neighbour's Envy*
iv. *You are Entitled to My opinion*
v. *Drive in the New and Drive out the Old (Car exchange ad.)*
vi. *Seven days without our butter makes one weak.*

Can you write catchy slogans for the following:

1. *For a business school*
2. *For a clean campus*
3. *A magic pen that will write exams*
4. *To prevent female infanticide*
5. *AIDS prevention*
6. *Save the Earth*
7. *For a logistics company*

VI. Writing Advertisements

Ads are mass communication efforts to persuade the customer to buy the product. Ads need to capture the attention of the audience and attract them in order to influence their choice. In the present-day world, business ads have become very important. It is said:

The medium is the message.

Or

The medium is the massage.

Consider the following ad of a computer company.

- *Small in size and Big in performance.*
- *Visual: A young boy throws down a sumo.*
- *Have you seen the zoo ads of Vodafone?*

Try your hand:

1. *Write an ad for a mobile phone company.*
2. *Write an ad for a life insurance company.*
3. *Write an ad for a bank to promote their savings bank account promotion.*
4. *Write an ad for a training centre in communication skills.*

VII. Play with Punctuation

A panda (a bear-like mammal, native to China) walks into a café. He orders a sandwich, tea, etc., eats and drinks all, then draws a gun and fires two shots in the air.

'Why?' asks the confused waiter, as the panda makes towards the exit. The panda produces a badly punctuated manual. 'Look it up, ' he says.

It is written 'Panda: Large black and white bear like mammal. Eats, shoots and leaves.'

The comma is the culprit!

Now you do it!

1. Punctuate and change the meaning.
   a. *My grandfather has a walking stick.*
   b. ______________________; ______________________
2.
   a. *I have a little used knife in my room.*
   b. ______________________; ______________________
3.
   a. *My friend is a sick-berth attendant.*
   b. ______________________; ______________________
4.
   a. *My father is a hard-working man.*
   b. ______________________; ______________________

5.
    a. The king declares Tenalirama is an ass.
    b. (Tenalirama added two commas). Guess.

6.
    a. My mother said, 'Govind is lazy'.
    b. (Make my mother lazy!)

7.
    a. 'Pardon impossible, to be sent to jail.'
    b. (Make the criminal escape!)

Case Study for Discussion

Sujit works in Perfect Solutions, a software company located in Noida, India. To keep abreast of latest software technology, the employees are required to attend conferences, make industrial trips, visit other companies, and invite experts for exchange of knowledge. To facilitate such exchanges and to build industrial relations, the company funds its employees' travel and other expenses to attend conferences, related to their expertise, in India and abroad.

Sujit attended a three day conference on 'Image Processing' in Goa. It was organized by the International Society on Image Processing. He received financial support from the company to attend this conference. Another senior colleague from the company, Aparna, also attended the same conference. On their return, they submitted their conference reports to their boss, Sanyog. In her report, Aparna claimed that Sujith did not attended all the conference sessions. Instead, he used his time to visit the city's tourist attractions.

Sanyog has to address this accusation. He is in a dilemma on how to handle the situation. As a boss, it is his duty to take omit action on the complaint filed by Aparna. At the same time, he does not want to accuse anybody without knowing the truth.

Questions

1. To know the truth, should he write a memo to Sujit, or an e-mail to Aparna, or visit Sujit personally?
2. Imagine yourself to be Aparna. Draft a letter to the boss accusing Sujit of neglect of duties.
3. Imagine yourself to be Sanyog. Write a memo to Sujit asking him to furnish the required information.
4. Write an e-mail or memo to your boss giving an explanation.

Unit X – Intercultural Communication

No two languages are ever sufficiently similar to be considered as representing the same social reality. The worlds in which different societies live are distinct, not merely the same world with different labels attached.

– Edward Sapir

OBJECTIVES:

After reading this unit you will be able to

- ✓ Define culture
- ✓ Examine intercultural and cross cultural discourses
- ✓ Identify imperatives for intercultural communication

Points to Remember

1. Intercultural communication is a symbolic, interpretive, transactional, contextual process in which people from different cultures create shared meanings.
2. After the Second World War (1939–1945) and during the Cold War (1947–1991) between the Western Block headed by the United States and the Eastern Block dominated by the Soviet Union, business transformed from individual-country capitalism, particularly American, to global capitalism; it necessitated the study of other cultures. The discipline 'cross-cultural communication', which was originally found within businesses and the government departments, expanded since business organizations and government departments also expanded globally. Language training was imparted by big businesses to their employees to make them competent for overseas jobs in the globalized market-place. Programmes were developed to train employees to understand foreign cultures.Thus began the concept of Cross-cultural communication.
3. In 1946, Edward T. Hall, an American anthropologist, was asked by the Foreign Service Institute in the USA to design 'preparedness' courses for overseas workers because materials about other cultures were scarce at that time. It was cross-cultural communication at that time. **Cross-cultural communication** involves a comparison of interactions among people from one culture to those from another culture; only certain aspects like marriage rituals, educational methods, child-rearing practices or comparing the systems in two languages were attempted; later, in the 1960s, it developed into the comparative study of a particular idea or concept in many cultures. Edward Hall's book ***The Silent Language*** is a good example of cross-cultural comparison. Cross-cultural communication is considered abstractly or even independently of any form of social interaction

in real life situations but intercultural communication considers communication when members of different cultural groups are directly engaged with each other in real situations. Edward Hall is considered the father of intercultural communication.

4. Intercultural communication is broader and includes all ideas and concepts like diversity training for students, business people, and corporate professionals. Now, in the globalized world and with all the technological developments, intercultural communication has become important and it has become an academic discipline.
5. Culture is a learned set of shared interpretations about beliefs, values, norms, and social practices which affect the behaviour of a relatively large group of people. Culture includes
   a) objective elements like rules and regulations, laws, behaviours, language (grammar, dictionaries, style manuals, etc.) and
   b) subjective elements like values, beliefs, attitudes, conventions, etc. Culture includes
      - ideology (values, beliefs, conventions, religion, etc)
      - forms of discourse like the functions of language, negotiation, etc.,
      - face systems like power hierarchy, kinship, concept of self, in-group-out-group relationships
      - interactions in socializing institutions like education, acculturation and enculturation
      - non-verbal communication.

   A person is born into a culture, a family, a gender, a generation and such other natural factors and acquires, unconsciously, and also through emulation and education, the culture of that society; this is called enculturation. Acculturation is the modification of an individual or group by adapting to or borrowing from another culture. For example, Indians adapting or borrowing American cultural ways is acculturation.
6. Even within one culture, there are sub-cultures and co-cultures; for example, within a culture there are inter-generational, inter-gender, inter-religious, inter-linguistic, inter-class/caste, inter-racial/ethnic, and inter-regional cultures resulting in intercultural communication and conflicts. Co-cultures exist side-by-side without any hierarchical implications that one is superior and the other is inferior like for example the way Hindus and Muslims lived together in the Pre-Ayodhya-Babri Mosque conflict days, or the way Hindus, Muslims and Christians lived in the Southern part of India or the way the Hindu culture and the Sufi culture co-existed in India during the Delhi Sultanate period and later for more than 1000 years, as a result of a spirit of accommodation adaptation, and piety. Sub-cultures are like gender, generation, caste/class, etc. that exist as components of a culture. So, intercultural communication may be at the national level as well as at the global level. For example, in India, there are several cultures – from Kashmir to Kerala- and within each many sub-cultures.
7. The study of intercultural communication has become necessary in the present-day context for the following reasons:
   a. **Identity imperative**: Understanding one's own culture has become a part of one's identity and location. This has become essential where globalization has brought in cultural waves, cultural colonization, and cultural hegemony; where one's identity is threatened, it is all the more imperative to be aware of one's own culture.

b. **The demographic imperative**: In the changing world of diversities, one must be aware of the culture (s) of other societies. Globalization has brought in more mobility, changing immigration patterns (people moving from one country to another, one State to another even within a country, and from rural to urban areas), seeking more opportunities. Countries and communities are becoming 'salad bowls' and not melting pots. So, any enlightened citizen must be aware of other cultures and ready to make adjustments. So, the ability to evaluate one's own culture and other cultures, omit critical cultural awareness, has become necessary.

c. **The economic imperative**: To reach the global market, to be mobile and to make use of the opportunities available, one must have intercultural competence. The recent trend towards globalization – the creation of a world market in goods, services, labour, capital, and technology-is shown dramatically in a Bangalore-based company asking for computers or TVs made in Japan, China, or Korea; probably they were co-designed by engineers in different countries. Cultural differences in business practices have implications not only when people from different companies do business with each other but also when people from different cultures work on the same team. Understanding cultural differences involves working with employees with diverse culture, recognizing markets in different cultures, developing new products according to local requirements.

d. **The technological imperative**: Modern transport systems, the internet and other technological developments, and ever expanding human interaction make intercultural communication a necessity. Increase in the volume of information, increased contact with people (those who are similar and those who differ), identity management and such other factors make intercultural communication imperative.

e. **The peace imperative**: The need to understand and appreciate each other has become more important in the face of cultural domination, neo-colonialism, linguistic imperialism and such other issues. In order to maintain peace and resolve conflicts, intercultural communication is essential.

f. **The ethical imperative**: Self-awareness, self-reflection, learning from others, being a universalist, social activism and fighting for social justice need interpersonal relationships and intercultural communication.

8. Intercultural competence includes components like motivations, attitude, knowledge, display of respect to other cultures, empathy, inter-discourse competence, tolerance of ambiguity, the willingness to be non-judgmental, and the skills in understanding and handling conventions and values.

   Motivations include feelings, intentions and actions; all these involve one's eagerness and willingness to experience other cultures, readiness to be positive and be accurate in making choices and act accordingly.

   Attitude means display of respect to other cultures through both verbal and nonverbal symbols. Expressing interest, concern, and understanding will show respect to others. This will show one's intercultural competence.

Proper orientation to knowledge about other cultures will be demonstrated in actions and words. For instance, North Indians often expressing personal attitudes or opinions about South Indians or South Indians making ill-informed/ sweeping statements about North Indians as if they were facts shows an ineffective orientation towards knowledge.

Display of respect is the ability to understand and show respect to the specific ways of showing respect in the use of titles, in the use of politeness rituals, body language, formalities in language, the tone of voice, etc.

Empathy is another important aspect of intercultural competence; empathy is the quality or the skill that makes one behave as if one understands the other culture or cultures as others do. Though it is not possible to put oneself in others' shoes, it is possible to show sufficient understanding of the feelings, moods, and thoughts of others.

Inter-discourse competence is the skill in learning the languages and body language of other cultures. With globalization, in a polyglot world, monolingualism is becoming a new form of illiteracy. Research shows that multilingual people are better at reasoning, at multitasking, at grasping and reconciling new ideas. A bilingual brain is proving to be a more flexible and more resourceful one and it is established that learning the lyricism of another language can make brains better. In intercultural competence, language and body language play very important roles in interactions and regulating conversations; starting, regulating, taking turns, sustaining and ending a discussion or conversation involves language management and body language management; it involves taking subtle cues and appropriateness. Task role behaviour and relational role behaviour are related basic elements in intercultural competence; these two refer to the abilities to contribute to omit problem-solving activities when working in a multi-cultural situation. Building and maintaining personal relations with group members, initiating new ideas, requesting more details or facts, seeking clarification, evaluating suggestions, etc. are important in the display of culturally appropriate behavior behaviour and it involves both verbal and non-verbal competence.

Tolerance of ambiguity means a person's response to uncertainty. When a person encounters new situations in a different culture, there will be many unpredictable encounters. One must be able to cope with new and unpredictable situations without being nervous or hostile to such situations. One must be able to adapt oneself without showing anger, sarcasm, or frustration. All such qualities add to intercultural competence.

9. **Language and culture:** There are at least three different opinions about the relationship between language and culture. Some argue that language is only 'an outer form of thought' and that all human beings have the same range of thoughts, which we express in different ways in different languages; this means that any thought can be expressed in any language, although some have more words and some fewer omit. For example, rice growing areas have more words to express different forms of rice than wheat growing areas. A dog is a dog though it may be 'kutha 'in Hindi 'kukka' in Telugu, and 'nay' in Tamil. Some take a relativist position, saying that language controls thought patterns and perceptions of reality; this hypothesis was proposed by Edward Sapir (1921),

a linguist, and his student, Benjamin Whorf (1956). According to them language is not merely an instrument for voicing ideas but is itself a shaper of ideas and language defines our experience. For example, in Indian languages there are many words to refer to family relationships but English has fewer words. This shows, according to the Sapir-Whorf hypothesis, that Indians think differently about family relationships because their languages have several words for family relationships. Can we say that Indians have no concept of 'nation' because there is no word for 'nation' in either Sanskrit or any Indian language? This may be an extreme position. The more recent position takes a more moderate view of the relationship between language and perception and argues that language *influences* our perception, and, ultimately, important cultural components, but does not *determine* them. It is better to assume that language and thought and, thereby, culture, are to some extent related but not completely. Now that a language like English has become global and different cultures are using English to express their own cultures, we have to say that language and culture are very closely networked. For example, Indians use English to express their own culture and use many words like 'shanti', 'eve-teasing', 'co-brother', etc.; some words have been borrowed and used in English by even native users of English.

Whatever position we take, language, as pointed out in earlier units (1 and 3), is ambiguous and vague. No word or sentence has a definite meaning and there are always differences between expression and impression because there is a lot of suppression in between. According to post-structuralist thinking, every word undergoes 'endless deferral', which means that no word has a fixed meaning and there is no 'signified' or fixed concept. In addition, communication styles vary from culture to culture. Edward Hall identified **high-context and low-context communication styles**; high-context communication emphasizes understanding messages without direct verbal communication; in other words, more of meaning is suggestive and implied. For example, a glance or a signal conveys meaning. In low-context communication, meaning is conveyed more in verbal form, directly without relying on non-verbal, implied, or contextual information. Styles can be elaborate, rich, ornamental, and expressive or understated, simple, and valuing silence. A common refrain is, "If you don't have anything nice to say, don't say anything at all." We must remember that communication style combines both language and non-verbal communication.

10. Moreover, meanings are interpreted in contexts. **Pragmatics** focuses on the actual use of language. We may call this 'the grammar of context', which is important in intercultural discourse. Many factors like the setting (time, place, use of space), purpose, topic, genre, who the participants are and the roles they play, the mode (speech, writing, silence, other media like video, email, mobile, etc.), sequence (set agenda or open agenda), co-occurrence patterns, styles (implicit, explicit, etc.) are essential to construct meaning.
11. Discourses are of different kinds: professional discourse, corporate discourse, generational discourse, gender discourse, religious discourse, class/caste discourse, etc. In intercultural communication and intercultural training all the components mentioned above are to be used in teaching, training, research, and consultation services in business and government sectors.
12. Intercultural conflicts occur as a result of many factors like economic, religious, cultural, class/caste, conflict of interest, value conflict, goal conflict, cognitive conflict, stereotyping, and political tensions, as well as lack of tolerance or mutual respect, empathy, non-judgementalism, non-

discrimination, forgiveness, ambiguity, language issues, and poor management styles. In addition, even differences in discourse styles cause conflicts. For example, the well-known statement that 'men are from Mars and women are from Venus' has some truth in it; there are differences in the communication patterns and styles between men and women. The differences between generations also pose many acute problems. Communication between men and women or two generations (called generation gap) may be due to the fact that while the words may be the same and 'understood', the meanings are inferred and interpreted differently creating communication gaps. Conflicts happen often between parents and children, teachers and students, and younger and older employees in companies. In the case of different generations within the same society and even of different genders within the same family, conflicts occur.

13. Conflicts may be destructive and confrontational, or productive if they are competitive. If cultural differences and discourse differences are properly understood, conflicts can be resolved amicably. Maintaining contact, staying connected, recognizing the existence of differences, identifying the preferred ways of conflict resolution, willingness to forgive and forget, and being creative in solving problems are some of the strategies in conflict management. Multicultural education at all levels will also be helpful as a long term solution.
14. Most importantly, we must know that only cultural patterns can be studied and not the behavior of every individual. We can only study and classify the dominant patterns of culture. For example, some cultures believe that institutional power should be distributed equally; some cultures can tolerate ambiguity and change; some cultures rely on and show allegiance to a leader or head; some cultures are assertive or 'manly'; some cultures are pleasure-seeking, etc. Individual variations cannot be classified.
15. Postmodern cultural spaces like cyberspace, the internet, SMS, blogs, face book, twitter, chat rooms, message bands, etc. have added new dimensions to intercultural communication. The social and cultural contexts in which our identity is formed, where we grow and where meanings are created have also been taken over by the postmodern cultural spaces, which are dynamic and tenuous.
16. Inspite of all the talk about globalization, intercultural communication is American and Euro-centric and not global. No Indian is asked to give a training course to Americans on how to communicate in India, or no Chinese is invited to instruct Europeans on business communication. Maybe, postcolonial and postmodern studies will change the trend and make intercultural communication truly global.

Online resources

1. www.intercultural.org
2. http://anthro.palomar.edu/language/default.htm
3. http://non-verbal.ucsc.edu
4. http://mediationchannel.com/
5. https://www.udemy.com/intercultural/
6. http://www.cmu.edu/icc/

Select Bibliography

1. Hall, Edward Twitchell. *The Silent Language*. Santa-Barbara:Greenwood Press, 1973.
2. English, Laura M. And Sarah Lynn. *Business Across Cultures: Effective Communication Strategies*. Boston:Addison-Wesley, 1995.
3. Holliday, Adrian and John Kullman. *Intercultural Communication: An advanced resource book for students*. London: Routledge, 2004.
4. Hofstede, Geert. *Culture's Consequences: Comparing Values, Behaviors, Institutions and Organizations Across Nations*. California: SAGE Publications Inc., 2001.
5. Hall, Stuart. Representation: *Cultural Representations and Signifying Practices*. London: SAGE Publications Ltd., 1997.

Unit X – Practice

1. Imagine a community where there are Asians (Chinese, Indians, Japanese, Koreans, Vietnamese, Indonesians, Singaporeans, etc.) Africans, Europeans, Latin Americans, North Americans, Middle Easterners, Australians, etc. Make a list of the religions, languages, food habits, dress patterns, etc. that may come into contact in such a global village.
2. Imagine that you are also living in that 'village' and list some of the issues and problems you may encounter. Identify some of the ways in which your life may be influenced by the presence of people from cultures different from yours.
3. Which of the imperatives for intercultural communication listed in the unit is the most important motivator for you? Give reasons for your answer.
4. One view is that 'People are born into a culture' and the other is 'One becomes a member of a culture through a process of enculturation'. What is your view? Explain.
5. What are the ways in which electronic communication and other technologies have influenced intercultural communication?
6. What is the difference between cross-cultural communication and intercultural communication?
7. Do you think that language – verbal as well as non-verbal-plays an important role in intercultural communication? Give reasons for your answer.
8. What are the ways in which we develop our cultural identities?
   (Think of many identities like age identity, class/caste, ethnic, religious, majority/minority, sexual, generational, spiritual, national, etc.)
9. Mention some of the non-verbal messages that we communicate with.
10. Do you know?
    In New Zealand the Maroi greeting, 'hongi', involves rubbing or touching of noses when two people meet. In Tibet, poking one's tongue out is the customary way to welcome people. In the Dutch part of Netherlands, friends and relatives greet each other with three air-kisses. The ethnic African tribe, Masai, greet their friends by spitting on one another. In the Southeast African country, Mozambique, people from the northern parts clap their hands three times before saying hello. In the Polynesian island of Tuvalu, the traditional greeting involves pressing one's face to the other person's cheek and then taking a deep sniff. Do you consider these customs weird? Why?
11. What are postmodern cultural spaces and how important are they in intercultural communication?
12. How do histories influence the process of identity formation and culture? Explain with reference to political, ideological, social, religious, national, intellectual, and other factors.
13. What are the relationships between one's language and how reality is perceived in culture formation?

14. What is 'culture shock' and how does it occur to people who make cultural transitions? Give examples.
15. What is the role of communication in the cultural adaptation process? Give examples.
16. Distinguish between 'tolerance' and 'mutual respect 'and 'assimilation' and 'co-existence'. Give examples.
17. Many Americans think that their way of life, their language, and their thinking is the best and only way of doing things and that is the standard for the rest of the world. Not only Americans but also many other cultural communities put on 'cultural blinders' and view the world. What are the consequences and problems arising out of such attitudes? Discuss with suitable examples.
18. Living in India teaches us to be more aware of diversity. Do you agree? Why or why not?
19. Why do people wish to be in the company of people of their own culture and language even when they move out of their own?
20. Some ethnic groups like the Sardarji's or the South Indians in the Bollywood films are stereotyped a lot. Why is it so and do you think it contributes to intercultural communication?
21. The RTE Act may create cultural conflicts or cultural harmony in our educational institutions. What is your view?
22. Categories to form stereotypes about people may be: regions of the world (Americans, Arabs, Africans, etc.), countries (China, Japan), regions within countries (Gujarat, Kerala, Bengal, Tamil Nadu, etc.), cities (Mumbai, Delhi, New York, etc.), race (Aryans, Mongols, African, etc.), religion, age, occupation, relational roles like father, husband, wife, etc., physical characteristics like fat, short, etc., social class or caste like Brahmins, the rich, middle class, etc. Many stereotypes are created by direct experience with one or two people or based on second hand information or inputs from media.
23. My father is a Hindu Brahmin and my mother is a Christian; both are Indians who migrated to the USA. I was born and brought up in the USA. My father wants me to be a Hindu Brahmin and my mother wants me to be an Indian Christian. I'm called 'Indian-American'. I don't know who I am! What am I supposed to do? Please advise me.
24. There is freedom in virtual space and traditions dominate the non-virtual space of family and society. Do you agree? Give reasons.
25. Code Switching (switching from one language to another in conversation) and Code Mixing (using words, phrases, and sentences from another language in conversation) is useful in establishing rapport in intercultural communication. What is your view? Explain with examples from Indian languages.
26. In a big multinational company, employees from different regions, countries, languages, and cultures work together. What are the problems that are likely to arise in such situations and what solutions can the management think of to prevent confusion and conflicts?
27. Construct an imaginary hilarious situation in which a Punjabi, a Bengali, and a Keralite, are talking about a business deal or are in social conversation in a club. Make it as humorous as possible.
28. Do you think intercultural communication has become truly intercultural including the cultures of various communities or it is only Euro-centric? Give reasons.

29. 'Young people are going to grow up in a global environment where they're competing not just against kids in Chicago or Los Angeles for jobs, but they are competing against folks in Beijing and Bangalore.' – Barrack Obama. Express your opinion on the statement.
30. List some of the stereotypes you have formed and the basis for them. Say how accurate they are.
31. In English, 'on time' means exactly at the arranged time. In your culture, how important is it to be on time and not late for appointments and meetings?

Case Study for Discussion

An Indian, Mr. Rakesh Kapoor, who studied in the USA and worked there in a multinational company, was posted as the manager of the company's branch in Chennai. When he took charge of the Chennai office, he wanted to get to know his employees and tell them that he is very friendly and interested in cordial work relationships. So, he decided to throw a party for all the employees in a less formal environment. He invited everybody to his house for a big party.

At his house, he arranged for a buffet of snacks and drinks so that the employees could help themselves to whatever they liked. He wanted the party to be very informal and everyone to move around and talk to each other.

But the party was not a success. The employees, mostly from the southern part of India, were very uncomfortable. They were not used to socializing and meeting people in a party atmosphere. They were used to talking to each other only about office matters. They thought that the manager was showing off his authority and power in inviting them to his house.

Questions

1. Collect information about the office culture in the USA and South India.
   - What differences in the two cultures affected the success of the party?
   - Who misunderstood who?
   - Can you suggest some solution to both the groups so that in future such misunderstandings do not happen?

Unit XI – Professional Communication

Leadership involves remembering past mistakes, an analysis of today's achievements, and a well-grounded imagination in visualizing the problem of the future.

– Stanley C. Allyn

OBJECTIVES

After reading this unit, you will be able to

- ✓ Acquire engineering and management skills
- ✓ Develop leadership skills

INTRODUCTION

In a highly competitive global environment, engineering and management professionals need to possess good inter-personal and intra-personal communication skills besides domain knowledge to succeed in the work place. Besides, they are required to be sensitive to the cultural background of their colleagues. Only when a professional has a thorough understanding of the dynamics of communication and cultural sensitivities of the work place will he be able to lead his team towards achieving the objectives of the organization.

I. Skills of an Engineer

A Good Engineer

- ➢ **Has excellent technical knowledge:** A good engineer is somebody who has expertise in his field as well as the knowledge of how the industry works. He is able to align his knowledge and skills to the needs of the industry. At the same time, he is always on the lookout for breakthroughs in his field and tries to implement the new knowledge in the practical domain.
- ➢ **Possesses good analytical skills:** Good engineers are naturally inquisitive and continuously thinking of innovative designs and products. They are trained to understand and analyze a situation from different angles and provide probable solutions. Good engineers always implement their suggestions in a time bound and systematic manner. They are constantly thinking of innovative techniques to solve a problem.
- ➢ **Fosters professionalism and trust:** A good engineer is a thorough professional at work. He likes to work in a team and is always looking for newer areas where his skill and

knowledge could be utilized. He believes in constructive suggestions and in translation of theoretical ideas into practical solutions.

- **Pays attention to detail:** It is important for an engineer to understand the minutest detail of the working of a project, be it the product or the process. Every clog in the machine is important for its working. An engineer understands the role of synchronization between different parts of a complex process in its smooth functioning.
- **Is proficient in soft skills:** Good engineers should have domain knowledge as well as expertise in soft skills or people skills. Ultimately they are dealing with people in real life situations. They should have in abundance qualities like empathy, honesty, sincerity and generosity. To be successful in their profession, they should be able to apply the theoretical knowledge they have acquired to the practical problems in day to day life.
- **Possesses good communication Skills:** An engineer possesses good written as well as presentation skills. He communicates with his team members in a clear and crisp manner. He is adept in writing reports, proposals, memos and letters. His writing is characterized by clarity, coherence, completeness, conciseness. His writing is simple, unambiguous, and jargon free. His communication style is audience-centric.
- **Works in teams**: He likes to work in a team. Most of the engineering projects are taken up by groups or teams. A team of people with creative minds can generate newer and better ideas on how to solve a problem. 'Silo Building' is discouraged in this profession. An engineering marvel is generally the outcome of team-work.
- **Sets realistic expectations**: Good engineers set challenging but achievable targets for themselves. They have the motivation, drive and enthusiasm to scale predetermined targets within well-defined time limits. They are ambitious to meet their targets quickly but do not get impatient or cranky if they do not get desired results. They are equally aware of the scope and limitations of their project.
- **Follows ethical behaviour:** An engineer works closely with society. His designs and products are used by common people. As his designs and products have far reaching effects on the users in terms of health and safety, it is the moral responsibility of an engineer to design safe products. An engineer has to think critically and independently about moral issues. He should also be bold enough to report any malfunction either in product or service before launching it in the market. It would be ideal if an engineer could strike a balance between safety and affordability while designing a product.

Key responsibilities:

Engineering education provides a wide range of specializations in areas ranging from Electrical to Mechanical, from Computers to Communication, and from Civil to Aeronautical engineering. Basically an engineer has four areas of responsibility:

- Acting as a nodal point between management, production and marketing divisions to discuss project specifications and overall working of the project. In this role, he develops and manages technical standards and service infrastructure. He also undertakes production

1.3 A liaison officer when he establishes and maintains contacts within and outside the organization to obtain information.

2. **Informational role**: The manager serves as the nodal point to receive all relevant information from inside and outside the organization and process it further in the interest of the organization. In this role, he acts as
   2.1 a monitor when he seeks and receives work related information from employees,
   2.2 a disseminator when he disseminates the information to others within the organization,
   2.3 A spokesperson when he transmits organizational information like plans, policies, and actions to outside agencies.
3. **Decisional role**: A manager has to take informed decisions within the organization. He may play the role of a decision maker for the company when he acts as
   3.1 an entrepreneur and generates new ideas and innovations for the growth of the company,
   3.2 a disturbance handler and deals with conflicts and disputes between individuals and groups and takes corrective measures,
   3.3 a resource allocator and acquires and allocates resources needed for smooth operations,
   3.4 a negotiator and negotiates with individuals, groups and other organizations for various resources for smooth operations of the organization.

To perform these roles, a manager establishes communication at various levels. These are called communication networks. In these networks, there could be Upward communication, Downward communication, Horizontal communication, and Multiple communication or Grapevine.

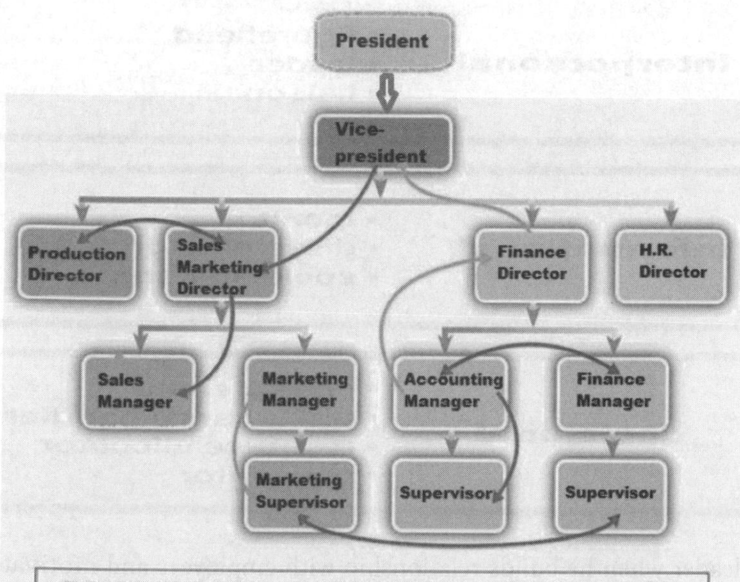

and management of technical documents and drawings. In a way, he acts as a reso
person taking care of various processes and products.

➢ Performing supervisory roles in coordinating and directing project related activiti
engineers or technologists; a technical advisory role in directing, reviewing and integra
technical activities for approving product design and specifications. In this role he prov
advice on technical issues, operations, maintenance and repairs.

➢ Coordinating with staff as well as clients to design and direct projects and make det
plans to accomplish goals. Under feasibility plan, analyzing current technology ne
resource requirements and market demand before finalizing any project. Providing upc
to the stakeholders on the work accomplished.

➢ Supporting the management in handling minor engineering projects; recruiting emplo
assigning and evaluating their work and making efforts towards development
maintenance of staff competence.

II. Management Skills

A Good Manager

According to *Henry Mintzberg*, an internationally acclaimed academic and author on busi
and management, a manager has three types of roles to play in an organization: Interperso
Informational and Decisional.

1. **Interpersonal role**: The manager performs the role of

   1.1 a figurehead when he fulfils social and legal obligations for the welfare of the comp

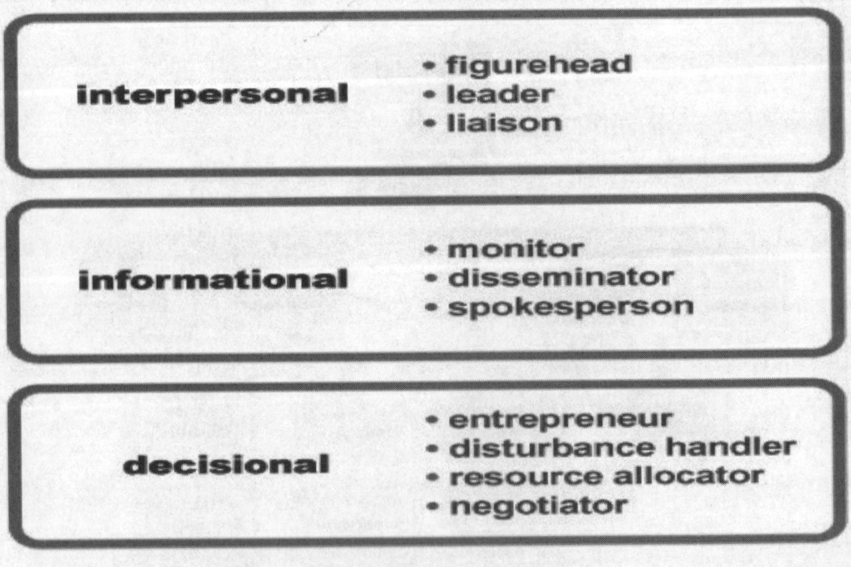

   1.2 a leader when he builds relationship with employees and motivates them to carr
   out various tasks,

1. **Upward Communication**: The flow of information is from lower to higher level. When a sales manager submits a sales report of electronic gadgets in a quarter to the vice president, sales, s/he is using an upward channel of communication.

   Advantages:

   ➢ **Builds trust**: When employees feel that they can easily make a contact with their seniors, they feel a stake in the company's progress and work with greater commitment to achieve targets. Ease of communication also facilitates timely redressal of grievances]. This in turn, builds mutual trust.

   ➢ **Provides feed back:**T he lower level employees provide genuine feedback to their bosses which could be used constructively. Employees' opinion could be instrumental in forming new policies or doing away with outdated ones.

   ➢ **Enhances morale**: Active participation in important company matters boosts up confidence of employees. This leads to high morale, which, if channeled in the right direction, works in the interest of the company.

   Disadvantages:

   ➢ **Inherent resistance:** The employees do not initiate communication as they are afraid to cxpress themselves openly in front of their seniors. They may not want to discuss issues which have a direct bearing on their job.

   ➢ **Fear of incompetence:** If the employee feels that his point of view or suggestion is unworthy of getting results, he may hesitate to communicate his views or work to his superiors.

   ➢ **Higher expectations:** When lower level employees start expecting a major role in decisional processes, upward communication takes a back seat.

   ➢ **Encourages sycophancy**: In extreme cases, it may lead to sycophancy.

2. **Downward Communication**: The flow of information from superiors to subordinates is referred to as downward communication. When the CEO of a company informs the employees about the new employment policy, he follows downward communication.

   Advantages:

   ➢ **Transparency**: Keeps the employees well informed about company policies and decisions which foster transparency and confidence building.

   ➢ **Sense of Belonging:** Helps establish confidence and a sense of belonging among lower level employees and instills faith in upper management.

   Disadvantages

   ➢ **Time Consuming**: It is not possible to share each and every bit of information with lower level employees. In situations of emergency, decisions are taken at the spur of the moment by the higher brass without involving anyone. This may create a feeling of dissent among employees.

- **High Expectations:** Expectations by lower level employees to get access to information which may be too sensitive to disclose. If such information is withheld, it may result in a loss of confidence in higher management.

3. **Horizontal Communication**: When the information flow is not only upward and downward, but also sideways, it is described as horizontal or lateral communication. This entails coordination and team work with people working at the same level too. For e,g., vice president production needs to coordinate with vice president sales and marketing to get input into product specification required by the clientele.

Advantages

- **Builds Camaraderie:** As people can freely exchange ideas and information across departments without any inhibition, a sense of camaraderie develops between them.
- **Boosts confidence:** As people can share their grievances with colleagues, it helps in cooling off tempers. It helps build rapport among people working at the same level.

Disadvantages

- **Lack of accountability:** The information is not authenticated by any higher authority therefore there is the danger of falsity.
- **Formation of trade unions:** At times people working at the same level get together against a common cause, andit leads to the formation of trade unions which is detrimental to the progress of any organization.

4. **Grapevine**: This is informal communication network of an organization. People transmit information to whoever they come in contact with at informal meeting places at the work place. Information sharing in this manner helps people in making social contacts. Good managers make the best use of grapevine to know what is happening in the organization at the grass root level and make constructive use of it.

Advantages:

- **Speeds up Communication**: Communication is fast as it doesn't have to cross formal barriers.
- **Creates social bonds:** It helps in creating social bonds where none existed before.
- **Fills communication gap:** It helps fill the communication gap.
- **Provides genuine feedback:**Managers at higher level get valuable feedback which they wouldn't get through formal communication channels.

Disadvantages:

- **Unverifiable information**: Information circulated is not verified.
- **May take the form of rumour:** Most of the times, it is in the form of a rumour and therefore cannot be believed.
- **May lead to gossip**: It sometimes takes the form of gossip which may ruin people's reputation, career or lives.

Roles and responsibilities of a manager

Global Management:

In the age of globalization, businesses have gone global; therefore, managers have to manage global teams. Such teams comprise people from different countries and cultures. Some cultures are individualistic cultures whereas others are collective cultures. Accordingly, there are issues whether a person would feel comfortable working independently or with people from across cultures. A manager's role is to maintain synergy between individuals and groups for smooth working in culturally diverse environments. With his knowledge and experience, he works similarities to his advantage and overlooks the differences, avoids stereotyping due to over generalization and thus acts as a conduit to bridge the cultural differences among people.

People working online from different time zones and speaking different languages could also pose a problem. Most of the BPOs operating from India schedule their working hours according to the time-zone of their western client.Indian employees working in BPOs also need to adopt the accent of their western counterpoint in order to be understood by them. People working in such circumstances may be working under different stress levels. A manager's role requires maintaining harmony in such circumstances.

Crisis Management:

Crisis is best dealt within teams. A manager's role is crucial in such situations. The manager needs to train his team on how to deal with a crisis. Training in team work is important to deal with situations of crisis.

Corporate Management:

A manager is responsible for projecting a positive and friendly image of the company to the outside world. This is done through good corporate communication which is the corporation's voice to project its image to the outside world. Ideally, it is an attitude or a set of mental habits that employees internalize. It is projected through the processes that the company employs in the form of speeches, reports, advertising, interviews and online communication. It has an influence on corporate reputation, corporate advocacy, investor relations, and government relations.

Employee Management:

Effective employee management and leadership skills allow one to capitalize on employee strengths for the progress of the company. One needs to understand what keeps the employees motivated and inspired to work consistently. Sometimes the manager has todeal with dissent among employees which may arise due to various reasons. Dealing with dissent is an art in itself which requires understanding, empathy and engagement with the employee in matters of his interest.Great leadership provides regular feedback on performance and compliments the employees on their achievements to boost their morale.

Media Management:

Media is one of the crucial elements in promoting the image of a company. Therefore, an appropriate and professional relationship with media is maintained by the management of all big corporations. In the age of internet and burgeoning social media, management of social media sites to showcase the company and its products has become of paramount importance. It has become crucial to maintain the company profile on social media and release latest updates on services and products for stakeholders. Further, communication through social media boosts global communication.

Ethics and Corporate Culture

According to Habermas' discourse ethics, every act should be a rational act. A person who performs an act should be able to justify the rationale behind it in an open forum. Ethics in corporate culture, ideally, should follow the same principle. All corporations are ethically and legally bound to engage in righteous speech and action.Since they are working in the public domain and their actions have a bearing on a large number of people, it is imperative for the leadership to develop ethical standards and follow them. They must also ensure that all employees follow personal and business ethics.

III. The art of leadership

A good leader

- **Is visionary by nature:**
  He has very clearly defined goals and objectives. He has a compelling and realistic vision set for himself. His focus is always on long term goals. He would let go short and temporary gains in the interests of long-term gains and mobilize people to adopt his point of view in a rationalistic manner. To do so, he would chart the future course of action and encourage people to follow that path.He maintains a balance between the well being of his people and the growth of the organization.
- **Creates an inclusive environment:**
  A good leader believes in transparency, inclusiveness, and leading by example. A leader is open and fair and lays down a clear operating philosophy with clearly defined roles and responsibilities. He does not have any 'favourites'. For him everybody is equal. His idea of reward is 'work' centric and not 'person' centric.
- **Trusts his people:**
  A leader sees things through the eyes of his people, which helps build trust among various stakeholders working for the organization. People work wholeheartedly for a leader in whom they repose their trust. A leader has faith in the capacity of his workers and motivates to bring out the best in them.

- **Believes in team work:**
  A leader embodies team spirit.He does not command his employees to carry out his orders; instead he goes that extra mile to lead from the front. He walks with his employees and instills a team-spirit in them. He is open to new ideas and ready to experiment with innovative suggestions. Great leaders share the profits earned by the organization with all the stakeholders because they believe that the happier people are, the better would be the growth of the organization.

- **Is compassionate by nature:**
  A leader extends his help and support to his people in adverse situations. He is sympathetic to the concerns and problems of his people and lends a listening ear in times of distress. He is empathetic and genuinely concerned about their problems. He is seen as a friend and a confidante by the employees in critical times.

- **Embodies humility and integrity:**
  A leader has integrity of character and a humble spirit.A leader places himself at the lowest position in the hierarchy of the organization to understand the mindset of people operating at that level. He does not hesitate to reach down to address their problems. He is simple in his thought, living and actions. He does not give credit to pomp and show. He is capable of lauding others for their efforts and laughing at himself for his follies. Integrity entails honesty, transparency and ethical decision making.

- **Demonstrates courage in moments of crisis**:
  Adept in handling crisis, a leader demonstrates courage and acts as a pillar of strength in situations of crisis. His visionary nature and rationalistic approach guide him in finding the best solution to the crisis. If the situation so demands, he is ready to shoulder the responsibilities of his people.In difficult times, his people draw strength from him.

- **The important roles that a leader must play**
  1. **Communicator:** The most effective leaders use all channels of communication to reach out to employees, clients and other stakeholders. They proactively encourage free and transparent exchange of information within the organization. All communication, whether verbal, written or online, is characterized by transparency and consistency and defines the motto of the organization. Successful leaders adopt personal communication styles that are open, fair and appropriate to the situation and people. Such leaders are open to a critical view and use it in a constructive manner for the growth of the organization.
  2. **Strategist:** A leader is a strategist who understands how different parts of an organization work together and how it can best respond to sudden or systemic changes. He foresees the requirement for organizational expansion in relation to evolving business needs. He makes a concerted effort to align the procedural operations with the objectives laid out for the organization in its vision-mission statement. He does not underestimate the competitors and deploys appropriate strategy to face the competition from current and future business trends. He has an awareness of the strengths, weaknesses, opportunities and threats facing the organization.

3. **Decision-maker:** A leader is a decision maker and takes decisions in the best interests of the organization as well as the stakeholders. He objectively considers the problem from various viewpoints before taking a decision. He does not shy away from taking tough decisions in the long term interests of the organization even if short term gains are insignificant or do not cater to a section of people. He chooses the best option available after weighing the pros and cons of all the options. He takes informed decisions on hiring, firing or retention of the employees.
4. **Team-builder:** Effective teams are built by ensuring that members are kept informed of all plans, issues and developments within an organization which may have a direct or indirect bearing on them. It serves to build trust among employees if they feel that they are involved in a meaningful way in the working of the organization. Confidence is also built when members are appreciated for their contribution towards positive growth and are appropriately rewarded. A leader's presence amidst the employees is tantamount to building confidence.
5. **Image-builder:** A leader is one who is always aware of the brand value of his organization. He is instrumental in building the brand by a consistent demonstration of integrity, honesty and professionalism which is recognized by the outside world. A leader is always unbiased, fair and open to his employees and is concerned about their well-being. A happy community of employees reflects a positive image of the organization.
6. **Coach:** As the word suggests, a coach is a person who teaches his team the tricks of the trade through intensive training. Effective coaching is a piece of team work which takes place in mutually beneficial environments. To build conducive environments, leaders engage the community in constructive dialogue by developing supporting networks. Good coaching entails delegating a task appropriate to the skills and capabilities of a person and explaining clearly the expectations from the delegated person. As a coach, the leader is always in control of the situation.

Roles of Managers Vs Leaders

Managers	Leaders
Coordinate people	Inspire and lead people
Provide instructions	Create self leaders
Maintain status quo	Are harbingers of change
Enforce organizational rules	Make or change rules
Enforce trust	Build trust
Are resource providers	Are visionaries
Pursue opportunities	Create opportunities

Online Resources

1. http://www.swlearning.com/management/wagner/ob5e/inet/
2. http://www.forbes.com/entrepreneurs/
3. http://leadership.uoregon.edu/resources/exercises_tips/skills/leadership_characteristics
4. http://www.todaysengineer.org/2007/nov/management.asp
5. http://theinstitute.ieee.org/career-and-education/career-guidance/from-engineer-to-manager-tips-you-need-to-know568

Bibliography

1. Bennis, Warren. *On Becoming a Leader: The Leadership Classic*. New York: Basic Books, 2003
2. Northouse, Peter G. *Leadership: Theory and Practice*. California: SAGE Publications, 2013
3. Kouzes, James M. and Barry Z. Posner. *The Leadership Challenge*, San Francisco: Jossey-Bass, 2007
4. Collins, Jim. *Good to Great: Why Some Companies Make the Leap... and Others Don't*. New York: HarperBusiness, 2001
5. AIMA. *Leaders on Leadership. New Delhi*: SAGE, 2012
6. Fleddermann, Charles B. *Engineering Ethics*. New Delhi: Pearson Education, 2004

Unit XI – Practice

1. How would you distinguish between the roles and responsibilities of a manager and a leader?
2. What do you mean by 'synchronization'? Is it important for an engineer to have an understanding of synchronization? Why/ Why not?
3. 'It is important for engineers, managers and leaders to have good communication skills'. Do you agree with this statement? If yes, explain.
4. What are the decisional roles of a manager?
5. In the engineering profession, how important is it to have practical domain knowledge.? What are the different ways in which one acquires it?
6. Could you think of an instance when you set out to achieve a challenging task for yourself? What was the method adopted and what was the outcome?
7. How can a leader be a good strategist?
8. Write a short note on ethics and corporate culture.
9. 'A leader in a true sense is a visionary'. Elaborate this statement.
10. Do you agree with the statement that 'All good managers are good leaders too'? Give reasons for your answer.
11. According to Socratic philosophy, good leadership entails three P's which are: possibilities, probabilities and priorities. As a leader of an organization, think of two questions under each of these three categories.
12. What are the advantages and disadvantages of upward communication?
13. Answer the following questions briefly:
    a. What is the importance of feedback for a manager?
    b. When does a manager perform the role of an entrepreneur?
14. Answer these questions critically.
    a. What does leadership mean to you?
    b. As a leader, what will you be afraid of?
    c. Can anyone become a leader? What are the special characteristics that make a person leader?
    d. Does every manager need to be a leader?
    e. Does a leader need power to fulfil his responsibilities?
15. In the movie 'Guardian' directed by Andrew Davis, the Academy of Coast guard Training trains recruits to work in teams. This is done through a rough training programme in handling crisis-situation. They ensure that their only way of work is team work. Nobody is permitted to do anything in isolation. They are taught quick and responsible ways of communicating in a crisis situation.

Watch the movie. After watching the movie, formulate your views on the strategy of handling crisis individually Vs in a team?

16. Read the passage below and answer the question that follows:
'As a group, we have always actively championed social responsibility. We have spent the last year exploring what we can do to further our commitment through 'shared value' initiatives that create both social and business benefits. In line with this, we are focused on playing our part in creating a more inclusive and greener India and have named this effort "Godrej Good and Green." As part of our Good and Green Vision, we aspire by 2020 to create a more employable Indian workforce, reach global standards in environmental sustainability, and innovate for products that address the under-served needs of Indians at the bottom of the income pyramid. I strongly believe that this vision will play a vital role in defining our contributions over the coming decade'.

– Adi Godrej (From *Leaders on Leadership*)

➢ Do you think the above initiative defines a genuine sense of corporate citizenship? Justify your answer.

17. **Read the passage below and answer the questions that follow:**
Good corporate governance entails Corporate Social Responsibility (CSR). CSR is a concept in which companies integrate social and environmental concerns in their operations on a voluntary basis. It has its own body of knowledge. In 2014, Tata Consultancy Services (TCS) promised to give an aid of Rs 200 crore to the Prime Minister's initiative of '**Swachh Bharat**' to build toilets across the country and to boost other cleanliness drives initiated by the Government of India. By this initiative, TCS fulfills its social responsibility towards making a cleaner India. Such initiatives are undertaken by most big corporations these days.

The advantages of CSR for a company are manifold. Besides philanthropy, it galvanizes media and public opinion in favour of the company which leads to better prospects in terms of social standing, better image and valued partnership with stakeholders. Such relationships in turn lead to long term financial gains.

➢ Could you identify five business houses in India which are involved in Corporate Social Responsibility (CSR) initiatives?

➢ These days almost all the big companies are involved in CSR initiatives? Do you think this engagement is actually beneficial to the society or the main aim is to get good publicity for the company?

➢ How do CSR initiatives help in the growth of the country? Cite some examples.

18. What is the difference between corporate culture and corporate philosophy? Illustrate by citing an example.

19. **Fill in the blanks:**

a. A---- at-----involving-----occurred today at-----. The incident is under investigation and more information is forthcoming. (Media Communication)
A (what happened) at (location) involving (who) occurred today at (time). The incident is under investigation and more information is forthcoming.

b. CSR stands for --------------------------.

c. When the CEO of a company informs the employees about the new pension policy, he follows ----------------- communication

20. N.R. Narayana Murthy says 'A plausible impossibility is better than a convincing possibility'. What does the statement reveal about the speaker?
21. 'The softest pillow is a clear conscience'. Elaborate the statement according to your understanding.
22. 'When in doubt, disclose', points towards which attribute of the speaker
    a. He is honest
    b. He is fearless
    c. He believes in transparency
    d. All of the above
23. 'Bedhadak bolo' is a phrase used by Adi Godrej to encourage employees to speak without inhibitions. Do you think it could be misused by people?

Case-Study for Discussion

Confederation of Indian Industry (CII) is a non-government, not-for-profit, industry-led and industry-managed organization, playing an important role in India's development process. It works to create and sustain an environment conducive to the growth of industry in India. It works closely with Government on policy issues. It creates business opportunities for industry through specialized services and strategic global collaborations. This case study traces the formation and working of CII in providing nationwide service. It also showcases the vision and values of CII which govern its employees and are instrumental in defining the success of the organization.

CII came into being after the merger of the Indian Engineering Association (IEA) and the Engineering Association of India (EAI) in the 1970s. With its headquarters in Delhi, it was expected to work differently. At a time, when everything was micro managed by the government, leadership at CII initiated new ways to project its capability and to earn the confidence of people.

It was a difficult time for the employees. There was shortage of finance, limited strength of staff, frequent changes in the political leadership and a bureaucracy that could not be held to account. The staff worked hard and tried to meet the challenges. Overseas offices were opened; overseas trade was initiated; the need for free economy, free trade and investment, and free import of technology was emphasized. In 1984–85, CII got into parternership with the World Economic Forum (WEF). All this happened at a fast pace in a relatively short span of time. This was made possible only with the team work of the office-bearers and staff of the organization and the acumen and insight of its leadership.

In the years 1991–1996, the organization came out with its vision, which was thus stated:

- To build an institution for change and development, going beyond past traditions
- Being the projector of Indian industry, its technology, and capability
- Being the presenter of confidence and the driver for change
- Being the bridge to the world and bringing the world to India
- Driving for policy liberalization, a freer economy, and openness not witnessed since 1947 and Independence.

These multiple vision-statements underlined the mission of the organization towards building a newer India. Based on these vision statements, support activities were undertaken at the organizational level. Positions of 'Office-bearers' and 'doers' were designated. Zonal offices were opened in various cities. MOUs were signed with international partners the India Economic Summit was organized with WEF, and trade fairs were planned. Proactive and competitive methods were adopted to generate more revenue.

Trained and experienced staff was employed. More women were inducted at the executive level. An open door policy was initiated to connect with the employees. Team work was encouraged to keep everybody on the same footing and 'Made in India' shows were organized abroad to project India and its capabilities. With growth, reviewing and restructuring was done.It helped in redefining ideas, objectives, and teamwork.

Today, with its focus on inclusive development across diverse domains like health care, skill development, education, livelihood, and empowerment of women, CII is constantly working towards building business leadership. It is striving to meet the expectations of the international business community as well as the aspirations of Today's India.

(Based on an article by Tarun Das in *Leaders on Leadership)*

Questions

1. The future of any organization depends onthe quality of leadership and retention of talent. According to you, what are the traits that define a leader? Do you possess those traits?
2. What do you understand by 'vision statement'? How does it define the culture and ethos of an organization?
3. What is the meaning of 'free economy'? Does India practise free economy currently?
4. Find out at least five projects initiated by CII in current times.
5. Do you think professional communication has a role to play in the growth of institutions like CII? Which of these projects have directly transformed the Indian village life?

Appendix I – Empower Your English

I. Speech Practice

Here are some tips for you to improve your speech:

I. Sounds and letters

- ✓ Note that there are only five letters in written English that are called vowels. But there are 20 vowel sounds in spoken English.
- ✓ There are 24 consonant sounds in spoken English but only 21 letters in written English that are called consonants.
- ✓ This means that each letter represents more than one sound and also that each sound may be represented by more than one letter.
- ✓ Here is a list of the sounds of English represented by their respective phonetic symbols along with key words.

Vowel sounds		**Consonant sounds**	
ɪ	pin	p	pen
i:	peel	l	led
e:	red	r	red
æ:	bad	b	bin
ɑ:	ask	t	tin
ɒ	got	d	din
ɔ:	door	k	kin
ə:	about	g	big
ʌ	cut	t͡ʃ	chair
ɜ:	word	d͡ʒ	jam
ʊ	book	t	tan
ʊ:	too	v	van
ei	fail	θ	thick
a ɪ	nine	ð	then
ɔi	oil	s	sim
əʊ	go	z	zoo
ɑʊ	cow	ʃ	ship
ɪ ə	hear	ʒ	vision
eə	there	h	hen

ʊə	poor	m	men
		n	nun
		ŋ	sing
		j	yes
		w	wet

a. **Homophones, Homographs, Homonyms [Home=same (Greek)]**

i. **Homophones:** Same pronunciation, different spelling and meaning

✓ brake (v) (stop by using a **brake**)	break (v) (shatter)
• feat (accomplishment)	feet
• in	inn
• air	heir
• mail	male
• pain	pane
• to	two, too
• bare	bear
• sea	see
• steal	steel
• meat	meet
• blew	blue
• peel	peal
• him	hymn
• write	right

ii. **Homograph:** *Same spelling, different pronunciation*

Example

a. Wind (n) (breeze)	wind (v) (to coil)
b. lead (metal)	lead (a) (dog's lead)
c. read	read (past tense)

Stress difference

• ‘address (N)	a’ddress (V)
• ‘export (N)	e’xport (v)
• ‘insult (N)	in’sult (v)
• lead (N)	lead (v)

• 'conduct (N)	con'duct (V)
• 'contest (N)	con'test (V)
• 'import (N)	im'port (V)
• 'permit (N)	per'mit (V)
• 'transform (N)	trans'form (V)
• 'discount (N)	dis'count (V)

iii. **Homonym:** *Same pronunciation same spelling, different meaning*

top (peak)	top (toy)
bear (animal)	bear (tolerate, hold)
bee (insect)	bee (meeting for continued work as in spelling bee)
fair (country fair)	fair (reasonable)
lie (untruth)	lie (put oneself flat on the ground)
well (a dug well)	well (to feel well)
mouse (rodent)	mouse (computer mouse)

II. Polish up your speech

A. Contractions: Statements

Contractions like I'm (for I am...) you'd (for you would...) etc. are part of speech; they are common and correct in informal writing too. So you must learn them.

Affirmative		**Negative**	
I am	I'm	I am not / I'm not	
we are	we're	are not / aren't	
he is	he's }		
she is	she's }	is not	isn't
she has	she's	has not	hasn't
I have	I've	have not	haven't
You had	you'd	had not	hadn't
You would	you'd	would not	wouldn't
They will	they'll	will not	won't
Other forms			
there is	there's	do not	don't
it is	it's	does not	doesn't
		did not	didn't

shall not	shan't
should not	shouldn't
cannot	can't
could not	couldn't
might not	mightn't
must not	mustn't
ought not	oughtn't
need not	needn't

Warning:

- *am not* is shortened to aren't only in questions.
  I'm late, aren't I?
  In other expressions the full form is used: I am not greedy I'm not greedy.
- The short forms *'re, 've, 'd,* and *'ll* are used in writing only after pronouns:
  She'll be coming here tomorrow. (used)
  Sheela'll be coming here tomorrow. (not used in writing)
- *Cannot* is always written as one word.

A. Conversational English: Questions

i. The language used in conversational English is very different from the language used in written English. What's normal in written English is not used in spoken English.

Written English	**Spoken English**
Is anyone absent?	('s/) anyone absent?
Is anyone listening?	('s) anyone listening?
Will you help me?	'll you help me?
Have you seen the movie?	've you seen the movie?
Do you understand me?	'd you understand me?
Did your brother do well in the exam?	'd your brother do well in the exam?

II. "Wh" questions

1. is

- When's.?=When is.. ?
- Which's..?=Which is..?
- Who's….?,
- Why's….?,
- Where's….?
- What's….?
- How's ….?
- Where's….?

2. are

- When're….?
- Where are….?
- where're….?
- What're….?

- Which're...?
- Who're....?
- Why're....?
- How're....?
- Whose're....?

3. **will**
   - When'll......? = when will---?
   - Which'll---?
   - Why'll---?
   - Where'll---?
   - Whose'll---?
   - What'll---?
   - How'll---?
     - How many'll---?
   - What time'll---?
4. **has**
   - When's---? = When has---?
   - Who's ---? = Who has ---?
   - Which as---?
   - Why's ---?
   - Where's ---?
   - What's ---?
   - How's---?
5. **have**

   Where've ? =Where have---?
6. **did**

   Where'd ---? Where did----?
7. **had**

   When'd ---? = When had ---?

   Where'd ---? = Where had ---?

Practice

1. When is the party?
2. What time will you arrive?
3. When is she going to leave?
4. Why is he absent?
5. What has she done?
6. When did they arrive?
7. Where did he go?
8. Who had he been talking to?
9. How often have you been absent?
10. What is she wearing?

One word questions in conversational English.

1. They are leaving today. When?
2. Something happened yesterday. What?
3. You are expected to work late. How often?
4. I usually get up early. How early?

III. Some useful expressions

- Hey! (Look out/be careful/watch out---)
- Excuse me? Pardon me? (= Please repeat what you said.)
- Excuse me. Pardon me. (= I'm sorry for what I did.]
- Sorry? What's that? Please say that again. (= i didn't hear you.)

- What? Say what?
- Oh? Really? Oh, really?
- So? So what?
- Hmm

Formal:

- I beg your pardon, sir/madam.
- Excuse me, sir/madam.

IV. Informal/Casual 'Yes'

- yeah
- um-hmm
- uh – huh ()
- Yep

Informal/Casual 'No'

- Hm-umm
- Huh/uh
- Nope
- Nah

V. Greetings

Casual

- Hi!
- Hey!
- Howdy!
- Polite
- Informal
- Hello!
- Hello there?
- Good morning/Good afternoon---

Very Polite/Formal

- How do you do?
- How do you do, doctor / Professor/Mr. –Name?
  Good/fine. Thank you.
- Good morning, Mr.-Name (Not Mis-ter)
- Good night/Goodbye.

Casual

- How's everything? Good/ So-so/Not bad
- How's it going?Not so well.
- How's it go-ing?Great/ terrific/fantastic
- How're things?Terrible/ awful/Really-bad
- How're you doing?
- How've you been?
- How's things?
- How's life?
- How're you today? (Polite)

B. Short expressions in speech

- I'm hungry. Me, too.
- I'm tired. So, am I.
- I have been working whole day. So, have I.
- I worked hard yesterday. So, did I.

• I'm not hungry.	Me, either.
• I haven't been worthy.	Neither, have I.

C. Fine tune your speech

The following words are often mispronounced by Indians. Learn the correct pronunciation.

Word	**Pronunciation**
oven (for cooking)	avan
suite (a set of rooms in a hotel)	sweet
suit (a set of outer clothes)	suut/syuut
sew (to join by stitches made with thread)	so
bury (someone)	beri
beat (the past tense of beat)	beat (same as present tense)
robot	robot
dais (a raised platform)	deis
drought	draut
demon	diiman
yacht	yaat
connoisseur	koniser
extempore	ekstempari
please	pliiz
laboratory	la'boratory
environment	en'vironment
percent	per'cent
demonstrate	'demonstrate

D. Note how the difference in sound results in difference in meaning. Pronounce the pairs aloud.

• Vine	Wine
• Vale	Whale
• Vet	Wet
• Vest	West
• Vent	Went

B. Vocabulary Enrichment

I. Enrich your Vocabulary

A. How well do you know your body? Name the parts with the help of the clues given.

1. The crown of the head. v--------x
2. The back of the head o--------t

3. The part of the face above the eyes and below the hair f--------d
4. The front part of the face where it stands out below the mouth c--------n
5. The lower part of the body below the waist and above the legs on both sides ----l----s
6. Thee narrow part of the body above the legs and hips w--------t
7. Either of the two upper limbs a--------m
8. The movable parts at the end of the arm, including fingers h--------d
9. The five movable parts at the end of each foot t--------es
10. The back bone v--------e
11. The heart muscles c--------c
12. The secretion produced by the glands in the mouth s--------a
13. Vessels taking blood away from the heart a--------s
14. Vessels taking blood to the heart v--------s
15. The nerves, brain and the spiral cord are called the system. n--------s

B. IIow well do you know the health words? Name the diseases with the help of the clues:

1. A disease affecting many persons at the same place and time. e--------c
2. A disease confined to a particular placc or arca. c--------c
3. A disease affecting widely scattered groups of people in. different parts s--------c
4. A disease affecting many people globally. p--------c
5. A medicine to counteract poison. a--------e
6. Free from infection i--------e
7. To place in an isolated place to prevent someone from infecting others q--------e
8. To cut off a part of a person's body which is infected a--------e
9. To be able to tell the nature of a disease by its symptoms. d--------e
10. A vehicle for carrying sick people to the hospital. a--------e
11. A cure for all diseases p--------a
12. A substance that produces insensitivity a--------c
13. A substance which destroys or weakens germs a--------c
14. A preventive measure for cholera, typhoid, etc. I--------n
15. Done to produce immunity against a specific disease v--------n

C. Are you interested in matrimony? Do some match-making. Match the words listed under Column A with their meanings given under B.

Sl No.	Column A	Column B
1.	Marriage within one's own clan, caste or tribe.	civil marriage
2.	Marriage between people of different clans, castes or tribes.	Polyandry
3.	Marriage performed by a registrar or a qualified civil official rather than by a priest or a clergyman.	solemnise
4.	Run away secretly with a lover, especially to get married.	matchmaker
5.	Celebrate a marriage and perform a ceremony with formal or religious rites.	exogamy
6.	Sexual relationship between close relatives in a family	betrothed
7.	Crime of being married to two or more people at any one time.	monogamy
8.	Custom of being married to more than one man at a time, as in some cultures.	hymeneal
9.	Custom of having more than one wife at a time, as in some cultures.	conjugal/ marital
10.	Custom of having only one marriage partner a time, as in most cultures	endogamy
11.	Engaged	incest
12.	Marriage song or poem	polygamy
13.	Person who is hired to bring a suitable pair together.	Wedding
14.	Concerning the relationship between husband and wife.	elope
15.	A marriage ceremony or service	divorce
16.	The legal ending of a marriage	bigamy

D. Name the ideologies:

Some ideologies have become so popular in the world that they have come to be known as "isms".

1. An ideology which believes in extreme patriotism even at the cost of other countries is ______________

2. An ideology which preaches extreme favouritism towards one's relatives regardless of their qualifications is ________________
3. An ideology that preaches that the motto of life is only to eat, drink and make merry is ________________
4. An ideology which says that there is no God is ________________
5. An ideology which advocates lawlessness and opposes every form of government is ________________
6. An ideology which advocates the system of private property and acquisition of wealth through private enterprise is ________________
7. An ideology which advocates that there should be no rich and poor is-
8. An ideology which says that we cannot know whether Goď exists or not is ________________
9. An ideology which advocates the rule of a dictator is ________________
10. An ideology which believes that anything can be done to safeguard and establish one's own religion is ________________
11. An ideology which advocates open-mindedness in political matters and favours democratic reforms is ________________
12. An ideology which advocates extreme changes in political matters and practices is ________________
13. An ideology which advocates that one should form opinions following reason is ________________
14. An ideology which advocates that the means of production should be owned by the state is ________________
15. An ideology which advocates an indifferent attitude towards both pleasure and pain in life is ________________
16. An ideology which encourages doubting of every established norm and doesn't assert anything positive is ________________
17. The principle of believing in only one god is ________________
18. The principle of believing in more than one God is ________________
19. The principle that God is not in man's image, but is a combination of all forces of the universe is ________________
20. An ideology which believes in the primary importance of human values and interests is ________________

E. Can you find the word that indicates human nature? Add an article where necessary.

1. A person who has a friendly and sweet nature is Amiable
2. A person who is always on the lookout for fighting is ____________
3. A person who feels sorry for his wrong doing is ____________
4. A person who has skilled hands ____________
5. A person who can use both hands skilfully is ____________
6. A person who has enormous knowledge is ____________

7. A person who has a gloomy nature is ____________
8. A person who is not educated is ____________
9. A person who is never tired is ____________
10. A person who is lazy in nature is ____________
11. A person who is educated is ____________
12. A person who talks a great deal is ____________
13. A person who is generous is ____________
14. A person who is clumsy with his hands is ____________
15. A person who is mean and cowardly is ____________
16. A person who is formal in etiquettes is ____________
17. A person who wants to be peaceful with others is ____________
18. A person who is cheerful by nature is ____________
19. A person who has a sad disposition is ____________
20. A person who is stubborn to admit his mistakes is ____________
21. A person who is rather informal in his dealings is ____________
22. A person who is well experienced in life is ____________

F. Name the subjects and their field of study:

1. The study of humans, their origin, development, customs and beliefs ________
2. The study of farming is ____________
3. The science of foretelling events by stars ____________
4. The study of ancient ruins ____________
5. The study of heavenly bodies is ____________
6. The study of life is ____________
7. The study of plants is ____________
8. The study of unborn babies is ____________
9. The study of insects is ____________
10. The study of words is ____________
11. The study of the art of hand-writing is ____________
12. The study of the earth is ____________
13. The study of languages is ____________
14. The study of prison reforms is ____________
15. T he study of manuscripts of written records is ____________
16. The study ofweather is ____________
17. The study of religions is ____________
18. The study of earth quakes is ____________
19. The study of planets is ____________
20. The study of speech sounds is ____________

G. Name the places of worship; use articles where necessary:

1. The living place of monks or nuns ____________
2. The chief church (big church) ____________

3. Christian place of worship ______________
4. A part of a church, a small church ______________
5. The living place of nuns ______________, ______________
6. The living place of monks ______________
7. The Muslim place of worship ______________
8. The Buddhist place of worship ______________
9. The living place of Buddhist monks ______________
10. A small Jewish place of worship ______________
11. The worshipping place of Hindus and others ______________

H. What's the word? Use articles as necessary.

1. A person who wants to do good to all ______________
2. A person who does things only for pleasure and not as a profession ______________
3. A person who wants to create lawlessness in the country ______________
4. A place where weapons and ammunition are stored ______________
5. A person blindly attached to any opinion, system or party ______________
6. One who is irreverent to God ______________
7. A person who eats human flesh ______________
8. An animal which eats flesh ______________
9. A person competent to pass critical judgement on anything ______________
10. One who is well versed in the science of skin ailments and skin diseases ______________
11. A place where one lives permanently ______________
12. A man who has the qualities of a woman ______________
13. One who is given to sensual enjoyments and the pleasures of life ______________
14. A speech made without any previous preparation ______________
15. One who cannot be easily pleased ______________
16. The murder of a brother ______________
17. The killing of a whole race ______________
18. The killing of one person by another person ______________
19. The murder of one's mother ______________
20. The murder of one's father ______________
21. The murder of a king ______________
22. Killing oneself ______________
23. A medicine that kills germs ______________
24. Animals living on plants ______________
25. That which cannot be corrected ______________
26. That which cannot be believed ______________
27. That which cannot be easily effaced or cancelled ______________
28. One who is not likely to make mistakes ______________
29. That which is quite harmless ______________

30. That which is bound to happen ____________
31. A person who talks too much or garrulous ____________
32. One who fights only for the sake of money ____________
33. The government or rule by the crowds ____________
34. That which is outdated ____________
35. A drug that produces sleep or stupor, etc. ____________
36. One who is all powerful ____________
37. One who is present everywhere ____________
38. One who knows everything ____________
39. A government in which the power is concentrated in the hands of a small group of people ____________
40. A thing through which light cannot pass ____________
41. One that lives on another ____________
42. One who flirts with women ____________
43. A government run by the rich and the wealthy ____________
44. A name assumed by a writer; not his/her real name ____________
45. The violation or profaning of sacred places and things ____________
46. One who takes pleasure in the suffering of others ____________
47. Talking to oneself ____________
48. The act of sleep walking ____________
49. A person who is indifferent to the pains and pleasures of life ____________
50. A person who changes sides ____________
51. Using more words than what are required ____________
52. One who acts against established religion ____________
53. A person more than one hundred years old ____________
54. One who is eighty years old ____________
55. One who is new to a profession ____________
56. One who treats eye diseases ____________
57. One who collects postage stamps ____________
58. One who retired from society to live a solitary life ____________
59. A cluster of houses; smaller than a village ____________
60. The ceremony at which one becomes a priest/nun/saint, etc. ____________
61. The act of spying ____________
62. Soldiers on horses ____________
63. Soldiers on foot ____________
64. Expressions that have been used too often ____________
65. A war of religion ____________
66. A writer who steals ideas from another ____________
67. One who lives for pleasure ____________
68. An imaginary ideal of world ____________

69. Commonplace remarks __________
70. A belief that nature is God __________
71. An excessive desire for oneself __________
72. Having a passion for stealing __________
73. A strong fear of water __________
74. A place where vegetables are sold __________
75. A place where household provisions are sold __________
76. The branch of science that deals with prevention and correction of irregular teeth formation __________
77. A person in charge of the works of art in a museum __________
78. A leather holder for a pistol or knife, hanging on a belt __________
79. The right to vote __________
80. One who mends pots and pans __________
81. One who makes iron tools __________
82. Attitudes that are already fixed __________
83. One who sells stockings, socks, undergarments etc. __________
84. A conceited showy person __________
85. The study of weather conditions or related matters __________

II. Are you a sophisticated user of English? Polish up your diction. Use a good dictionary and find out the differences.

1. Alter: These clothes are too large; they must be altered.
   Change: Through alchemy you can change one metal into another.
   Modify: You'd better modify your tone.
2. Allow:
   Permit:
3. Reply:
4. Answer:
5. Admit:
   Confess:
6. Amusement:
   Recreation:
7. Abstain:
   Refrain:
8. Addicted:
   Accustomed:
9. Accept:
   Acknowledge:
10. Autocratic:
    Despotic:
11. Apprehend:
    Comprehend:
12. Accident:
    Incident:
13. Avenge:
    Revenge:
14. Anticipate:
    Forestall:
15. Astonishment:
    Wonder:
16. Battle
    War
17. Begin:
    Commence:
18. Crime:
    Vice:
19. Character:
    Reputation:
20. Custom:
    Habit:
21. Confer:
    Bestow:
22. Common:
    Mutual:
23. Comply:
    Conform:
23. Compulsion:
    Obligation:
24. Drown:
    Sink:
25. Deny:
    Refuse:
26. Delightful:
    Delicious:
27. Distinguish:
    Discriminate:
28. Doubt:
    Suspect:

29. Envy:
    Jealousy:
30. Enough:
    Sufficient:
31. Forgiveness:
    Pardon:
32. Falsehood:
    Lie:
33. Grateful:
    Thankful:
34. Probable:
    Possible:
35. Protect:
    Defend:
36. Part:
    Portion:
37. Rural:
    Rustic:
38. Recollect
    Remember:
39. General:
    Universal:
    Global:
40. Loyalty:
    Allegiance:

III. Do you know the meanings of the following foreign words and phrases?

1. a la carte (Fr)
2. a priori (Lat)
3. ad hoc (Lat)
4. adieu (Fr)
5. aide (Fr)
6. alias (Lat)
7. alma mater
8. alter ego (Lat)
9. alumni (Lat)
10. annodomini (Lat)
11. bon voyage (Fr)
12. bona fide (Lat)
13. bourgeoise (Fr)
14. carte blanche (Fr)
15. caveat (Lat)
16. charge d' affairs (Fr)
17. coup detat (Fr)
18. de facto (Lat)
19. de jure (Lat)
20. en masse (Fr)
21. en route (Fr)
22. enfant terrible (Fr)
23. errata (Lat)
24. etcetra (Lat)
25. eureka (Greek)
26. ex officio (Lat)
27. ex parte (Lat)
28. extempore (Lat)
29. fait accompli (Fr)
30. fiesta (Sp)
31. lateas corpus (Lat)
32. in absentia (Lat)
33. incognito (Lat)
34. intoto (Lat)
35. ipso facto (Lat)
36. laissez faire (Fr)
37. macho (Sp)
38. magnum opus (Lat)
39. malafide (Lat)
40. mein kampf (Ger)
41. per capita (Lat)
42. peon (Sp)
43. per diem (Lat)
44. persona non grata (Lat)
45. post meridium (Lat)
46. proforma (Lat)
47. quid pro quo (Lat)
48. quo vadis (Lat)
49. sanctum sanctorum (Lat)
50. siesta (Sp)
51. sine die (Lat)
52. sub judice (Lat)
53. abula rasa (Lat)
54. tete-a-tete (Fr)
55. via media (Lat)
56. viva voce (Lat)
57. viz (Lat)
58. volte-face (Fr)
59. impasse (Fr)
60. juvenile (Sp)

61. lingua franca (Italian)
62. locus standi (Lat)
63. maestro (Italian)
64. modus operandi (Lat)
65. par excellence (Fr)
66. per annum (Lat)
67. post mortem (Lat)
68. salve (Lat)
69. ultra vires (Lat)
70. de luxe (Fr)
71. donna (Italian)
72. ex gratia (Lat)
73. per se (Lat)
74. pro rata (Lat)
75. prime facie (Lat)
76. quasi (Lat)
77. QED
78. provogue (Fr)
79. ad nauseam (Lat)
80. bona fide (Lat)

Confusables In each pair one word is explained; give the meaning of the other

1. i. sociable: fond of and friendly in company
   ii. social:
2. i. tasteful: in good taste
   ii. tasty:
3. i. incapable: lacking in ability; not capable
   ii. unable:
4. i. valuable: of great value
   ii. valued:
5. i. vigorous: full of force and energy
   ii. rigorous:
6. i. historic: significant;deserving to be noted in history
   ii. historical:
7. i. reputed: generally supposed, but with some doubt;reported to be
   ii. reputable:
8. i. prescribe: to be followed as a course
   ii. proscribe:
9. i. sensual: excessively gratifying the senses
   ii. sensuous:
10. i. contagious: spread by direct contact (of diseases)
    ii. infectious:
11. i. award: (something given by way of recognition as a prize)
    ii. reward:
12. i. all together: all in one place or time
    ii. altogether:
13. i. alternate: occurring by turns, first one then the other
    ii. alternative:
14. i. affect: influence, often adversely
    ii. effect:
15. i. discreet: judiciously reserved
    ii. discrete:

It makes a lot of difference!

Given below are pairs of words; a small difference in spelling makes a lot of difference in meaning. Find out the words from the meaning given.

1. i. A male pig:
   ii. One who causes others to lose interest in him/her by dull talk:
2. i. Something that completes:
   ii. An expression of praise:
3. i. A musical performance:
   ii. The wife or husband:
4. i. consisting of two parts:
   ii. A fight or argument between two:
5. i. An extract from a book:
   ii. Exclude from:
6. i. A typical of ornoticeable quality
   ii. Time yet to come:
7. i. A hundred thousand:
   ii. To be without
8. i. Afterwards:
   ii. The second of the two:
9. i. Something seen or to be seen:
   ii. A place where something particular happens or happened:
10. i. Concerning marriage:
    ii. Concerning war, soldiers and fight:
11. i. The head of a government/council:
    ii. A former example of rule for further action
12. i. Something to make one remember:
    ii. The rest:
13. i. The pattern of doing things in a religious ceremony:
    ii. The social advantages in which one has a claim:
14. i. Something that is not bent
    ii. A narrow passage of water connecting two seas:
15. i. Standing still
    ii. Material for writing:

Confusing Couples!

Given below are pairs of words that sound similar. The meaning of the first word is given. Find the meaning of the second.

1. i. ballet (pronounced balei) : a form of dance in which a story is told without words
   ii. ballot:
2. i. birth: the act of being born
   ii. berth:
3. i. barren: not able to reproduce
   ii. baron:

4. i. allay: to make less (fear, doubt, etc.)
   ii. alley:
5. i. allusion: indirect mention
   ii. illusion:
6. i. accomplish: to succeed in doing something
   ii. accomplice:
7. i. adopt: take an idea or custom and use
   ii. adapt:
8. i. descent: going down
   ii. dissent'
9. i. disease: illness
   ii. decease:
10. i. dying: expiring:
    ii. dyeing:
11. i. queue: a line of people
    ii. cue:
12. i. magnet:a piece of iron that is able to attract iron
    ii. magnate:
13. i. story: short fiction
    ii. storey:
14. i. tier: a row (as in 2-tier/3tier)
    ii. tear:
15. i. berry: fruit
    ii. bury:
16. i. elementary: simple, rudimentary
    ii. elemental:
17. immigrant: one who enters a country

What a subtle difference! Dictionaries may not help you; A lot depends on use. Try.

18. i. eminent: distinguished
    ii. imminent:
19. i. suffering: subjection to pain
    ii. suffrage:
20. i. gourmet: a connoisseur of food who eats with discrimination
    ii. gourmand:
21. i. graceful: beautiful in form and styly
    ii. gracious:
22. i. hale: healthy
    ii. hail:
23. i. hoard: stock, store
    ii. horde
24. i. intensely: ardently, extremely
    ii. intently:
25. i. metal: mineral substance such as iron etc.
    ii. mettle:
26. i. alter:
    ii. change: Turtles alter nesting dates due to temperature change.
27. i. Allow:
    ii. Permit:
28. i. Reply:
    ii. Answer: You reply to a question but answer a question
29. i. Admit:
    ii. Confess:
30. i. Accident:
    ii. Incident:
31. i. Battle:
    ii. War:
32. i. Beautiful:
    ii. Handsome:
33. i. Crime:
    ii. Vice:
34. i. Character:
    ii. Reputation:
35. i. Custom:
    ii. Habit:
36. i. Confer:
    ii. Bestow:
37. i. Common:
    ii. Mutual:
38. i. Compulsion
    ii. Obligation

39. i. Drown
    ii. Sink
40. i. Deny
    ii. Refuse
41. i. Distinguish
    ii. Discriminate
42. i. Doubt
    ii. Suspect
43. i. Rural
    ii. Rustic
44. i. Protect
    ii. Defend
45. i. Accept
    ii. Acknowledge
46. i. Ancient:
    ii. Old:
47. i. Anticipate:
    ii. Forestall:
48. i. Autocratic:
    ii. Despotic:
49. i. Apprehend:
    ii. Comprehend:
50. i. Astonishment:
    ii. Wonder:
51. i. Delightful:
    ii. Delicious:
52. i. Amusement:
    ii. Recreation:
53. i. Abstain:
    ii. Refrain:
54. i. Addicted:
    ii. Accustomed:
55. i. Avenge:
    ii. Revenge:
56. i. Begin:
    ii. Commence:
57. i. Comply:
    ii. Conform:
58. i. Delightful:
    ii. Delicious:
59. i. Envy:
    ii. Jealousy:
60. i. Enough:
    ii. Sufficient:
61. i. Forgiveness:
    ii. Pardon:
62. i. Falsehood:
    ii. Lie:
63. i. Grateful:
    ii. Thankful:
64. i. Probable:
    ii. Possible:
65. i. Protect:
    ii. Defend:
66. i. Part:
    ii. Portion:
67. i. Recollect:
    ii. Remember:
68. i. General:
    ii. Universal:
    iii. Global:
69. i. Loyalty:
    ii. Allegiance:

II. Usage

"Please", "Thank you", and "Sorry" are three little magic words in English. Use them as often as you can, as appropriate. This will make your language pleasant.

i. Complete the following poem by putting in the contracted forms of the verbs given in the box.

he is	he has	we have	cannot	I will	there is	you have	he would	that is

Mother, 1 a strange man
Waiting at the door
With a familiar sort of face
You feel 2 seen before

Says his name is Jesus.
Can we spare a couple of bob?
Says 3 been made redundant
And now 4 find a job.
Yet I think 5 a foreigner
Egyptian or a Jew.
Oh aye, and that reminds me
6 like some water too.

Well, shall I give him what he wants,
Or send him on his way?
OK 7 give him 5 p
Say 8 all 9 got today.

– *Roger McCough: Three Rusty Nails*

*A couple of bob: a little money
[Question: Who's this strange man?]

ii. How good are you in understanding subtle jokes? Try.

a. Three men met on a highway-one American, one British and one Indian. The American asked the Englishman, 'Do you have children?' the Englishman said, 'It has not happened to me, so far, but I can't say anything about the future'. The Indian said, 'I'm having three children.'
b. Sign board: 'Alcohol kills you slowly.' Somebody wrote under that: 'I'm not in a great hurry'.

iii. Idioms

Do you know the origins of these common expressions?

1. Baker's dozen
2. A feather in your cap
3. Leave no stone unturned
4. Let the cat out of the bag
5. Lion's share
6. Make ends meet
7. Mind your P's and Q's
8. The Naked Truth
9. Red-letter day

10. White elephant
11. OK

iv. Common Errors

Learning from mistakes

You can also learn from mistakes. Be Indian, but beware of Indianisms, which are generally used in the non-standard variety.

Correct the following and record them.

1. Fire broke out in our village.
2. Andamans are a group of islands.
3. The boys leave the school at four o'clock.
4. I'm not on talking terms with my friend.
5. There was pin-drop silence in the hall.
6. Boarding and lodging is provided here.
7. We have discussed about the matter.
8. The meeting has been pre-poned.
9. Have you given key to the clock?
10. This road is more shorter than that.
11. This paper is superior than that.
12. My sister has gone for shopping.
13. Ravi uncle is very kind to me.
14. We go to the hostel mess every day.
15. My friend speaks chaste English.
16. I went home by walk.
17. My brother brings two milk-bottles from the booth, every morning.
18. We have chit-chat with our neighbour.
19. Please shut the window; it is fairly cold.
20. Please consider me as your friend.
21. Drinking tea is a Chinese habit.
22. She shut the TV and then opened the taps.
23. The weather is too hot – I enjoy it like this.
24. The magistrate issued order for his arrest.
25. May I take your leave?
26. I'll avail of this opportunity to meet you then.
27. I'm living in Bangalore.
28. She has left painting.
29. She asked me where was I going.
30. Will you kindly open this knot?
31. Will you kindly mend his pencil?
32. Please write your name with ink.
33. We got down from the bus.

34. They have no issues.
35. Life is full of miseries.
36. Colleges should be established in every town of some importance.
37. Each and every time it happens, some statement is issued.
38. We want something to cover us with.
39. Last month I had been to Delhi.
40. The student has been conferred a degree.
41. Do you know to dance?
42. We are not able to cope up with the cost of living.
43. I feel badly about the delay.
44. Lentils are equally as nutritious as black beans.
45. To none of these questions a reply can be given.
46. Kiran as well as Kamal are leaving for England.
47. Cinema has no other aim but entertainment.
48. I enquired of his health.
49. There are many worth seeing places in Kerala.
50. The children are learning their alphabets.
51. I and my wife went to a movie.
52. I haven't got some money.
53. This tea is very hot to drink.
54. This is somewhat true.
55. They lived here since three years.
56. She covered her head by a shawl.
57. The child died from fever.
58. I doubt that she will succeed.
59. We are used to live here like this.
60. We are living in Mumbai since 1990.
61. All the furnitures were destroyed.
62. He is my older brother.
63. We went for a picnic and enjoyed very much.
64. Each one of them were presented with a gold watch.
65. This house costed me a lot of money.
66. The teacher hanged the map on the wall.
67. She was awoke by the sound of the alarm.
68. Knowledge is more preferable than riches.
69. Do not go out with your head open.
70. Mohan and myself will come.
71. Yourself did it.
72. My mother always cooks herself in the morning.
73. I thanked her for her sweet words.
74. You can lift it slowly, slowly.

75. She resembles to her mother.
76. In terms of rank, a captain is underneath a lieutenant.
77. One student only came in late yesterday.
78. Not a line of these lectures have been prepared.
79. My wife wants that I come home early.
80. Have you breakfast at eight?
81. I enjoy to learn English.
82. We shall look forward to seeing you.
83. I was tired of the life, but I love the travel I crossed the Atlantic to united states and stayed in the New York.
84. Her autobiography is more interesting than any book I have read.
85. If the baby does not thrive on fresh milk, it should be boiled.
86. He was so afraid that his knees knocked one another.
87. Is the old always wiser than the young?
88. What a nonsense to go out in such a bad weather?
89. We saw them before one month.
90. Do not go to other shops to be disappointed, but come to us.
91. The college may refuse admission to anyone they think proper.
92. Fried in oil, the guests enjoyed the potatoes.
93. She went to her village to sell the land along with her husband.
94. When we breathe in we inhale; when we breathe out we expire!
95. After attending my classes for two years, the student knows nothing.
96. Would you like to try on the dress in the window?
97. Being an architect, his home was designed by himself.
98. He broke open the door with his wife.
99. You are not allowed to cut jokes in the class.
100. I have headache.

v. What's wrong? Can you give the standard version of the following sentences?

a. Very good morning.
b. What's your good name?
c. Where do you come from? Ans: I'm coming from Mumbai.
d. You must be knowing Mumbai very well.
e. Do you know the concerned officer?
f. We have seen this report last year.
g. The terrorist is absconding.
h. Boarding and lodging will be provided in the campus.
i. Please pass order for this.
j. Indians have black hairs.
k. We're learning the English alphabets.
l. In the family, there are four daughter-in-laws.

m. I and my brother went to see a movie.
n. This road is more shorter than that.
o. I did nothing but laughed.
p. She told to me that she was not interested in that.
q. We got down from the bus.
r. I doubt that he will succeed.
s. We have just taken our meals.
t. We are living in Bangalore since 2000.
u. We saw her before one month.
v. Why you are coming late?
w. He died from fever.
x. You can avail for this facility.
y. You are leaving back your luggage.

D. Composition

i. Rewrite the following in Standard English

Goodbye party for Pushpa Miss

'The poem was written by Nissim Ezekiel as a parody of 'Indian English.

Friends,
our dear sister
is departing for foreign
in two three days,
and
we are meeting today
to wish her bon voyage.

You are all knowing friends,
What sweetness is in Miss Pushpa.
I don't mean only external sweetness
but internal sweetness.
Miss Pushpa is smiling and smiling
even for no reason
but simply because she is feeling.

Miss Pushpa is coming
From very high family.
Her father was renowned advocate
In Bulsar or Surat
I am not remembering now which place.

Surat? Ah, yes.
once only I stayed in Surat
with family members
of my uncle's very old friend –
his wife was cooking nicely.....
that was long time ago.

Coming back to Miss Pushpa
she is most popular lady
with men also and ladies also.
Whenever I asked her to to do anything,
she was saying, 'Just now only
I will do it.' That is showing
good spirit. I am always
appreciating the good spirit.

Pushpa Miss is never saying no.
Whatever I or anybody is asking
she is always saying yes,
and today she is going
to improve her prospects
and we are wishing her bon voyage.
Now I ask other speakers to speak
and afterwards Miss Pushpa
will do the summing up.

Appendix I – Answer Key

II. Vocabulary Enrichment

i. A. 1. *vortex*
2. *occiput*
3. *forehead*
4. *chin*
5. *loins*
6. *waist*
7. *arm*
8. *hand*
9. *toe*
10. *vertebrae*
11. *cardiac*
12. *Saliva*
13. *arteries*
14. *veins*
15. *nervous*

B. 1. *Epidemic*
2. *endemic*
3. *sporadic*
4. *pandemic*
5. *antidote*
6. *immune*
7. *quarantine*
8. *amputate*
9. *diagnose*
10. *ambulance*
11. *panacea*
12. *antiseptic*
13. *anaesthetic*
14. *innoculation*
15. *vaccination*

D. Ideologies:
1. *Chauvinism*
2. *Nepotism*
3. *Epicureanism*
4. *Atheism*
5. *Anarchism*
6. *Capitalism*
7. *Communism*
8. *Agnosticism*
9. *Fascism*
10. *Fanaticism*
11. *Liberalism*
12. *Radicalism*
13. *Rationalism*
14. *Socialism*
15. *Stoicism*
16. *Scepticism*
17. *Monotheism*
18. *Polytheism*
19. *Pantheism*
20. *Humanism*

E. 1. *Amiable*
2. *Bellicose*
3. *Compunctious*
4. *Dexterous*
5. *Ambidextrous*
6. *Erudite*
12. *Loquacious*
13. *Magnanimous*
14. *Maladroit*
15. *Pusillanimous*
16. *Punctilious*
17. *Pacifical*

7. *Despondent*
8. *Illiterate*
9. *Indefatigable*
10. *Indolent*
11. *Literate*
18. *Sanguine*
19. *Melancholic*
20. *Obdurate*
21. *Unceremonious*
22. *Veteran*

F. 1. *Anthropology*
2. *Agronomy*
3. *Astrology*
4. *Archaeology*
5. *Astronomy*
6. *Biology*
7. *Botany*
8. *Embryology*
9. *Entomology*
10. *Etymology*
11. *Graphology*
12. *Geology*
13. *Linguistics*
14. *Penology*
15. *Philology*
16. *Meteorology*
17. *Theology*
18. *Seismology*
19. *Cosmology*
20. *Phonetics*

G. 1. *Abbey*
2. *Cathedral*
3. *Church*
4. *Chapel*
5. *Convent, Nunnery*
6. *Monastery*
7. *Mosque*
8. *Pagoda*
9. *Priory*
10. *Synagogue*
11. *Temple*

H. *What's the word?*

1. *Altruist*
2. *Amateur*
3. *Anarchist*
4. *Arsenal*
5. *Bigot*
6. *Blasphemous*
7. *Cannibal*
8. *Carnivorous*
9. *Connoisseur*
10. *Dermatologist*
11. *Domicile*
12. *Effeminate*
13. *Epicurean*
14. *Extempore*
15. *Fastidious*
16. *Fratricide*
17. *Genocide*
18. *Homicide*
19. *Matricide*
20. *Patricide*
21. *Regicide*
22. *Suicide*
23. *Germicide*
24. *Herbivorous*
25. *Incorrigible*
26. *Incredible*
27. *Indelible*
28. *Infallible*
29. *Innocuous*
30. *Inevitable*
31. *Loquacious*
32. *Mercenary*
33. *Mobocracy*
34. *Obsolete*
35. *Narcotic*
36. *Omnipotent*

37. *Omnipresent*
38. *Omniscient*
39. *Oligarchy*
40. *Opaque*
41. *Parasite*
42. *Philanderer*
43. *Plutocracy*
44. *Pseudonym*
45. *Sacrilege*
46. *Sadist*
47. *Soliloquy*
48. *Somnambulism*
49. *Stoic*
50. *Turncoat*
51. *Verbose*
52. *Heretic*
53. *Centenarian*
54. *Octogenarian*
55. *Novice*
56. *Oculist*
57. *Philatelist*
58. *Recluse*
59. *Hamlet*
60. *Ordination*
61. *Espionage*
62. *Cavalry*
63. *Infantry*
64. *Hackneyed*
65. *Crusade*
66. *Plagiarist*
67. *Hedonist*
68. *Utopia*
69. *Platitudes*
70. *Pantheism*
71. *Egomania*
72. *Kleptomania*
73. *Hydrophobia*
74. *Greengrocer*
75. *Grocery*
76. *Orthodontics*
77. *Curator*
78. *Holster*
79. *Franchise*
80. *Tinker*
81. *Blacksmith*
82. *Mind-set*
83. *Hosier*
84. *Coxcomb*
85. *Meteorology*

iii. Foreign words and phrases

1. Dishes with a stated price for each
2. From cause to effect, deductively (applied to reasoning)
3. Temporary
4. Farewell, goodbye
5. Helper
6. Otherwise known as
7. The institution where one is educated
8. Another self
9. Old students of an institution
10. In the year of the Lord (abbr: A.D.)
11. Have a good trip
12. In good faith
13. The middle class
14. Full power or authority

15. Let him beware, a warning or caution
16. A deputy or temporary substitute for an ambassador
17. A violent or illegal change in the government of a country
18. Really
19. By right
20. As a group
21. On the way
22. A child who always makes inopportune and embarrassing remarks
23. Errors
24. and the n---??
25. I have found it
26. By virtue of one's office
27. From one side only
28. Without preparation
29. Something surely (already) established or done
30. Party, feast, festival
31. A writ requiring a person to be brought before a court or judge
32. In or during absence
33. In disguise
34. On the whole, entirely
35. By the fact itself, in the nature of the case
36. Letting events take their own course
37. Male
38. A great work
39. With bad faith, treacherously
40. My struggle or battle
41. For each person
42. Unskilled labourer
43. By the day, daily
44. An acceptable or welcome person
45. Afternoon
46. as a matter of form
47. Something in return, compensation
48. Where do you go?/Where are you going?
49. The holy of holies
50. An afternoon nap
51. In parliamentary procedure without appointing a day to assemble again
52. Under judicial consideration
53. Clean state
54. Head to head confidential conversation
55. A middle course

56. By word of mouth, orally
57. Namely
58. Reversal
59. Deadlock
60. Youthful, Juvenile
61. Language of the masses
62. A right to participate in something
63. Master, teacher, instructor
64. Manner of working
65. Pre-eminently, outstandingly
66. Annually
67. After death, an autopsy
68. Hail
69. Not valid, not within powers
70. Luxurious, elegant
71. Madam
72. Payment not legally binding but for which some moral obligation is felt
73. By or in itself
74. In proportion
75. At first consideration, before there has been time for inquiry or examination
76. As if, as it were
77. Which was to be shown or demonstrated
78. Bring to an end without dissolving it; some unfinished business may be taken up again
79. To the point of disgust
80. Genuine

iv. Confusables

1. social: relating to society: a social evening, club or circle brings one into contact with other people in society.
2. ii. tasty: having a pleasant flavour
3. ii. unable: lack of ability in specific circumstances
4. valued: highly regarded and esteemed
5. rigorous: full of rigour, strictness, severity
6. historical: belonging or pertaining to history or its study (historical research/novel etc)
7. reputable: respected, of good repute
8. proscribe: forbid (by law), reject as dangerous
9. sensuous: affecting or taking pleasure in the senses, as one might derive sensuous pleasure in skiing.
10. infectious: spread by micro-organisms (in air, water etc.)
    Figuratively, they are interchangeable – contagious enthusiasm, infectious laughter
11. reward: something given by way of recompense or return for service or merit
12. altogether: in total; completely; on the whole

13. alternative: affording a choice, implies choice
14. effect: (n) result; bring about (v) (effect an improvement). (n) influence (his protests had no effect on her)
15. discrete: separate; consisting of distinct parts

v. It makes a lot of difference

	i.	ii.
(1)	boar	bore
(2)	complement	compliment
(3)	concert	consort
(4)	dual	duel
(5)	excerpt	except
(6)	feature	future
(7)	lakh	lack
(8)	later	latter
(9)	sight	site
(10)	marital	martial
(11)	president	precedent
(12)	reminder	remainder
(13)	rites	rights
(14)	straight	strait
(15)	stationary	stationery

vi. Confusing couples

(1) ticket used in secret voting
(2) sleeping-place ina train, a ship or an aircraft
(3) nobleman
(4) a narrow lane
(5) that which does not really exist
(6) helper or companion
(7) make suitable for a new use, need, situation etc.
(8) right and suitable; respectful
(9) (a person's) death
(10) colour, usually by dipping in a liquid
(11) hint about how to behave, what to do, etc.
(12) person who has power through wealth, position, business or industry
(13) floor or a level in a building
(14) drop of salty water coming from the eye
(15) place (a dead body) in the ground, in a graveyard
(16) adj. (1) of the four elements (2) of the elementals
(17) a person who goes away from one's own country to another to settle there
(18) (of events, esp. dangers) likely to come or happen soon
(19) consent expressed by voting

(20) lover of food
(21) kind, generous, courteous
(22) (n) frozen rain drops falling from the sky; (v) greet, give a welcoming cry to.
(23) (n) wandering tribe, gypsy
(24) eagerly, earnestly
(25) quality (e.g.) in persons, horses of endurance and courage

IV Idioms

1. A Baker's Dozen
   Consumer protection is nothing new. Even in the late 16th century in England, tradesmen were subject to heavy penalties for cheating customers-selling shoddy goods, short weighing, etc. So, bakers always gave an extra roll or loaf to compensate for any eventuality like underweight rolls, etc. They gave 13 instead of a dozen – a baker's dozen.
   The original baker's dozen was 13 rather than 12 loaves or rolls.
2. A feather in your cap
   In olden days, a feather was regarded as a badge of honour for the hunter or warrior. A hunter who killed a bird would pluck a feather from it and wear it as a mark of achievement. American Indians did it. Soldiers in Europe paraded feathers in their caps to symbolise battle honours. Chinese governments did it. Indians also wore peacock feathers on their crowns.
3. Kick the bucket
   Bucket= Old French, for a wooden beam of frame from which a live pig would be suspended in the abattoir. When slaughtered, the pig would kick the frame.
   Or, while committing suicide by hanging on an upturned bucket.
4. Leave no stone unturned
   Latin or Greek tradition. In 479 B.C. a Greek army defeated the Persians but failed to discover a treasure buried by the Persian general. The Greek commander went to the Oracle at Delphi. The oracle, a priestess, as cryptic as ever, advised him to 'turn every stone'. Maybe the treasure was found under the stone floor of the Persian general's tent.
5. Let the cat out of the bag
   Dishonest traders would offer prepacked sack at a discount. Instead of a pig or piglet, there may be something dead or it may be something else like a cat. The careful buyer would untie the sack only to let the cat out of the bag – 'to reveal a trick or secret'.
6. Lion's share
   In Aesop's fable – a lion went out hunting with some other animals. Once the hunt was over, the lion laid down his claim – one share for himself, another for his courage, a third for his lioness and for his cubs. The fourth and last quarter was for the one who can fight with him for it.
7. Make ends meet
   To make the two ends of the year meet. Live within your means during the year. Otherwise, you will be in debt at the end of the year.

8. Mind your P's and q's.
Similarity of appearance between the letter p and q. Young children get them mixed up, just as they mix up b and d. So they were urged to mind their p's and q's.
9. The Naked Truth
Goddess Truth and Falsehood go swimming together. Falsehood comes out first and wears the clothes of goddess Truth to parade as Truth. When goddess Truth came out, the clothes of Falsehood were there. But she preferred to walk naked rather than look like Falsehood.
10. Red-letter day
Religious calenders used the red colour to indicate holy days. So,]any memorable day in one's life.
11. White elephant
In parts of south and southeast Asia, elephants with an unusual whitish hide were regarded with veneration.
India's Iravatham, for example.
The ancient kings of Siam (now Thailand), would take subtle revenge on any high ranking official by gifting a whole elephant. They were very expensive to maintain. So, a showpiece became a source of high cost and inconvenience.
So, a white elephant is anything that is not very useful but costs high.
12. O.K.
A humourous spellinh of 'oll korect' that was used in the late 1830s
Or
A railway clerk Obadiah Kelly put his initials OK for acceptance for all packeges he approved for shipping put his initials OK. So, OK
Or
'OK club formed' in 1840 to support the election of a US president. His town was Old Kinderhook and the initial letters were used in honour of the town.
13. Between the devil and the deep sea – Choice between two equally unwelcome options.
The plank of seam on a pirate ship was called 'devil'
So, a captive walking on the plank would have this choice.

iv. Common Errors

i. Correct the following and reword them

1. A fire
2. The Andamans
3. Leave school
4. Speaking terms
5. Complete
6. Board
7. Discussed the
8. Advanced
9. Wound
10. Shorter/much shorter
11. Superior to
12. No 'for'/ gone shopping
13. Uncle Ravi
14. Dining hall
15. Flawless
16. On foot

17. Bottles of milk
18. Gossip
19. Rather cold
20. No 'as'/me your friend
21. Custom
22. Turned off; turned on
23. Very hot
24. Orders
25. Take leave of you
26. Avail of myself
27. Live
28. Given up
29. Where I was
30. Untie
31. Sharpen
32. In ink
33. We got off
34. Issue (=children)
35. (No plural) misery
36. Any importance
37. Every time
38. Cover ourselves
39. Went to
40. A degree has been conferred upon the student
41. How to dance
42. Cope with
43. Bad
44. Just as
45. Can a reply be
46. Is leaving
47. Than entertainment
48. About or after
49. Many places worth seeing
50. Alphabet
51. My wife and I
52. Any money
53. Too hot to
54. Partly true
55. For three
56. With a shawl
57. Of fever
58. Whether
59. Living
60. From; have been living
61. Furniture was
62. Elder
63. Enjoyed it /enjoyed ourselves
64. Was
65. Cost
66. Hung
67. Awakened
68. Is preferable to
69. Bare
70. And I
71. You yourself
72. My mother herself cooks food
73. Kind words
74. Very slowly
75. Resembles her
76. Under
77. Any one
78. Has been
79. Wants me to
80. Do you have
81. Learning
82. We look forward
83. Life, travel, the United states
84. Any other book
85. The milk should
86. Each other
87. Are the ---
88. What nonsense
89. A month ago
90. Crack (Answers to items 91-99 may vary)
100. a headache

Unit IX Answers to the questions

III Reference Skills

1 (a); 2. (a); 3. (c); 4. (b); 5. (b); 6. (b); 7. (a); 8. (a); 9. (a); 10. (b); 11 (c); 12 (b); 13. (b); 14 (b); 15. (c); 16. (b); 17. (c); 18. (b); 19. (c); 20. (a)

IV. Find the origins of the following words:

1. Arabic
2. Hindi
3. French
4. Spanish
5. Japanese
6. French
7. Sanskrit
8. Hindi
9. Hindi
10. Urdu
11. Arabic
12. German
13. German
14. Arabic
15. Persian
16. Tamil
17. Portuguese/Spanish
18. Portuguese
19. Dutch
20. Chinese
21. Persian

Appendix II – Towards Gender-Sensitive Communication

Man Made World/Word

For centuries men, meaning 'males', ruled over language and they were not sensitive to the sentiments of women. It was a male-made world and it is said that those who rule the word rule the world. Look at what even the great men said.

Aristotle (384–322 B.C.), the great Greek philosopher, said: " We should look upon the female state as being, as it were a deformity, one which occurs in the ordinary course of nature... on account of its weakness it quickly approaches its maturity and old age since inferior things all reach their ends more quickly" (*Generation of Animals*), trans by Peck). (Obviously, Aristotle is wrong since women outlive men, a well-known fact!) A Roman Catholic scholar like Thomas Aquinas (13th century A.D.) said that the female is a 'misbegotten' male. Freud, a well-known psychologist, made women envy some parts of a man. Nietzsche, the great German philosopher, says 'man is for women a means: the end is always the child. But what is woman for a man ... a dangerous toy. He continues, 'Man shall be educated for war, and women for the recreation of the warrior; everything else is folly' (*The Will to Power*, 1889).

Now, look at some of the so-called 'funny sayings' about women:

"Here lies my wife:
Here let her lie!
Now she is at rest, and so am I."

– Dryden

Here is another from a 17th century British churchman:

"A woman, a dog, and a walnut tree,
The more you beat them the better they are."

– Thomas Fuller

Here is one by the famous poet Kipling:

"For the female of the species is more deadly than the male."

Ambrose Bierce, an American satirist, says in a toast: " Here is to woman– who came after man, and who has been after him ever since."

Many more can be cited.

In India too, we do not lag behind. The mythical Markandeya said: " By serving their husbands only can women win heaven"; the saint Vyasa through Draupadi advises another women Satyabhama saying], " keeping aside vanity and controlling desire and wrath, I always serve with devotion the sons of Pandu and their wives") *Mahabharata*, trans. By P.C. Roy). One can see that irrespective of religion, country, race, the period in which people lived, more or less the same perception about women prevailed. The Bible teaches that women brought sin into this world and that she precipitated the fall of the human race.

Many religious myths perpetuate this kind of mind-set to demean women and create a historical conditioning. For example, in Hindu mythology, only the birth of boys is mentioned. Parvathi gave birth to two sons and Sita too two. (We don't know if they had daughters or not.) In the Ramayana, Rama had an elder sister but we never hear of her because King Dasarata gave her in adoption to the king of Angadesh; Dasarata did not want a girl as the eldest child. In the *Mahabharata,* Kunti and Madri gave birth to the Pandavas and Karna; Gandhari mass-produced one hundred sons and it is said there was only one insignificant female (Dushala). Look at the ratio 100:1. No wonder there is population imbalance! One often wonders where all the girls have gone!

Birthdays seem to be only for boys – be it Ram Navami or Krishna Jenmashtami. Since girls were not born, obviously, there can't be any birthdays for them! All the ten avathars called Dasavathar that appear to establish Dharma on this planet, are males, though everybody knows only women are culture-preservers. In Christianity, all the twelve apostles of Christ are men. It is the same story in all religions. In Hinduism among the twelve Vaishnavite Alwars, there is only one woman – Andal; among the 63 Shaivite Naynmars, there are only one or two, perhaps, like Karaikal Ammayar. A woman even today may become the president of a country or the head of a political party (as it has already happened in India and some other countries), but no woman can ever become a Pope or an Ayatulla or a Sankaracharya. No religion will allow this though in our contemporary world women are at the top in politics, in business, in the corporate world, in scientific research, in art and culture, and so on.

The burial of women takes place even in language. Otto Jespersen, the well known Danish Grammarian, in his book '*Language, its Nature, Development and Origin*' (1922, p.27) says women by virtue of their sex shrank from coarse and gross expressions and had a preference for veiled and indirect expressions which precluded from being as effective as men; therefore, women had a debilitating effect upon language and it was reasonable for men certainly with great justice to object: there is a danger of the language becoming languid and insipid, if we were to content ourselves with women's expressions. For centuries this kind of stereotyping continued in all cultures.

Many language scholars have stated that men's speech is forceful, efficient, blunt, authoritative, serious, effective and masterful while women's speech is weak, ineffective, tentative, trivial and hesitant, and is often marked by gossip and meaningless expressions. They go in circles like a labyrinth. Robin Lakoff's book '*Language and Women's Place*' (1975) confirms this. She says the word 'shit' is more commonly found in male vocabulary and the expression "Oh dear' in female vocabulary;

She further adds that women use more question tags and hedges like 'well', 'you know', etc. since they are unclear and uncertain about what they say. It is said that there is no humour in the language of women and the level of pitch is high in women's speech.

This asymmetry in the representation of men and women in language is often reflected in the order of precedence given to males and females in many expressions: husband and wife, son and daughter, brother and sister, king and queen, and Adam and Eve.

Eakins and Eakins (1976) suggest that women more often than men are referred to in terms of their partners: 'John's wife', 'Harry's daughter, and so on; a woman whose husband is dead is 'Edwin's widow, but the man whose wife is deceased is not referred to as 'Rosie's widower'.

If we compare the following pairs of words, we can see that the masculine gender has been not only stable in the English language but also dominant: mister/mistress (an illegal one); sir/madam (a brothel keeper); governor/governess (a tutor in a private house); courtier/courtesan (a woman who takes payment for services rendered); king/queen (sexual connotations); wizard/witch (derogatory); Lord/Lady (a doll like decorative object); dog/bitch (derogatory), etc. In other words, words that denote the feminine gender have a lesser value. Words like 'whore' and 'harlot', which were used to refer to both the sexes, are now used to refer only to women. When we say 'He is a professional', it is respectable; but 'She is a professional' has a bad odour. The process of semantic degeneration shows the evaluation of women over the years.

Expressions like 'the proper study of mankind is Man' (Pope), " The child is father of the man' (Wordsworth), " Man is a noble animal" (Pythagoras), etc. clearly show that "man" is generic. The pronoun 'he' is also generic. For example, **'He** who laughs lasts longest'; 'A teacher should do whatever **he** thinks best'. Linguistic conditioning is used as a powerful tool for keeping women in the 'right place'. Even while abusing men, expressions used are all targeted towards women. For example, 'son of a bitch', and many other expressions that cannot be expressed are often used. Many proverbs perform the same function.

The educational curriculum too is a tool to perpetuate the gender bias in every subject. Most of the school textbooks portray women doing all the time only domestic chores like washing, cleaning, cooking, etc. Even today, the electronic media portrays women only in stereotyped roles. Goffman's (1976) analysis of more than 500 pictorial advertisements, depicting women, men and children leads him to the conclusion that 'advertisers conventionalize our conventions'. For example, 'Drivers: belt the wives and kids – and keep them safe', advises a road safety poster. Another ad.for a car says, 'If I were a lady, I would get its bottom pinched'. We must've all seen the frequently repeated ad. for the perfume 'AXE'; the main objective is to attract women. Whatever be the product – be it a washing powder, a dishwashing cake, a chewing gum or a car, only women are used as exhibits. In most of the TV shows the mangal-sutra or some other symbol of marriage is projected as the most sacred fence for women though in reality the story is very different. Incidentally no need of a fence for men because we all know they stray anyhow! In short, the educational system through the curriculum and the text books, the print and electronic media, the beauty industry, the language and all the other possible instruments are only used to project and retain the patriarchal order. Like the pre-Copernican Geo-centric world, the word and world have become andro-centric (i. e. male-centred).

The Changing Scenario

Now, with globalization, the advent of information technology, and women empowerment this depressing picture is somewhat changing. Women are getting educated, learning English and getting more and more job opportunities and becoming economically independent. The old stereotype that girls are good at learning languages has now come to their advantage; they learn English easily with élan (better than boys) and, as a result, the job market has opened up; they are everywhere; they go abroad; they are independent and quite a few prefer to be happily single. In America, women have become a major work force. For the first time, there are more women managers (51.4%). Women hold half of banking and insurance jobs. In the West, for every two men who got a college degree three women did. India is also not legging behind. It is fast catching up and the trends are emerging; changes are taking place and they are visible in urban and semi-urban areas. Gitls do very well in examinations, even better than boys.

In the corporate sector, for example, Indira Nooyi is the CEO of Pepsi Foods and M.S. Koachar the CEO of the ICICI bank; Kiran Majumdar Shah, Kiran Bedi, and a host of others have pushed the margins, bringing women more and more close to the centre. In politics, Sonia Gandhi, Mamta Banerjee, Sushma Swaraj, and many other have made a mark. In sports, Sania Mirza, Saina Nehwal, and Mary Kom are breaking all records. Even in religion, the hugging mother, Mata Amurthaanandamayi, is a force to reckon with. Thus the entire scenario is fast changing and along with that language also changes rapidly. It is becoming non-sexist, gender-neutral, and gender-sensitive.

Gender-neutral language

If you want to become a successful communicator in the present-day world, you must learn how to make your language gender-neutral. Gender-neutral language or gender neutrality aims to eliminate (or neutralize) reference to gender in communication. In your communication or narrative style, do not use gender-specific words. The use of gender-specific language also called sexism in language has become a thing of the past. Although the extent of this may still vary from country to country, it is now becoming more common and acceptable to use gender-neutral terms when writing and speaking in English.

Here are some hints for making communication gender-sensitive:
Guidelines for gender-neutral language

1. Replace generic masculine pronouns (*he, his*) by rewriting your sentence in one of the following ways:
   a. **Recast your sentence in the plural.**
      Example: *Each participant* must present *his* ID badge at the door.
      Revised: *All participants* must present *their* ID badges at the door.
   b. **Use both pronouns without parentheses (e.g. she or he, her/him**, his/hers, herself or himself).
      Example: The client should receive *his* invoice in two weeks.
      Revised: The client should receive *his or her* invoice in two weeks.
      Note: Most sources agree that the construction *s/he* should be avoided.
   c. **Use neutral words like individual or *one*.**
      Example: The stage manager must delegate all the tasks; *he* is therefore responsible for the show's success.

Revised: The stage manager must delegate all the tasks; this *individual* is therefore responsible for the show's success.

d. **Eliminate the pronoun altogether.**
Example: The incumbent is expected to edit a variety of documents. *He* must also prepare weekly updates.
Revised: The incumbent is required to edit a variety of documents *and prepare* weekly updates.

e. **Repeat the noun.**
Example: The student must submit the course registration papers by July 1. *His* guidance counsellor will send confirmation by mail.
Revised: The student must submit the course registration papers by July 1. The *student's* guidance counsellor will send confirmation by mail.

f. **Use sentence fragments where appropriate** (e.g. work descriptions, c.v.'s).

g. **Address your reader directly, using you and your.**
Example: The tenant must keep *hi s*APARTMENT clean and tidy.
Revised: *You* must keep *your* apartment clean and tidy.
Note: Although plural pronouns (*they, them, themselves*) are sometimes used as gender-neutral singular pronouns in informal writing, they are not fully accepted. Use this practice with caution.
Example: If your *child* is expecting you after school, please don't make *them* wait.
Better: If your *children* are expecting you after school, please don't make them wait.

2. Avoid patronizing expressions, and use *woman* instead of *girl* or *lady* unless you are referring to a minor.
Example: One of the *lovely ladies* in the office will answer your call.
Revised: One of the *administrative assistants* will answer your call.
Example: If you need anything, just let *the girl* at the desk know.
Revised: If you need anything, just let *my assistant* know.

3. Use gender-neutral occupational titles.

Don't use	**Use**
businessman, businesswoman	businessperson, people in business
chairman, chairwoman	chair, chairperson, convenor
cleaning lady	office cleaner
foreman	supervisor
headmaster, headmistress	director, principal
mailman	mail carrier, letter carrier
policeman, policewoman	police officer
salesman	clerk, salesclerk, sales associate, salesperson

4. Avoid the generic term man, generic words and expressions that contain man and the use of man as an adjective or verb.

Don't use	Use
average man	average person, ordinary person
best man for the job	best person for the job
layman	layperson, non-specialist
man (when referring to humanity)	human beings, humanity, humans, individuals, people
man and wife	wife and husband, partners
mankind	Humankind
man-made	artificial, handmade, manufactured, synthetic
manpower	personnel, staff, workers, workforce
to man	to operate, to staff
workmanlike	skilful

This table provides a list of gender-neutral generic terms to use instead of the generic term man, generic words and expressions that contain the word man and the use of man as an adjective or verb.

Example: Please get a clerk to man the front desk.

Revised: Please get a clerk to staff the front desk.

Note: You should also avoid expressions like career woman. Instead, be spe-**cific:** artist, director, doctor, professor, etc.

5. Avoid irrelevant references to details such as a woman's marital status, role or physical appearance.

   Example: Widow, 58, rescues kitten from tree

   Revised: Woman, 58, rescues kitten from tree

   Example: The always elegant Vice President, Sharmila Goel, accepted the award on behalf of the organization.

   Revised: The Vice President, Sharmila Goel, accepted the award on behalf of the organization.

6. Avoid generalizations about men's and women's personality traits and social roles.

   Example: *Hysterical* women and *angry* men

   Revised: *Angry* women and men

   Example: The *nurse* should bring *her* stethoscope to the training session.

   Revised: *Nurses* should bring *their* stethoscopes to the training session.

7. In correspondence, use parallel constructions.

   When using *Mrs.*, use *Ms.* unless you know the preferred title (*Miss, Mrs.*) of the person you are addressing or referring to.

   Example: Dear *Ms.* Shaheen

Note: If you don't know the sex of the addressee, use *Dear* followed by the person's initials and surname. Similarly, if you do not know the name of the addressee, use the form *Dear Madam or Sir* or *Dear Sir/Madam*.

8. Alternate your word order.

   Examples:

   Each student must submit her or his paper by noon tomorrow.
   Dear Madam or Sir:
   In India, women and men are equally susceptible to heart disease.
9. More on pronouns
   a. Avoid unnecessary male pronouns by using plural pronouns "they", "them", etc.
      "Someone has left their briefcase behind."
      "If anyone phones, tell them I am in a meeting."
   b. Replace male pronouns with combinations such as "she or he", "him or her", "her or his".*
      "A fashion model is usually obsessive about her or his diet."
      "The journalist must be accurate when she or he reports interviews."
      (* these combinations can sound rather awkward. They should not be re-peated often in a piece of writing or conversation. The written form s/he, he/she, her/him is acceptable.)
   c. Use other words when referring to both men and women.
      "People are ..."
      "Human beings must protect ..."
      "Who's staffing the office?"
   d. Use expressions or pronouns that do not support sexist assumptions about jobs.
      "Teachers must not be late for their classes."
      "A chairperson should be fair to all her or his colleagues."
   e. Use job names that apply equally to men and women.
      "The chairperson handed out notes of the last meeting."
      "Mary is a very experienced camera operator."
      "James is a nurse and Barbara is a doctor."
      "We offer language courses for business people."

(Source: Adapted from the Internet.)

Following is a list of gender-specific words/terms with their recommended gender-neutral equivalents. The words/terms that are included on the list are the one that we most frequently encounter in day-to-day writing and speaking. You must learn to use them in your communication

Instead of this...	Use this...
actress	actor
airline stewardess	flight attendant
airman, airwoman	pilot, aviator, flier, flight crew
alderman	council member/person

Instead of this...	**Use this...**
alumna, alumnus	graduates, alums
anchorman, anchorwoman	anchor
blind man	blind person
bondsman	bondsperson, guarantor, insurer
brakeman (train)	brake operator
brew master	brew director, chief/head brewer
bridesmaid	bride's attendant
brotherhood	fellowship, camaraderie
brotherly	kind, helpful
brotherly love	charity, goodwill
businessman, businesswoman	businessperson
cabin boy	cabin attendant
cameraman, camerawoman	camera operator
career woman	career professional
cavemen	cave dwellers, cave people
chairman, chairwoman	chairperson, chair
chambermaid	housekeeper
chorus girl, chorus boy	chorus singer, chorus member
city fathers	city leaders
clergy men, clergy women	clergy, clerics, ministers, pastors, etc.
common man	average person, commoner
conductress	conductor
confidence man	swindler, crook
congressman	member of congress, congress person
contact man	contact person, contact
councilman	council member
countryman	compatriot
cowboy, cowgirl	cowhand
craftsman	artisan, craftsperson
crewman	crew member
dairyman	dairy farmer
deliveryman	deliverer, delivery clerk, courier
doorman	doorkeeper, door attendant

Instead of this...	Use this...
Dutchman	Dutch person
elder statesman	senior statesperson
Englishman	Englander, Briton
fall guy	scapegoat
fatherhood	parenthood
fraternal twins	non-identical twins
fatherland	homeland
fireman	Fire fighter
flagman	flagger
floor man	floorwalker, duty person
forefathers	ancestors, forebears
foreman, forewoman, forelady	supervisor, boss
founding father	founder
Frenchmen	the French, French people
freshman	first year students, undergrads
gateman	gate keeper, gate attendant
gentlemen's agreement	unwritten agreement
goddess	god
governess	child caretaker, child care worker, nurse
guardsman	guard, soldier
gunman	shooter, killer, assassin
handyman	fixer, maintenance person
headman	boss, chief, president, leader
headmaster	principal
heiress	heir
henchman	partner in crime
heroine	hero
horseman, horsewoman	rider, equestrian
hostess	host
housewife	homemaker
infantryman	infantry soldier
inside man	insider
insurance man	insurance agent

Instead of this...	**Use this...**
Irishmen	Irish people
jack-of-all-trades	handyperson
jazz man	jazz player, jazz musician
journeyman	experienced tradesperson
juryman	juror, jury person
key man	key person
king-size	huge, very large
layman	layperson
lineman	line technician, football player
maid	house cleaner
maiden name	family name, birth name
mailman/ postman	letter carrier, mail carrier
maintenance man	janitor, caretaker
male nurse	nurse
man among men	outstanding person
man of action	go-getter, human dynamo
man of distinction	person of distinction
man of letters	scholar, academic
man of the year	newsmaker of the year
man on the street	average person, ordinary citizen
man (verb: to man)	operate, staff
man's best friend	dog
man's work	work, hard work
man-to-man	head-to-head, face-to-face
manageress	manager
man-eater	flesh eater
manhandle	rough up, move roughly
manhole	utility access hole, maintenance hole
man-hours	work hours
mankind	humankind, humanity
manlike	humanlike
manmade	hand made, hand built, manufactured
manpower	workers, workforce, staff

Instead of this...	Use this...
man of the house	husband, father
marked man	targeted person
marksman	sharpshooter
masculine	male
masseuse	massage therapist
master	expert
master key	passkey
master plan	main plan, primary plan
masterful	skilful, expert
masterpiece	great work of art
master's degree	graduate degree
matron of honour	honoured attendant
medicine man	spirit healer, faith healer
men working	people working
middleman	go-between, intermediary
Miss	Ms.
modern man	modern people
mother country	homeland
Mother Earth	earth, world, planet earth
Mother Nature	nature
mother tongue	first language, native language
motherhood	parenthood
Mrs.	Ms.
murderess	murderer
newsman	reporter, newscaster
newspaperman	reporter, journalist, editor, writer
night watchman	night security guard
no-man's-land	uninhabited land, neutral zone
nobleman	noble person
number-one-man	head, chief, leader
number-two-man	second in command
oarsman	rower, crew member
odd-man-out	person not included

Instead of this...	Use this...
office boy	messenger, clerk, support staff
old wives' tale	superstition
organization man	team player, loyal company person
outdoorsman	outdoors person
paperboy	paper carrier
patrolman	police officer
penmanship	handwriting
playboy, playgirl	pleasure seeker, partier, carouser
postman	letter carrier
postmaster/ postmistress	post master
prehistoric man	prehistoric person
priestess	priest
prodigal son	returning child
publicity man	publicist
radioman	radio broadcaster
Renaissance man	Renaissance person
repairman	repairer, maintenance specialist
rifleman	shooter, sharpshooter
right-hand man	main assistant
salesman, saleslady	sales person, sales associate/agent
Scotsman	Scot
sculptress	sculptor
seaman	sailor, mariner, sea farer
seamstress	tailor, sewer, mender, needle worker
seductress	seducer
serviceman	sailor, soldier, airman
serviceman	repair person, maintenance person
shipmaster	captain, commander
showman	actor, performer, entertainer
showmanship	stage presence
signalman	signal operator
sister ship	partnership
snowman	snow person

Instead of this...	Use this...
songstress	singer
sorceress	sorcerer, enchanter
spaceman	astronaut
spokesman, spokeswoman	spokesperson
sportsmanlike	sporting, sporty
starlet	star young actor
statesman	leader, senior politician, diplomat
stewardess	flight attendant
straw man	test theory
switchman	switch operator
taskmaster	supervisor, tyrant
temptress	tempter, enticer
toastmaster, toastmistress	toast maker
trash man	trash collector
tribesman	tribe member
Uncle Sam	U.S., United States
usherette	usher
waitress	server
watchman	security guard, lookout guard
weatherman	weathercaster, meteorologist
Welshman	Welsh person
workman	worker
workmanlike	skillful, efficient
workmen's compensation	workers' compensation
yes-man	avid follower, supporter
young man	youth, teenager

(Source: Adapted from the Internet.) The above list is not exhaustive, You can add to it whenever you come across a new word.

References

Books and Style Guides

1. Eakins, B., and G. Eakins. 1976. 'Verbal Turn-taking and Exchanges in Faculty dialogue.' In B.L. Dubois and I. Crouch (eds.) *The Sociology of the Language of American Women*. San Antonio, Texas: Trinity university press.
2. Goffman, E. 1976. *'Gender Advertisements.' Studies in the Anthropology of Visual Communication*, 4:65–154.
3. Jespersen, Otto. 1922. *Language: Its Nature, Development and Origin*. Allen and Unwin.
4. Kakar, Sudhir. 1981. *The Inner World: a Psycho Analytic Study of Childhood and Society in India*. Delhi: OUP.
5. Krishnaswamy, Revathi. 1998. *Effeminism. Ann Arbor*: The University of Michigan Press.
6. Lakoff, R. 1975. *Language and Woman's Place*. New York: Harper and Row.
7. Nandy, Ashis. 1983. *Intimate Enemy: Loss and Recovery of Self under Colonialism*. Delhi: OUP.